The War-Bond
of Davishill
FP

THE AIREDALE

FOR

WORK AND SHOW

BY

A. F. HOCHWALT

...AUTHOR OF...

"Dogcraft," "The Pointer and the Setter in America," "The Modern Pointer," "The Modern Setter," "The Working Dog and His Education," "Practical Dog Keeping for the Amateur," "Arrows of Ambition," Etc.

Reprinted by Boxer Books

To order contact:
Boxer Books
P.O. Box 523
Lavonia, Georgia 30553
Tel: 706-356-8877
Fax: 706.356.8877 (call first)
1-800-583-5396
Email: wertan@alltell.net
Web Site: http://www.alltel.net/~wertan

ISBN: 0-9653624-2-6

Reprinted in 1998 in the United States of America by
Morris Publishing • 3212 East Highway 30 • Kearney, NE 68847

TO THE READER

The Airedale For Work and Show was originally published in 1921. The author, A. F. Hochwalt, however, was a product of 19th century culture and education, having been born in 1869. A. F. Hochwalt was a 19th century man with 19th century sensibilities. Therefore, along with archaic spelling and atavistic forms of English, you will also find an extremely different view of nature than the one we hold today. The roll dogs played was seen as almost totally utilitarian. Nature was viewed as a hostile enemy and the dog was man's ally in survival. The concept of dogs as pets and the subject of maudlin fiction is almost a completely 20th century phenomenon.

The Airedale For Work and Show is filled with interesting facts and lore about the early Airedale. It also provides a window to a world that no longer exists.

Special care was taken to reproduce the photographs as carefully as possible. Please note the initial quality of some the photographs was very poor.

<u>NOTE</u>: Do not try any of the remedies or cures offered in Chapter XV without first consulting a veterinarian. Dog medical care before the advent of modern veterinary medicine after World War Two was as much as much myth as medicine. Only the strongest and the luckiest dogs survived to pass on their genes.

To aid catalogers and collectors, this title is printed in a small limited edition.

Foreword to the reprinting

Many years ago, after acquiring my first Airedale, I started to collect as many early books about the breed as I could. The first of these happened to be Hochwalt's superb work, *The Airedale for Work and Show*, first written in 1921. This was, and is, one of the finest breed books ever written. When recently assessing the breed literature, I wrote that Hochwalt maintained "a judicious balance of discussion about pre-show history, analysis of various strains, showing, breeding, health and working ...There is an abundance of photographs depicting the breed at work and at play...(It is) among the very best of the breed literature."

Very few books can stand the test of time. Three-quarters of a century later, Hochwalt's book remains a classic. Until this time, however, it has remained virtually unattainable. It can be found in the hands of a very few fanciers who have been fortunate to find copies, usually at high prices. Understandably, these lucky few people are reluctant to part with their treasures.

Today, this has changed. We are very fortunate that we have, in Lawrence Wertan, a breed fancier whose passion for the breed runs deep. Mr. Wertan is an acknowledged writer and the author of two highly acclaimed novels about the Airedale. He is a true student of the breed. Now, the Airedale fancy is more indebted to him than ever, for he has offered to the world this reprint of the one of the earliest and finest pieces of writing about the world's greatest breed - the Airedale. Thank you, Larry.

Bryan Cummins
Bolton, Ontario
May 8, 1998

TABLE OF CONTENTS

FOREWORD

A number of books have been published on the Airedale; so many, indeed, that the reader may ask, "Why another?" The query is justifiable under the circumstances.

The aims of the author of this book have been, however, to investigate those by-paths hitherto but little trodden by his predecessors. While he endeavors to present a comprehensive history of the breed from its origin to the present date, to point out the leading winners at bench shows and to give the stories of outstanding families and individuals, the keynote of this book is that the Airedale is primarily a dog for real use in any sphere where one may wish to place him.

He was evolved from an allround sporting and general utility dog and he is intended to remain such even in this day of numerous bench shows, if he is bred right and brought up properly. He is the dog par excellence for the sportsman who can keep but one to fit all purposes; he is the guardian of the home, and the playmate of the children; he is the watchful automobile dog and above all he is the farmer's dog; as useful for herding cattle, sheep or swine as he for hunting squirrels, rabbits or upland game.

It is the hope of the author that the breeder of many years may find some information in these chapters on Airedale history and genealogy that may interest him, but it is his still greater desire that the novice may, by a study of these pages, be able to breed or buy the kind of dog that he wishes to own; whether it is for show, for sport, for home guardian or a dog for allround work on a farm.

Dayton, Ohio The Author.

THE AIREDALE FOR WORK AND SHOW.
BY A.F. HOCHWALT.

INTRODUCTION

In the latter part of the seventies a group of boys living in a Southern Ohio town owned a dog named "Jack." That is, the dog came to them one day, a homeless wanderer, seemingly and evidently dropping in from nowhere. At least that is the supposition. He was seen around the haunts of these five boys for several days, making efforts to become acquainted or at least showing every evidence that he like to romp with boys, and before long he found a responsive willingness on the part of these red-blooded youths to take him in as one of their own company. Jack seemed to play no favorites: he was a diplomatic dog and a wise one. Sometimes he stayed at the home of one of the boys for a few days, then at the home of another for the same period or a little longer, and again at still another's; and so he made the rounds, for all five of the boys were to him a master and he obeyed each and every one with equal alacrity. He was treated with the same consideration by all of them and he was in every sense a community dog; that is, he belonged to the boys of this particular locality and came to be recognized as their property wherever the boys and the dog went. And Jack was loyal to his five masters, taking no commands from anyone but them and resenting any interference by lads not connected with this particular set. During vacation days when the sun beat down hot from out of the clear summer skies, Jack was always at the heels of one or the other boys. Usually all five were together and their destination was the old swimming hole down at the "Clay Banks." This was Jack's great delight. He would remain on shore and watch the clothes, it is true, and never once did he attempt to come into the water of his own volition, but it required only a word from one of the boys and in he was, disporting with them in all the unalloyed glee and pleasure that boys and dogs know how to make the most of. How he would go after sticks were thrown for him retrieve! How he would dive for stones and invariably go to the bottom and bring up the identical stone that was thrown in, delivering it to the one of the five who had given the command to fetch. Those were great days for boys and dog; days that passed all too quickly now that one looks back over a span of years to them, but they left memories that are pleasant to dwell upon. Jack knew his own boys under any and all conditions and woe to the stranger who dared to interfere with any of them! Woe also to the strange boy's dog who thought he had a fighter and "sicked" him on

Jack! Jack was not a quarrelsome dog; he never started a fight , but when it came to finishing one, he was generally the top dog. The community dog soon acquired a reputation among the dogs and the boys of the town and it was seldom necessary for him to fight for the honor of his five masters or for his own. So the summer days went by and fall came on. Here also Jack was always busy. As a rabbit dog, few could equal him routing them out and chasing them to a standstill. As a squirrel dog, he could spot them from afar, and when Jack's sharp bark was heard from away back in the deep oak woods, it was certain that he had one treed. How he could rout out woodchucks and other "varmints"! Verily, he was a pastmaster the way he grabbed them and with a toss or two put them out of misery. Along the old canal banks he dug rats and chased them back and forth across the water until he finally tired them out and caught them, and in fights with raccoons, he had some hard experiences on several occasions, but he never came out with discredit to himself. As a retriever of ducks he was equally expert, though it was only on rare occasions that he had an opportunity, for the community "Zulu" gun which the boys used in turns, only brought down a mallard or a pintail occasionally. On quail, however, Jack was clever. He could find them and point them, not with the style of the modern field trail winner, but with the accuracy of much more aristocrat dogs. And then on Saturdays and holidays how the boys would hitch him up to their wagons! He became the "draught horse" for them all, carrying loads in the little wagons that seemed to be almost impossible. In the winter, when the snow was on the ground and the boys went to the hill to coast, Jack enjoyed it as much as they, and after running down the hill alongside one of their sleds and barking gleefully all the way, he was there at the finish, taking the end of the rope between his strong teeth and literally pulling boys and sled all the way up the hill, incidentally gaining as much enjoyment out of it as the boys.

Jack was a mysterious dog; no one knew from whence he came; no owner ever claimed him and no one ever professed to know what kind of a dog he was until the boys decided among themselves the breed he belonged to. Some called him a shepherd dog, some thought him part setter, some said he was a rough-coated hound, until at last one of the community boys, a little better posted on canine matters than the others, having read of various breeds of dogs in an old book that came into his possession, christened him a "Siberian Terrier." The dictum was accepted by the four others as the most fitting breed for Jack to be affiliated with and henceforth he was a Siberian Terrier. No one questioned the name or breed, for certainly it sounded formidable as well as erudite.

Jack weighed about fifty-five pounds; he carried houndy ears with the regular side carriage, but set somewhat higher than the ordinary hound breeds carry theirs. His eyes were rather large and yellow, but he looked out of them intelligently and their general demeanor betokened intelligence. Long hair in whisker shape decorated his muzzle. His skull was flat and rather wide, but his head was not wedgy in the real sense and came down to a mouth that possesses a most punishing jaw. His coat was on the crinkly order, very dense, with a harsh outer coat and a soft, pily fur underneath. In color he was grizzle or greyish blue on the back and faded-out tan on the legs, underbody, feet, and head. Some might call tan, but it was more the color of a well-used piece of chamois leather. His tail was docked to the length of about three inches. He was a big-boned fellow, and altogether, to the stranger he looked formidable, not to say vicious, but Jack had a big heart underneath that uncouth exterior and no one knew it better than his five self-selected masters.

Jack might have been a mixture of a dozen or more breeds, as far as the boys knew. No doubt he was something like "Topsy" in "Uncle Tom's Cabin," he "jes' growed." If he had any pride of ancestry, no one knew it; not even himself, and as for leaving his name to posterity, Jack had numerous sons and daughters, the result of untold affairs d'amour, but none of them as far as anyone was aware, looked the least like him, which is only more evidence of the fact that like does not always beget like, especially when it comes to canines of heterogeneous composition as Jack no doubt was, and from whence his marvelous intelligence, courage and stamina came from.

The years passed; Jack grew old. The quintet of boys was dispersed; some going to other places, taking up commercial pursuits, others went to college: and so Jack disappeared as suddenly and mysteriously from that community as he entered it a number of years before. One of the boys attempted to get tidings of him when he came home on one of his vacations, but nothing definite was ever learned. Jack simply passed out of existence as dogs sometimes will; perhaps in obedience to the eternal law of survival of the fittest.

Fifteen or more years after those days just described I was passing down the aisles of a dog show in the East and saw several dogs that brought Jack back to my mind very vividly. I looked in the catalog and found they were called Airedale terriers. Their heads had more refinement of finish, it is true, but one of them in particular had the yellow eye of rather goodly dimensions and both had the grizzle backs and the washed-out tan, like old chamois leather.

The hardy Yorkshire working men in their endeavors to secure a dog good for all-round purposes succeeded in evolving one like Jack of our boyhood days, but whether or not they had any thoughts of ever popularizing him into a bench show idol I have my doubts. Certainly they had a variety of types those early days even after they once became popular in America. They have made a handsome dog of the Airedale now and he is one of the most popular breeds on the show bench. Whether they have retained the gameness and the all round utility of the "chance-bred dog" of fifty or more years ago, may be a question, but at all events the story of this "biggest and best of all terriers," as he called, is an interesting one. Years after seeing my first Airedales, when I thought them to be nondescripts, like the community dog Jack-during the early years of the present century, to be exact-I met C. P. Hubbard, of Atlantic, Iowa, at one of the Middle West shows. He had with him one of his big, handsome, gamy dogs that looked like fire in the face, and splintered steel in bone and muscle. He had the marks of refinement in breeding and still he was not bred down to effeminate uselessness. C. P. Hubbard was one of the early breeders in the West, and for that matter, one of the very early successful breeders of big-game hunting Airedales in the country. I traveled with him through the circuit of shows in the East and then back to Chicago, and during that time we looked at Airedales of every description; we talked Airedale day and night. The result was that I not only learned much about the breed, but I resolved to own some of the kind that are useful-and I have had them ever since.

CHAPTER I.

The Predecessors of the Airedale-The Otter Hound-The Old-Fashioned Rough-Coated Terrier-Other Supposed Crosses-What Early Authorities Thought of the Airedale.

No one knows positively from whence he came, nor where, but it is now generally conceded that the Airedale originated among the hardy Yorkshiremen living in the valley of the Aire and its tributaries. They are a sport-loving race, these Yorkshire mill workers and factory hands, and they must have their diversions just as the laird of the manor indulges in his sports and pastimes on a more elaborate scale. For that matter, one seldom encounters an Englishman who is not somewhat of a sport or sportsman, as the case may be, no matter what his walk in life.

In that well-populated locality of Yorkshire, the superficial observer would imagine that there is little opportunity for sport with dogs, but the residents of that country make the most of their opportunities. There, amid its fells and glens one finds the sweet and the foul mart, and among the rocky caverns of the broken-up country, the badger has its lair. Along the river banks one can always obtain a half day's excitement hunting the rats that frequent these water courses and also the otter which makes his home here. And then, not far away is the preserve of the laird and of a dark night when the moon is hidden, why, is there anything quite so exciting as to pick up a hare or two if it can be cunningly done by evading the game keepers? In his walks of a holiday the resident of that country would not be content without a tyke at his heels and then to cap it all, he must have a protector for the family, when he is away attending to his labors that bring to him and his the weekly pittance that goes toward feeding the babies-and the puppies.

A dog, to fill these varied requirements did not exist fifty years ago, and so these sport-loving workers proceeded to manufacture one; they produced a dog which as the saying goes, "could do anything any other dog can do and then lick the other dog."

The elements varied, no doubt, and we have no hesitancy in saying that no preconceived plan was laid out, for while the Airedale is the evolution of artificial selection, he is the result of more or less haphazard breeding just as the community dog Jack, referred to previously, was the result of unknown processes, with this difference, however, that the breeders in the Valley of the Aire continued on with their experiments until a real dog was manufactured that could reproduce himself with added improvements from generation to generation. Now, with less than fifty years of history, the Airedale has developed into the most popular breed in existence today. He has won the admiration of the populace because he is equally at home in any line of endeavor. As a retriever he has few equals, and when it comes to bringing wild fowl out of the water, few specialists in this line are his superiors. We, of course, refer to the dogs from the working strains; dogs that have been bred and brought up from generation to generation to do the all-round work of the all-round sportsman. Such a terrier is not only an excellent ratter, a good squirrel and rabbit dog, but a night hunter par excellence, and in his engagements with the raccoon he is there to the finish. In the Rockies, few dogs can equal him in his fights with mountain lions, the grizzly and various other varmints of that wild and mountainous country. In the South he is equally adroit in handling the black bears, the cats and other game of those latitudes. For upland shooting he points the quail, the pheasant or the prairie chicken and he retrieves them to a nicety.

On the farm he makes a splendid cattle dog, and when it comes to guarding the master's home, no dog twice his size can do as well. Such is the usefulness of the many-sided Airedale in his working aspect. On the show bench he brings down the admiration of the galleries, but whether or not the out-and-out bench show fanciers will create of him a breed suited for nothing but the sawdust ring is problematical, though it is quite certain that history will repeat itself in respect to the Airedale as it has with the pointer and the setter, in that the larger following will retain the interest in the usefulness of the dog rather than in his show qualities alone.

The fathers of the breed, when they began crossing with the idea of establishing an all round dog, probably had not the remotest idea of ever making a show dog of their product. They bred for utility and hard work; for dogs equally good on land and in water and the weather-resisting under coat, together with the outside pigskin-bristle jacket, made him impervious to water under any conditions, and to cover, no matter what its nature.

The generally accepted theory now is that the Airedale is the offspring of the otter hound, quite well known in Yorkshire fifty or more years ago, and a dark-coated, broken-haired terrier which was also indiginous to that locality a half century ago. Some say that these two breeds, and these two alone, are responsible for the Airedale, but these assertions are based more on assumption and speculation than on facts. Theories founded in such manner are more or less elastic and debatable.

Some claim that four or five breeds entered into the composition of the Airedale and that his predecessors are numbered among various breeds. No doubt this is nearer the truth than the first assumption. The harrier of that part of England was in those early days a hardy sporting dog with a harsh bristly jacket, and many of his characteristics are to be found in the Airedale of today, both temperamental and physical. Perhaps also the sheep dog of some variety was used as an occasional cross, for why the frequent occurrence of sheep-coated ones even at this day? In the earlier days, breeders were likely to get four or five different types in one litter that might have passed with impunity as so many different kinds of dogs, and had they so minded, they could have shown them on the bench under all these various breeds and probably won with them. This indicates the diversified lines of the Airedale and gives indication of his prehistoric days, but it also shows that the breed has no mongrel blood in it - that all the breeds used in his manufacturer were pure and well established, otherwise atavism would not have asserted itself with such pronounced activity.

The yellow eye, the houndy ear, the sheep coat, all have their significance and will crop out occasionally in the most carefully bred litter, but on the whole, it is surprising how in the remarkably short space of time a definite and sure type has been fixed in the Airedale. This much the bench show enthusiasts must be given credit for, and if they are only satisfied now let well enough alone and not endeavor to "fine" down the Airedale to the size of an Irish terrier or breed away his gameness by non-usage, then their deeds will go on record as a most successful feat of accomplishment.

Going back to those fountain-heads of the breed, the otter hound indubitably plays the most important part and it is quite certain that the Airedale inherits his great love for water from this prehistoric ancestor of his. The otter hound, during the middle of the past century, was kept in packs in Yorkshire; he was used to fight the otter in his own haunts, and water battles were a common thing; in fact, the principal thing in the otter hound's life.

It may be interesting at this date to read what "Stonehenge,' in his "Dogs of the British Islands," fourth edition, published in 1882, says of the otter hound: "Packs of these hounds possess a great advantage in being able to show sport during the summer, and by some it is alleged that otter hunting and angling may be made to dovetail with each other on alternate days of the week; but this scarcely seems practicable, inasmuch as the artificial preservation of the otter in any considerable numbers is antagonistic to the preservation of the fish on which he wastefully feeds. The angler consequently shows him no mercy, and on 'good rivers' the appearance of an otter is the signal for a foray against him with gun, trap and spear. In Cumberland, Devonshire, and some parts of Wales, there are however, many large brooks and embryo rivers, where the fish run too small for good sport with the rod, and yet afford the otter sufficient food. Here hunting him is prosecuted with great zest and no one can possibly object to such an amount of preservation as will not supply the adjacent districts with more than a casual visitor, whose appearance is soon signaled to the master of the nearest pack and a short shift is given him when once his 'spraint' is discovered there. . . . . The otter hound is no doubt a lineal descendant of the southern hound, with his coat roughened by a long process of selection and breeding. He evidently has not crossed with any breed other than the hound, or he would have lost some one or more of the characteristics peculiar to the hunting dog, either in shape of body, length of ear, style of hunting, or tongue. In these qualities he is the southern hound to the letter, with the addition of a rough coat, the history of which is not known. In many cases a pure-bred foxhound has been used with success against the otter. As far as the mere hunting goes, he fulfills the task set him admirably; but it has usually been found that in a very short time the wet tells on him, and he either becomes rheumatic or is attacked by disease of the chest in some shape.

"It is not the long hair of the true otter hound which saves him from these penalties, but *the thick under-coat, with which he is furnished* for the same purpose as the collies and the Dandie Dinmont terrier. He also strongly resembles the southern hound in his style of hunting, which is low and slow, but very sure, his nose being of the tenderest kind and often owning an air bubble or 'vent' at the distance of some yards. Like him he is apt to sit down on his haunches and throw his tongue with delight at first touching on a scent, in a most characteristic manner. . . . .

"The points of the otter hound are like those of the bloodhound, except as to coat, which should be composed of hard and long hair, somewhat rough in its lying, and mixed with a short, woolly under-coat, which serves to keep the body warm even when wetted by long emersion. The color differs also in not being confined to black-and-tan or tan, the former, however, being often met with."

From the above description the inference may easily be drawn that the otter hound gave to his new terrier representative many of his characteristics, as for instance the physical points in the matter of color, coat and ears; keenness of nose and gameness, were the other attributes that were handed down.

The terrier to which the evolution of this new breed is attributed is not a dog of the present time; in fact, from what can be learned, he was a goodly-sized animal, hard-bitten, game and energetic, with a coat and color that blended admirably with those of the otter hound. As for the other breeds entered, or were supposed to enter into the Airedale's composition that, of course, is mere speculation, although most of the authorities on the Airedale are agreed that a dash of bull terrier was used and perhaps also some of the sheep dog blood that was extant at the time, as well as the dash of harrier, which gave him his desire for rabbit hunting.

Thus this composite dog lived and flourished for a number of years, cherished only by those ardent supporters of the valley of the Aire. Bred for the purpose of an all-round dog, his owners had no desire to exploit him to the outside world, for in those early days there was little uniformly of type. His owners selected the individuals in making their matings and in thus doing it was invariably the dog which proved his utility in his many-sided calling that was used, which accounts for the intelligence of the breed for a composite of pure blood of various breeds will invariably beget intelligence.

At first the Airedale was known by various names. In the very early days he was called the "Waterside terrier" because he was used to work to waterways principally. This was all very well as long as he was known only as a local celebrity, but when the attention of the outside world began to be attracted, then, also, a new name was suggested. "Stonehenge" ventured the name of "Bingley Terrier," as this is the name of one of the principal towns in the vicinity of the Airedale's inception, and for a time this was used, but Bingley had no more right to the credit of the discovery of this new breed than any of the other towns in the valley of the Aire, and so jealousies grew out of this and the name was dropped. In 1883 a class was provided for this breed for the first time at the Birmingham show, and the new breed was known as the "Airedale or Waterside Terrier," which clung to him for two years, when the dual name was dropped and he became known as the Airedale terrier.

Official recognition was long in coming, however, and for a number of years the dog fanciers of Great Britain looked with suspicion upon this new large, so-called terrier; rightly denying him the name of terrier, for on account of his size he could not go to earth and was, therefore, not a terrier in the true acceptation of the term.

After a lapse of forty years it is rather amusing to read what "Stonehenge" said of this new breed as late as 1882, when his fourth edition of "Dogs of the British Islands" was published. "Stonehenge," or J. H. Walsh, was then the editor of the *London Field* and the leading authority on dogs in Great Britain. His views were naturally drawn from those of others, but it is quite clear that he went for his authority to those who were not much in favor of the "biggest and best terrier," for he received but scant praise and considerable condemnation from all the correspondents whom Stonehenge quotes. However, it only serves to illustrate that it is not always wise to make predictions, as did Mr. Walsh, for in the light of the unprecedented popularity that this breed now enjoys, his statements look ridiculous. For the benefit of the present-day readers I shall quote what is said of the Airedale in the work alluded to :

"Most visitors to the North of England shows must have been struck by the appearance of the large, rough-coated dogs which it is now the fashion to style Airedale terriers. The animal itself is simply the old Yorkshire waterside terrier, a little improved in looks by careful breeding, rechristened and brought before the public as the 'coming breed.' Many ideas are prevalent as regards the origin of the variety, but as it has for years been in the hands of a class of men whose pockets are not deep, and whose ideas of breeding up to a standard are somewhat vague, the Airedale ancestry is decidedly mixed and all hopes of disentangling the ramifications of the family tree are positively futile. In fact, a north-country authority on the breed writes as follows:

"'They (the Airedales) are the produce of sires and dams put together without any idea of breeding to a standard of excellence, but simply to produce a dog useful to the semi-rural sports suited to the tastes and pocketbooks of the somewhat impecunious class to which their admirers mostly belong. It is almost impossible to trace the origin of the breed to any particular source. Some districts claim to have a breed with nearly forty years' pedigree, but in several attempts that have been made to trace one of these strains, it has invariably happened that, beyond a generation of two, all trace of individual dogs get merged in so-and-so's breed, which were descended from a bitch from so-and-so, which was put to a dog from such a place and so on.'"

"In my opinion," continues Mr. Walsh, "both otter hound and Irish terrier are largely responsible for the existence of the so-called Airedale terrier, and no doubt the aid of some or other of the various breeds of terrier was enlisted from time to time. Many authorities aver that bull blood was used; others maintain that it was Scotch or Dandie blood that was resorted to; whilst others still declare that the animal is made up of an *olla podrida* of Scotch, Dandie, Bedlington and bull terrier, mixed up with the otter hound.

"So far, I am aware that my endeavors to supply information about the origin of the Airedale have not been attended with success, but upon the merits of the breed *I can speak with more authority, having had the benefit of the experience of a gentleman who took it up some short time back from the glowing accounts he had heard of its gameness and bottom*." (The italics are ours.) Mr. Walsh rambles on in his authoritative air: "The result was most mortifying. He could make nothing of the dogs and was heartily glad to get rid of them. Form what he tells me concerning Airedales, I have no doubt that they potter about the banks or a river and take water well, and that they will kill rats, which, as they scale from forty to fifty pounds, is not much in their favor. I will even go further and admit that specimens may be produced which will tackle a badger under protest; but not another step will I go in favor of the Airedales as a game, hard-bitten race.

"In support of my view, I shall quote from a letter just received from a gentleman who has owned Airedales, and whose opinions are identical with what I have stated above. He writes:

"'Airedale terriers are a failure. The result of my experiences of them is that I find them to have good noses, they will beat a hedge row, and will find and kill rats and rabbits and will work well with ferrets. They are good water dogs and companions, possessing a fair amount of intelligence. This is the sum total of their excellence. They came to me with a great reputation for gameness, but out or fourteen that I have personally tried at badger and fighting with a bull terrier of twenty-four pounds, I have never found one game-at least to my idea of the word.'

"This is strong speaking, but the gentleman's experiences corroborate every word that has gone before, and the woeful exhibition made by some Airedales when tried at a badger at Wolverhampton last January, was literally the laugh of the show.

"Summing up the merits and demerits of the breed, it must be said of the Airedale that his want of heart, his size, the diversity or types and the tendency to throw back in breeding, are great drawbacks which his fondness for water scarcely outbalances. Therefore, when we find, as I believe we can, that a wire-haired Scotch, Dandie Dinmont, Skye, Irish, or small bull terrier possesses all the gameness of the Airedale (in addition to which they take up one quarter the room and can go to earth) the question only remains, 'Why keep an Airedale?'"

Unfortunately Mr. Walsh does not give the names of his correspondents, hence his statements are like many others connected with this breed and practically all others: they are founded on hearsay. His writings of nearly fifty years ago prove several things, however. First, that as little was known of the origin of the breeder as later research has developed and secondly, that much depends upon what particular strain one has experience with. There are a number of strains in this country that are practically worthless as far as working dogs are concerned because they have been bred from probably just such dogs as Stonehenge describes-dogs that were intended to improve bench type and consequently their real utility was lost sight of for generation after generation. We have dogs of this type in the United States today, but on the other hand, we have strains that are as game as any breed that ever lived and we are wondering what Stonehenge might say were he able to witness some of the work of Airedales in the packs of some of the guides of the Rocky Mountains or those in use in the South or those with the Rainey Exposition in Africa. Perhaps he might wish to revise his opinion of the Airedale as expressed in 1882.

No doubt the bad character given to the Airedale by Stonehenge and a few of his contemporaries was greatly due to not knowing the breed. A dog may be ferocious and still not be game when it comes to a finish fight and he may be vicious and still lack the real quality of courage. The Airedale being a dog slow to take offense, and holding himself aloof from the ordinary fighting dog, gained a reputation for lack of gameness mainly on this account. This was, and still is, the outstanding character of the Airedale. He is not, figuratively speaking, going about with a chip on his shoulder, but the close observer will note the smoldering fire in the dog's eye when danger is near and once drawn into combat that fire is like the sparks from a charged battery. Occasionally there is a coward among his kind, but the average Airedale, once he is aroused, will fight to the finish whether his antagonist be a raccoon, a lynx, a jaguar, a lion, a bear or one of his own race.

CHAPTER II.

The Dawn of Authentic Airedale History-Some of the Early Pillars.

It was in the seventies that the hardy Yorkshiremen began holding shows at Otley and in other towns in the locality where the new breed had his inception, and these events were keen in the extreme, but even prior to this, these industrial workers of that locality succeeded in having considerable sport in matching their dogs one against the other, in a species of field meet which consisted of working a brace of dogs for a given distance along the banks of the rivers infested with rats. In this sport they gained considerable pleasure and excitement and of a Saturday afternoon when a well-known pair of dogs were put down, the countryside turned out to see the work. The dogs were worked by their owners or handlers along the banks under a set of rules formulated for the purpose; as for instance, the dog spotting a hole that eventually yielded a rat scored two points. A ferret was then placed in the hole and when the rodent bolted into the water the sport was on. The dog making the kill scored one point. Thus if one dog of a brace scored on marking, his competitor still had a chance of scoring one point on the kill, but the excitement was great as the two dogs worked down along the stream for a distance of a mile or more. Sometimes it was one and then the other which scored. Thus the points were run up, frequently, at the conclusion of the working distance, the score was a tie, when another heat was necessary to decide the winner and these mill workers, though short of purse in comparison with those who followed field trials of bird dogs, frequently wagered their week's earnings on the result of the matches. It may, therefore, be imagined how important these matches were, to not only the owners, but to others as well, for each dog had his admirers.

It was at the shows, however, where the crowd gathered and several of those Yorkshire towns held regular events for their favorite breed. It may be taken for granted that the work of the adjudicator was not an easy one, for around that ring were men and women, who probably knew as much about the breed, if not more, than some of the judges, and it not infrequently happened that a judge was compelled to make a hasty retreat after giving a decision that did not meet with the approval of the crowd. Those lusty mill workers of the Aire Valley were not the class to stand on ceremony on such occasions. They took themselves and their dogs seriously and it was all that the officials could do sometimes to keep order. Real Airedale history began making, however, when the regular show-giving clubs recognized the Airedale terrier as a breed. As stated in the previous chapter, it was at Birmingham in 1883 that classes were provided for the breed under the name of Airedale or Waterside terriers. It was not until 1886 that the English Kennel Club recognized this big, strapping terrier from the North as a distinct breed, but in that year the stud book was opened for them and something like two dozen were registered, of which all but three were pedigreed. The show fancy began taking them up after this, and it is surprising what rapid improvement resulted in a few years. The heads became longer and leaner, the ears smaller, the coats closer and less woolly, but in breeding for show points sometimes other qualities were sacrificed, as for instance, in the endeavor to get the harsh pig-bristle texture and the rich black and tan, the pily, water-resisting undercoat, which has always been considered the leading physical attribute of the Airedale, began disappearing, though sometimes the other extreme was encountered and dogs of the decided sheep coat texture were coming more and more into evidence. Breeders soon realized, however, that to breed good-looking coats, the best results came from bitches which were nearly smooth and thus a happy medium was struck. Size was also beginning to suffer and the breeders of the south of England were perhaps mainly responsible for this, endeavoring to breed quality into the dogs at the sacrifice of many of the working qualities. It is right here at this early period that the handwriting was seen on the wall; that is, the line of demarcation between the working and the show dog began to appear. Naturally, it is easier to breed a good little one than a good big one, and the breeders in the southern part of the Tight Little Island were going in strong for the smaller ones. They were careful, however, to keep in mind that the Airedale was a sporting dog by breeding and instincts; furthermore, they were just as painstaking in keeping this thought before the public, but nevertheless most of the South of England breeders lost sight entirely of what the breed was created for up north and bred for the show bench alone. No doubt their endeavors had the advantage of fixing type, for which we should be thankful at the present day, for it is remarkable how rapidly the looks of the Airedale improved, especially after the first ten years from the time he was admitted into the stud-book fold as a regular breed, but there is such a thing as going too far along this improvement line and in some of the families of the present day we can already detect the signs of deterioration, for sporting instincts have been sacrificed for type, which is only natural when one thinks of strains which have been bred in bench show kennels, generation after generation, never having the slightest opportunity for real work, until the characters most useful in the Airedale have become latent.

During those early days an Airedale Terrier Club was formed which did a certain amount of good for the breed, although it was somewhat lethargic in many respects, allowing matters to run in a rather go-as-you-please fashion. The South of England Airedale Terrier Club, organized some time later, was composed of a more active set and probably did more to popularize the breed in its own country as well as in America than all of the work of the early pioneers. Many of these South of England members, however, were dealers; they exploited their wares and sent them to all parts of the world especially to the United States or "Dollar Land," as W. J. Phillips expresses it in his book on the Airedale; and Dollar Land it was to them, for we doubt not that many a dog was sold that perhaps might be worth all that obtained for him, but on the other hand, more than one unsuspecting native of this so-called Dollar-land bought a "pig-in-the-poke" from these astute buyers and sellers, who knew how to extol their wares, "counterfeits," though many of them were.

The average veteran in any sphere is prone to turn his lamps in the reverse direction and look upon the achievements or the things of the past in a roseate, reminiscent light that makes present-day ideals look ordinary in comparison; so it is with the old field trial man when he makes a mental comparison of the dogs of thirty years ago with those of today; so its is with the average fancier of the other breeds; the more distant the perspective, the more concentrated is the light of the present thrown upon things of the past! With the Airedale, however, one does not find much of this. His history is still too recent to create a perspective, and as one looks back in the dawn of the breed's beginnings he recalls very well such dogs as Airedale Jerry, Tommy Tucker, and later, Rustic Twig, Tanner, Young Tanner, Newbold Fritz, Rustic Lad, Venom, Vixen and Rustic Kitty, the latter becoming a great influence on the breed. But in recalling the appearance of the dogs enumerated no one who saw them would have the temerity to say that they were better dogs, from the viewpoint of type and conformation, than are best of today. One has only to scrutinize the pictures of some of the old timers, to note the improvement. For instance, in

Stonehenge's book "Dogs of the British Islands," there is a cut made from a drawing of the Airedale bitch, Fracture, supposed to be a typical representative of her tribe. Long and low, large in eye, too much stop and weak in foreface would describe her at the present time. Newbold Test and Vixen II were great dogs in their day, although from a scrutiny of the illustrations that are now to be found of them one would readily agree that there has been a vast improvement. Newbold Test, however, is a dog which occupies an important place in Airedale history, for he proved to be a great influence on the breed, this blood being valued not only by the bench show element, for the good results obtained in fixing type, but also by the sporting element, for through him came gameness and fighting ability. The sire of Newbold Test was Guess, a houndy dog, rather full in skull and sheep-coated, so it is said, but Jenny his dam, was a terrier all over; and while on this subject I wish to digress long enough to say that my experience has been that the small typy bitches with fiery eye, and the characteristic varminty expression; those with sparse, not to say smooth coats, usually brought best results. Hockwell's Tess, a small good-coated, good-colored fiery bitch, game as a pebble and ready for anything at any time, produced several good ones in her short period of life. When bred to Teddy the Terror, a dog representing all that a working Airedale should be, she produced on the two occasions that she was mated with him, litters in which not a bad one was to be found. This was particularly true of her daughters, among them being Peggy the Rough Neck, which afterwards, when bred to Caswell Warrior, produced the good War Bond, which won so consistently during the season of 1920 and '21, and at this writing her winning career is far from being over. I have found that the more fiery and terrier-like the dams are the more likely one is to get type as well as working qualities, for it has always been my method to use good large, heavy-boned dogs on these small bitches and the results were always as anticipated.

Reverting again to Newbold Test, he was bred to Chesterfield Kitty another terrier-like bitch, on the small order, from which union came a bitch called Rosamond. Cholmondeley Briar bred to Rosamond produced Briar Test, and the appearance of this dog marks an epoch in the history of the Airedale. Cholmondeley Briar was a great dog in every respect himself and was never beaten on the bench in his early days; in fact, it was only very late in life when he was obliged to give away to the younger and fresher Clonmel Marvel, of which more anon. In 1891, Mr. H. T. Bryans, then one of the leading breeders of the Airedale in England, had the proud distinction of winning with his team over eleven other teams of various terriers in the variety classes at the Crystal Palace show. It was the first time that an Airedale team ever won in variety classes and naturally not only did the owner of the dogs feel much elated, but all lovers of the Airedale as well. The dogs with which Mr. Bryans achieved this victory were Cholmondeley Briar, Briar Test and Cholmondeley Bridesmaid. In those days Mr. Bryans was at the height of his fame as a breeder and be it said to his credit that he did more toward fixing and maintaining type and terrier quality than any other man of that period, for he was a breeder first of all, which is in direct contradistinction to the dealers who spring up later on, frequently shows for "pickups" which they often bought for a song and sold to American fanciers at prices that in those days were considered fabulous. It is no wonder that some of the Airedale dealers of a decade or two ago named the United States "Dollar Land," for to them it meant an easy living.

Briar Test was always considered one of the best terriers of his day, but like many men who, though they have the ability, never attain their highest ambitions, just so it was with Briar Test; he never became a champion, although he was undoubtedly better than many of his contemporaries which achieved this distinction on far less merit. Briar Test sired many good sons and daughters, but perhaps the greatest of his scions was the wonderful (for his day and ours) Master Briar. It was in the year 1897-the Jubilee Year of Queen Victoria-when this event transpired. The dam of Master Briar was Betty, a long, lean-headed bitch, well filled up before the eye, well set, small ear, varminty in expression and terrier in every movement. In size she was scarcely larger than an Irish terrier, but in temperamental qualities she had the stamp of her family. Betty was by a dog called A. P. Bruce, which was by Rock. Bruce is described as a big dog with good utility legs and feet and a nice length of head as heads went in those days. In respect to size, Master Briar resembled his sire and not his dam. This is an experience I could also always depend upon when breeding to such bitches of the type of Betty, but too much of this kind of breeding would naturally result in offspring possessing all the essential fire and terrier character, perhaps, but many would be weedy, undersized specimens; therefore, one must of a necessity be on his guard. It is because of the persistent following of this theory that some of our strains are now too small. Master Briar, however, was just the kind of a dog to appeal to the man looking for a real man's dog. He was slow to mature, it is true, and under a year old-in fact until he was practically past two-one did not realize just what manner of dog he was, but that also is a well-known fact; dogs that are slow to mature, usually wear well and Master Briar was one of the kind which over in England they call "lasters." Other dogs whose history in this respect was similar to that of Master Briar were: Colne Crack, Willow Nut, Clonmel Bedrock, Tone Master Piece, known in this country as York Masterpiece, Tone Jerry and probably half a dozen more whose names do not come to mind at the moment. Master Briar at ten ears of age looked as clean as a two-year-old. He stood on the best of legs, straight as the proverbial gun barrels, with bone and substance that were the delight of the sportsman accustomed to seeing the Airedale in his battles with the big game of this country. There was no suggestion of weakness about the pasterns fore or aft, the bone seemingly coming down without break to the toes; his feet were small and cat-like and even in his old age his shoulders were clean. In this respect one finds an Airedale occasionally which never goes heavy in the shoulders, and a dog that I have in mind as I write is Teddy the Terror, which at seven years of age, is as clean as a yearling in every way and Teddy is a lineal descendent of Master Briar on both sides of the house. In ribs, Master Briar could not be excelled and in back, which was short and sound, with loin and quarters to match, he was perfection. For the size of his bone and his substance generally, perhaps Master Briar would have looked better with just a trifle more length of leg, but taking the dog as a unit, he was a remarkably well-made-one. His head was level; long from occiput to the tip of the nose, the right proportions from the corner of his eyes to the end of his muzzle, and his foreface was well filled-in. The eyes were small and well set, with all of that much-desired smoldering fire, ready to leap into flame at the slightest pretext. These attributes are the marks of prepotency and have gone down through generations to the present day in certain lines of Airedale breeding. Another character which, however, was not always handed down, was his coat of close, hard texture, his deep, black saddles and his rich tan markings. It is true that Master Briar's offspring in many instances displayed the sheep coats, but when bred to certain lines, the harsh texture of coat was retained in the progeny down through generation after generation. Still another quality that has come through him is his powerful loin and quarters, which in an Airedale of the working type is so essential and which many of the present-day Airedales are losing, a fact that is very apparent in looking over some or our winners of the period, for it is easy to note how many of them possessing grand heads, fronts and coats are lacking in the most necessary quality of the working dog, viz., strength of back, loin and quarters. The lineal descendants of Master Briar, however, even to this day still possess this character. The soft coats which were transmitted largely through this family were greatly overcome when the daughters of Clonmel Marvel appeared on the horizon and were bred to Master Briar. It was through this cross that Clonmel Monarch was produced, but this is coming into the period of the middle age history of the Airedale, and connecting link between the early days and the modern times; and before touching upon this we must take a brief survey of other families which were contemporaneous with the dogs of the family just described. Among these the name of Warfdale Rush is vividly recalled, for his name appears in quite a few pedigrees of the present time, but as a direct factor in the struggle for improvement he was not a great contender. Warfdale Rush was a dog of good color and type, but rather houndy in ear carriage and general appearance; a characteristic, however, that was by no means uncommon in those days.

Clip was another dog which gained considerable notoriety in his way. It was because of this dog that a miniature riot was almost created. This was at the annual Otley show, when the judge put up Clip over dogs which some of the ringsiders thought should have beaten him and in that district, for Otley is in the heart of the Airedale country, the mill hands and industrial workers who make up the greater part of the audience do not stand on ceremony and the judge was obliged to beat a hasty retreat, although most of the cooler heads deplored the demonstration and admitted that the judge was not far wrong in placing Clip up. It is said by those who knew Clip well that he was a dog with splendid dark eyes which he transmitted to all of his progeny and that he did much toward stamping out the hound characteristics which were so prevalent during that period. In a direct line perhaps he never succeeded in producing a specimen of the first flight unless it was Marsden Rush, not so well remembered at this date, but he was a very game dog. Rush and Clip were owned for a time by the firm of Mills and Buckley, those famous purveyors of the Airedales to American buyers under the kennel prefix of Clonmel.

Clonmel Marvel was a purchase of Messrs. Mills and Buckley and eventually the dog found his way to America-at a long price. But Marvel did much for the breed when his daughters were crossed on Master Briar as previously indicated. Clonmel Marvel was by Clipper, a son of old Clip, just referred to. There seems to be considerable haze associated with this dog, Clipper. A dog was brought over to this country about that period know as Hastings Clipper, and many on this side have claimed that he was the sire of Clonmel Marvel, but it seems that there was another Clipper over in England which never came to America, and he is the sire of the dog in question. The Clipper sent to America was known as Hastings Clipper, but the breeding of his dam is entirely different from the Clipper which is really the sire of Clonmel Marvel.

Clonmel Marvel had a romantic history and much as has been said of the science and the perspicacity of English breeders, most of which is also true, here is one instance where a very high-class dog was produced through accident, and Holland Buckley tells it on himself in his book, "The Airedale Terrier." It seems that a bitch by the name of Cholmondeley Mona was shown by a farmer named F. C. Brown at a small show held at Lewisham. At this same show was Holland Buckley with his dog Crack Royal and a Mr. Russell with the dog Clipper previously referred to. Crack Royal won first, Clipper, second and Cholmondeley Mona, third. Mr. Brown, the owner of Mona, went to Buckley after the judging and desired to make arrangement with him to breed Mona to Crack Royal. Mr. Buckley, however, was only concerned in the jingle of the coin of the realm and would not deviate from the stud fee demanded for Royal's services, which evidently was too high for the owner of Mona. As a consequence, Mr. Brown arranged with the owner of Clipper, at a much lower fee, to breed to that dog, and thus considerable Airedale history was changed because of a money consideration, for in course of time Cholmondeley Mona whelped a litter of nine from which Mr. Brown selected one to show at Reading, more to test out the quality of the litter than with any idea that he had a real flyer. As a matter of fact, he selected a three pound selling class for this puppy, now seven months old, to make his debut in. The puppy was called and entered as Warfield Victor and he won second place in the class. The puppy, it is said, refused to show, which the reason he did not go to the top, but he was promptly recognized as a good one by "Jack" Holgate, than whom no keener man exists in England, when it comes to picking "Diamonds in the rough,"in the shape of winning dogs; and many an honest penny has he thus turned, not only in selling these pickups at home, but many more of them at still longer figures here in America. Brown, realizing that he had a better dog than he supposed, wished to keep the dog when he saw how keen Holgate was, but the latter claimed the puppy at the catalog price and took him home where he soon put him into real shape. The sequel is told in Buckley's own words: "In twenty-four hours Mr. Roysten Mills and myself had an imperative summons to come to Surbiton and buy the best Airedale alive. We had in the past seen so many 'best alives' that our frame of mind leaned strongly to the pessimistic. Five minutes, however, sufficed to change the ownership for the largest cheque ever written in this country for an Airedale and never was a better investment made, for after one or two setbacks, Marvel downed every dog or bitch in the strongest competition, frequently being the recipient of cups for best dog in the show." While still under the ownership of the Clonmel firm, Marvel won eighteen championships in England, among his victories being his defeat of Cholmondeley Briar, but this was when the latter dog was already well up in years and Marvel was at his best.

J. L. Lorillard proved to be the American buyer of Clonmel Marvel, at which time he also purchased Ch. Clonmel Sensation and Clonmel Veracity, which three figure in quite a number of our American pedigrees, Marvel in particular doing much for the breed on this side.

Clonmel Marvel, in addition to the quality and type with which he impressed his progeny, also was a factor in reproducing gameness and the sporting instinct. Himself a terrier all over, he was strong and powerfully built for his inches, and his descendants, which have been continued as working dogs, have all proved good. Personally I always like to see an Airedale pedigree with an abundance of Marvel's blood in the background, for it stands for all that an Airedale should be and, as previously stated, when this blood was given the opportunity to show its quality in the business of big game hunting it seldom failed to make good. Of course, there were many of Marvel's descendants in this country that were relegated to bench shows only and they had no opportunity to prove their prowess in hunting, but this fighting blood of Marvel's was only latent in these strains and always asserted itself in later descendants when fused with the strains that have been kept for work as well as show purposes.

It was about this time that the bitch, Dumbarton Lass, was unearthed. She was shown at Woolwich in a rather rough and unkempt form, but the judge was Fred Gresham, who promptly recognized her worth and put her up in her classes. She was promptly claimed at her catalog price of twenty-five pounds by A. E. Jennings, who showed her regularly and won consistently. Lass was somewhat soft in coat and rather light in color, but aside from this she was difficult to fault. Dumbarton Lass passed into the hands of Stuart Noble at the dispersal of Mr. Jennings' kennel and from this time, for a short period, Mr. Noble had one of the very strong kennels of England, among which at the time were such dogs as the aforesaid Dumbarton Lass, Master Briar, Arthington Tinner and Briarwood, all of which became champions in short order, except the latter, but he had all the qualities of a champion and it was only through a series of untoward circumstances that he did not become one. Dumbarton Lass with a number of others eventually became the property of the Canadian fancier, Joseph A. Laurin, of Colne fame, and it may be said here, that Mr. Laurin spent many pounds in bringing over the best to be found in England. For a number of years the Colne Kennels, of Montreal, were the leaders in America. And so we might go on indefinitely relating the activities of those breeders who assisted in making the Airedale the leading breed in the United States as well as in England.

Another bitch which was quite a factor in Airedale history about this time was Bath Lady and her name stands for much, even in present-day pedigrees. She became the dam of a number of good ones among them being Briarwood, previously mentioned. Hyndman Briar was the sire of Briarwood, the latter being a son of Willow Nut. Hyndman Briar, it may be said in passing, was a very superior terrier, but for some reason he never got anything of real first-class merit except out of Bath Lady.

During that period of the middle nineties, Airedale breeders were springing up everywhere in England and one of the kennels which deserves particular mention is that of Leaver Brothers, of Blackburn, who adopted the Crompton prefix which was destined to play such an important part in the making of Airedale history. Still another well-known prefix was the Barkerends of Herbert Croft, of Bradford, Yorkshire, but it was perhaps the fusion of the Crompton and the Midlands which were the leading factor toward bringing the Airedale down to modern times; at least their part in the drama is an important one. However, there were still others which figured conspicuously in the evolution of the breed, as for instance the Legrams, the Rustics, the Huckleberrys, the Tones and the Primroses-all kennel prefixes that are well known to breeders, with possibly half a dozen more lesser lights.

This brings us down to the "Middle Ages of the Airedale" and the epoch when American interests began taking such a decided place and proved to be such a lucrative market for the English breeders.

CHAPTER III.

The Middle Ages of the Airedale.

We now come to that period, which as a matter of convenience might be designated the "Middle ages of the Airedale." It is an epoch in the breed's history that was critical. I have already shown in earlier chapters that some of the leading writers, among them "Stonehenge," did not take kindly to this new breed and great influence that he was upon the kennel mind of England and even America, it is but natural that the breed did not become popular rapidly, but remained in the hands of but a few. The Airedale Terrier Club, formed in the North of England, was lethargic in its movements. It did little to counteract the sentiment and prejudice that was created through writers who were either ignorant of the merits of the breed or willfully misrepresented it, and so, even though a small coterie of the faithful continued on and produced a few good ones it was not until the formation of the South of England Terrier Club, that the breed obtained a decisive impetus. Through the efforts of such enthusiasts, however, as G. H. Elder, Holland Buckley, E. Roysten Mills and a few others, this club began to draw attention and did more toward attracting people to this breed than anything that could have been done. The attention of the world was thus brought to the new breed from the North, and America was a large part of that world. Messrs. Mills and Buckley formed a kennel partnership, which under the kennel prefix of "Clonmel" did a thriving business in the States as well as in other countries, but it was to the land of the Stars and Stripes that this enterprising firm Airedale dealers directed their main efforts. I say dealers in the real sense, for they were buyers and sellers rather than breeders, and they were constantly on the qui vive for "pickups" in their own country which they could turn over to fanciers in America at a good price, all of which was perfectly legitimate and proper, and even though some may sneer at the method and remark that the ethics of sportsmanship are thus lowered, it is quite certain that the business acumen of this firm of Clonmel did more toward popularizing the Airedale in all parts of the world than any one, or any other force could have done. One thing is quite certain. The firm was after good, sound American dollars and they held nothing back.

They sold the best in the land as well as the worst, but to their credit, be it said, that they seldom sent over a "rotter." America was stocked with the best to be had to such an extent that many breeders in England began to fear for the future of the breed. In this respect English Airedale breeders and dealers were different from their bird-dog-loving brethren. The latter-it is quite well known by their own assertions-sent over to America their culls, keeping the best ones for themselves with an eye to the future of the breed at home, but Airedale fanciers were different. Nothing was too good to send to America provided the price was paid, and Americans were glad to pay the price for the best.

Aside from the class who bought Airedales for show purposes only, was that other element; those who hunted big game. The fact that the Airedale was primarily a sporting dog was never lost sight of, neither was this part of the publicity neglected by the English promoters who were so instrumental in selling dogs to this country, consequently there were two separate and distinct markets for the breed. Conflicting statements concerning the dog were heard in respect to his qualities as a big game fighter, but the preponderance of evidence from reliable and experienced huntsmen seemed to be greatly in his favor, hence many breeders, especially those in the West, began to breed for the working qualities primarily, and that is why the line of demarcation became greater in this country than in England. We are not, at present, concerned in this phase of the Airedales' history, however, let us, on the other hand, trace the progress made through that period. We have already referred to Bath Lady, which in England was called "a gold mine," because of her prepotent qualities in producing winners. One of her daughters which went to fame quickly was Champion Clonmel Kitty, which was bought by Holland Buckley for the small sum of four pounds and was sold afterwards for many times that price. Clonmel Kitty was a terrier in every respect and one of the type which last well. Although bearing the Clonmel prefix, it was G. H. Elder who was responsible for campaigning and making a champion of her. While on the subject of great bitches of that period, there was also Chippenham Daisy, which won frequently, and Clonmel Veracity, which but for the fact that she was almost impossible in the ring, due to the fact that she failed utterly to show, might have won considerably more than she did. Coming somewhat later was Walton Victory, bred by Marshall Lee, who at the time was president of the South of England Airedale Terrier Club. Victory was by Master Briar and her dam was none other than the famous Bath Lady, already referred to as the peerless mother of winners. At Birmingham she met an exceptionally good lot of bitches and the judge had a long time deciding, finally, however, awarding her the coveted honor over Gainsborough Duchess and Rock Ferry Vixen. Duchess was considered a good one with the exception that she was somewhat masculine in head. Vixen was described as having remarkably good shoulders, splendid legs and feet and an excellent coat of proper texture and color. Delph Girl was another good bitch coming out at Otley in 1902, which really brings us up to modern times. Later on she came to America. Claverhouse Enchantress is another which played an important part in history, becoming the mother, among others, of Dumbarton Sceptre, but her story also comes into the modern period.

It was Mr. Elder who was responsible for the Tone Kennels, from which place many noted ones came, among them several which in this country proved to be quite successful. Theodore Offerman it was who imported Tone Masterpiece, which on our show benches was known as York Masterpiece. Among the others that Mr. Elder brought into prominence were Champion Tone Jerry, Champion Tone Crack, Champion Tone Chief and Champion Tone Regent, nearly all of which figure in our later pedigrees. Among the north of England breeders of that period was E. Bairstow, whose prefix, Rustic, was very much in evidence up to within a few years ago. Among the dogs coming from these kennels that were best known are Champion Rustic Kitty, Rustic Lad, Rustic Twig, Rustic Twilight and others.

From the north country also hailed J. R. Cooper, who had among his winners such well-known ones as Champion Rock King, Champion Rock Princess and Champion Rock Salt. The latter had a number of friends and admirers, but there seemed to be a great difference of opinion concerning him. He made his debut as a show dog at Derby under Marsden Midgley, when he was still but a rough, unfinished puppy. However, he was promptly recognized, which at the time created some comment, but Mr. Marsden's estimate of him was borne out by later events, for he was shown fearlessly and beat the best of them with the possible exception of Clonmel Monarch. The principal criticisms against Rock Salt was that, while he was a good, sound dog in every way, he seemed to be lacking in real terrier character. A native of Otley was (Mr.) Maude Barrett and Otley was the storm center, as it were, of the Airedale terrier, for in this town the great shows of the early days were held. Mr. Barrett did much for the success of these shows not only in promoting the interests of the fixture but also in promoting the breed. He owned some good terriers himself at various times, among others being Champion Otley Chevin and

Champion Tommy Tucker.

While the North was responsible for the production of the Airedale terrier and made a brave fight toward his recognition and the upholding of the breed's traditions it was the South which went on constantly toward improvement in looks, perhaps at the expense of working qualities, but it must be admitted that type should be fixed in any breed, particularly in a new one, as the Airedale unquestionably was at that period. It is also quite true that sometimes in the mad desire for type and show points there is danger of sacrificing some of the physical as well as the temperamental qualities. Whether or not the Airedale suffered by too much improvement just at this time is a mooted question, but the fact remains that at least in some strains, quality (so-called) was becoming greater, but size, bone and substances were suffering along with the inherent qualities of the Airedale-namely, gameness and sporting instincts. Thus, fortunately for the breed, some of the fanciers, particularly those of the North, still kept in mind that the dog was originated primarily as an all round working breed and the extremests both ways met on a common plane with the result that neither could go too far.

The South of England, however, outstripped the North in numbers of kennels and perhaps in financial resources, hence it was the southern breeders who began to dominate the situation to a great extent, although there were many among these who also kept the fact before them that the dog must be, first of all constructed on such lines so as to be able to do the work for which he was originally designed.

The Broadlands Kennels, owned by A. Clarkson, were among the southern kennels which for a time were very successful. Among the dogs emanating from here being Broadlands Bashful, Broadlands Royal Descendent, Broadlands Bunkum and others nearly as good. Royal Descendent coming along among the later ones, he being a son of Clonmel Monarch, which comes into Airedale history at the beginning of a new epoch, especially as far as this country is concerned.

The prefix, Rock Ferry, was also frequently seen along about this period, and at one time it was a name to conjure with; the kennel bearing it being operated by Messrs. Baines & Dodwell. Among the dogs that they brought out was Accrington Rough, described as an extraordinary good youngster, possessing shoulders and neck that were far above the average. The owners, however, did not keep him long and very early in his career sold him to an Australian fancier, where he said to have been a success at stud, as far as this was possible with his limited opportunities. It is freely stated that had he come to the States instead, his name would have lived a long time in the records of winners.

Studholme is another name that was seen more or more or less and again coming along at the present time, but in those days the dogs represented were Studholme Spark, the sire of Legrams Prince and Briarwood, both well known, especially the latter, in this country, although they were never in the first flight as far as shows were concerned. The dog himself did not wear well, as is the case with some Airedales. As a young dog he was attractive and well put up, but grew coarse with age. Despite this, however, he became the sire in England of Broadlands Bashful and Dumbarton Rattler.

In 1896 Studholme Sherry began a rather brilliant career, but after that one season he did little more on the bench. Nevertheless, despite the fact that as a show dog he was unable to hold his own with the company that was out at the period in which he thrived, this dog would have been a great influence on the breed had he been used at stud as frequently as his merit and his blood lines warranted. He was by Briar Test out of Red Linnet, and traced back in direct lines to Rustic Rushlight, the dog which did so much for color and coat to say nothing about the game qualities that he transmitted. Marsden Rush, also of this breeding, left England before his worth was recognized even by his owners, Messrs. Mills and Buckley, his ultimate destination being Ceylon.

Banes Condy, of "Huckleberry" fame, gained considerable notoriety principally through Huckleberry Lass, which in marked contrast to Briarwood, was an extremely good "laster" and at six years old took the championship with something to spare at the Bristol show, despite the fact that she was in a large company of much younger competitors. She was not one of the kind that one would go into ecstasies over, but nevertheless it was just as difficult to fault her seriously. She was of good type and what is more for a bitch, she had an abundance of bone and substance. E. L. R. Hoskins was the owner of Legrams Lass and Lance Corporal, the latter becoming a champion, but he was severely handicapped with an exceedingly light eye, which should at all times be a bar to real first-flight company. As a matter of fact, in my own experience I always thought the light eye an abomination, for of all the characters that are easily transmitted and difficult to breed out, it is this very same light eye. This I found, not only held good in Airedales, but in pointers and setters as well.

Still another kennel that was going along consistently, if not with the blare of trumpets that heralded the sales of some of the others, was that of W. H. Chandler. His kennels were not of the meteoric kind to flash upon the kennel world firmament with temporary brilliancy only to die out after a short life. On the other hand, the Primrose prefix which Mr. Chandler adopted proved a lasting one. It was as early as 1887 that he became interested in the breed and from that time on, for a number of years, Primrose Airedales were very much in evidence and as a breeder he was one of the most consistent in England. With a definite purpose in view he hewed along those lines and established a strain that for uniformity of type and excellence stood well with any in their native country and what is more, the Primroses in addition to their excellent quality, bred up to size and substance, together with that gameness and terrier fire that is so essential in the breed. We could name a long list from these kennels, but it is only necessary to say that he began to find a place in the sun with that good bitch, Young Primrose, which won three firsts and special for the best Airedale bitch at Crufts in 1889. Young Primrose in her very first litter produced Cholmondeley Bridesmaid, which won two challenge certificates and more than fifty firsts during her career, and so on the Primrose success continued. Among others of the earlier days was Cholmondeley Byrony, Brigand, Nutcracker, Bottington of Clipstone, Admiral of Clipstone, Rajah of Clipstone, Champion Watlands Marvel, Primrose Rebound, Primrose Regent and many others which cover a span from the early days, down through the Middle ages and into the modern history of the breed.

One essential which Mr. Chandler always bore in mind and which seemingly was lost sight of by many breeders in both countries, is that first of all, the Airedale must, in addition to quality possess size and substance. Naturally, as I have pointed out frequently, it is easier to breed a good little one than a good big one, but the owner of the Primrose prefix always kept in mind that the Airedale was essentially a dog for hard work and in addition to type, he made it a rule to secure substance; this essential he never lost sight of. Take his Primrose Regent of more recent years, for instance. This dog is a short-backed, sound-bodied animal, with a wealth of bone, possessing excellent loin, quarters and stifles; the essentials for any dog that is to stand the wear and tear of mountain work in the West or the arduous labor of bear fighting in the cane brakes of the South. Mr. Chandler was called upon frequently to judge at various shows, but the fancy soon discovered that it was labor lost to bring the "quality weeds" which were becoming prevalent among certain strains, before him.

Writing of Mr. Chandler and the Primroses calls to mind one of his predecessors at whose lamp he lighted his own torch which was to diffuse its light over the Airedale world. This is none other than Colonel E. Newton Deakin, of Mosley Hall, Cheadle. The Colonel became interested in the breed at a very early date and began with a dog and a bitch which led to the purchase of other good ones emanating from the kennels of Walter Fathan, of Rochdale. In this lot were four champions, namely, Rover II, Vixen II, Wharfdale Rush and Newbold Test, in addition to various other lesser lights. Living in this locality, Mr. Chandler had excellent opportunities to study the breed with which he soon became infatuated.

Another name which is recalled in those early days is that of John C. Horrocks, of Lancashire. No doubt to the present-day American breeders, his name is all but forgotten, but it was he who owned that famous Airedale, Jerry, one of the old pillars of the breed. Mr. Horrocks has ever remained a lover of the breed, but never did much showing or winning, although in 1891 he brought out that good bitch, Tonic, which did some winning. Because of business cares and ill health Mr. Horrocks was compelled to part with his kennels in later years.

Coming down to the latter nineties, American and English history merge into each other, for importations were coming to the States in large numbers and the breed began making more rapid strides than ever. It was the dawn of the modern era of the Airedale.

CHAPTER IV.

Early American History-Airedale Activities on both sides of the Water.

While the firm of Mills and Buckley, of Clonmel fame, was responsible for sending the great majority of the Airedales to this country in the early days and through their clever exploitation had more to do with the breed becoming popular outside of their own country, but particularly in America, it was not they who sent the first dog to the United States. On the other hand, to E. Bairstow, of Bradford, belongs that distinction. Far back in the breed's early dawn he sold the dog, Bruce, to C. H. Mason as one of his collection of prize dogs comprising every breed known in the British Islands. These, Mason brought to this country in the early eighties and Bruce represented the Airedale breed, which at that period was not even recognized as a distinct variety by the English Kennel Club. Bruce was a one-eyed dog, according to Mr. Bairstow's own statement, but a game and courageous animal. In this country he gained the reputation for viciousness, but he was no doubt as good a specimen of the breed as one found those days. In addition to that, he became the sire of Champion Brush before leaving England. In this country Bruce was probably not greatly appreciated, for we learn of him that he eventually found a home in a New York livery stable where he died in 1885. Several other desultory importations were made during the years following, but it was in the last decade of the past century-the middle age period of the Airedale in England-that American breeders began to really take notice of the breed which was so rapidly attracting world-wide attention.

It is not the author's intention of tiring the reader with a long list of details about dogs that have practically passed out of history leaving no impression. As a matter of fact, such details under the circumstances would not only be impossible to collect; but of little interest. The activities of Airedales in America until nearly the close of the past century were of such an exceedingly limited nature that one can well pass over that period. Then came the sudden rise in popularity. American breeders began awakening to the possibilities of this new dog. A number of them stood ready to spend good gold to obtain the best, and it may be safely taken for granted that the breeders over in England were just as ready to part with their best for this acceptable commodity. Such men as Barclay and Newbold in Philadelphia, Jos, E. Laurin in Montreal, Theodore Offerman in New York, J. L. Lorillard, of Arden, Russel Johnson, of Philadelphia, Arthur Mettir and many others seemed to take the fever almost simultaneously. Merritt, of Boston, imported The New King among the first great ones. He was a good, sound dog, needing very little in the way of artificial aid to put him in shape for the show ring. In stud he did considerable good, but he soon became a champion on the bench also.

Mr. Laurin, of Montreal, was bringing them over quite consistently during these days, among the best were Master Royal and Mistress Royal, though it must not be forgotten that he also imported Dumbarton Lass and a host of others. The appearance of Clonmel Marvel in this country, however, was the signal for other importations, for the latter dog came over practically as an unbeatable proposition and that he remained until he met another importation-Clonmel Monarch-which defeated him at Philadelphia some years later under George Raper, who declared that Monarch was easily the best Airedale in England or America. Clonmel Floriform was another dog which marked an epoch in this country but he came somewhat later, just preceding York Masterpiece, which, like Floriform, was an Offerman importation.

It is Clonmel Monarch, however, which may rightly be styled the father of the Modern Airedale in America, if indeed, not in the world, for though he was imported when just past two years old, he left his mark in England both as a winner and a sire. Like many another good one, it was the Clonmel firm of Mills and Buckley who discovered this dog, brought him to the front in England and finally sold him to Clement B. Newbold, of Philadelphia, for the largest figure that was ever paid for an Airedale up to that period. But Mr. Newbold made the best investment in buying this dog that anyone ever made in dog flesh, for when records are compared it will be found that Clonmel Monarch's name figures in practically all the pedigrees of good ones, even up to this day, and it is a guarantee of all that an Airedale terrier should stand for.

The history of Clonmel Monarch is rather unique, but like Clonmel Marvel, he was a "find"; on this occasion, however, the discovered was Holland Buckley himself, consequently the dog did not pass through several hands before reaching the Clonmel firm. Clonmel Monarch was bred by Berkinshaw Smith, was sired by the great Master Briar and owned as his mother, a daughter of Clonmel Marvel. As we have seen in an earlier chapter, Master Briar was considered one of the best, if not the very best Airedale of his day, being by Briar Test, the son of Cholmondeley Briar, the son of Newbold Test, which was by Guess out of Jenny. The dam of Clonmel Monarch was Richmond Peggy, by Clonmel Marvel out of Richmond Nell.

Monarch's breeder, however, unlike the breeder of Marvel, knew what he had and was not to be parted from him for a song. When he was shown by Mr. Smith the first time he was but six months old and bore such a look of quality that he captivated the Clonmel firm at once, who promptly made overtures with a view to purchasing. Mr. Smith, who knew an Airedale as well as anybody, was obdurate and refused to part with his dog. It was at the Leicester show where Monarch, then under another name, was shown the first time and despite his tender age went through his class, taking reserve winners to Rock Salt, which was in his best form on that occasion. The puppy remained in Mr. Smith's possession for a short while longer, but business conditions made it imperative to part with his dogs and the youngster was offered to the Clonmel firm. It is needless to say that the sale was soon negotiated and the dog which caught Holland Buckley's eye at six months old now became an inmate of the Clonmel kennels, winning everywhere, never again taking defeat. He won the championship from his sire, the latter, however, then well up in years, and continued on through his successful, but short career in England, winning among other noted trophies, the Midland Counties challenge cup in competition with ten other champions of various breeds and under three of the best allround judges in England.

In his early days Clonmel Monarch was small and undersized, his weight at twelve months being about thirty-six pounds. There was a finish and refinement about him that could not be ignored and that is why he won so consistently. Some of the critics at his first appearance and in fact until he was nearly two years old said he was bitchy, which in a measure was true, but it is surprising how the dog furnished and rounded out in growth. He was slow to mature, being just about at his best when he was sent to Mr. Newbold in Philadelphia, and at that time he had passed the two-year-old mark and weighed very close to forty-five pounds.

In his description of him Holland Buckley in his book waxes eloquent over this dog and indeed he has good reason to hold him sacred in his memory when he looks back over the dog's achievements and those of his progeny and his relatives of succeeding generations.

The dog was well up in years when I saw him, but I always had a great fancy for his blood lines and the stamp of noblesse which he placed on his get. One other thing I liked about him and which he has never been valued at its true worth; Clonmel Monarch imparted gameness, terrier fire, character and the instincts that all working dogs should have, namely, the desire to hunt and follow the calling for which the Airedale was originated. I always wanted to see an abundance of Monarch's blood in pedigrees of working dogs; the more that was present, the more likely was such progeny to make good at their avocation. Since his days I have seen one of two leading bench show strains that imparted the hunting to a decidedly greater degree than others, but of the early strains, Clonmel Monarch always impressed me most and during the first decade of the present century I had ample opportunity to see how the Airedale took to the business of bear and other big game hunting. Buckley, naturally, only saw Clonmel Monarch from the viewpoint of the bench show fancier; whether or not Monarch or his progeny could impart hunting instincts was a secondary consideration, but if one were to look over the pedigrees of some of those early Airedales which made names for themselves in hunting the mountain lion and other big game of the Rockies, he would find that the blood of Clonmel Monarch figures very substantially in them.

Monarch's outstanding victory before leaving England was at the great annual Airedale terrier function which takes place at Otley. The judge was F. M. Jowett, a north country-man who knows terriers of the broken-haired varieties as few know them; as a matter of fact, Mr. Jowett served in this country several occasions, giving the greatest satisfaction. It was at this show that Monarch met his conqueror of the early days, but the latter was obliged to go down in defeat. Monarch won the gold medal for best of all and in awarding the prize Mr. Jowett remarked, according to Mr. Buckley's statement, that "he absolutely fills the bill."

Clonmel Monarch's very last show before coming to Philadelphia was at Cruft's, and it was a happy farewell. He beat Tone Masterpiece (York Masterpiece in this country) and then met Broadlands Bashful for the mixed special, once more proving the victor.

The sale of Clonmel Monarch to America created considerable discussion and adverse criticisms on the part of fanciers in England. Naturally the departure of such a good dog from Albion's shores meant the depletion of the best breeding stock and as Clonmel Monarch had already shown in the short period of his life what a success he was as a sire, the action on the part of Messrs.. Mills and Buckley in selling him was all the more commented upon. The most direful prophecies were heard, for Clonmel Monarch was not the only good one that was sent to

America. They were coming over by almost every boat. No doubt the Clonmel firm had some misgivings in allowing their best to depart, but American gold outweighed their qualms and thus what was a distinct loss to England proved to be of estimable value to the United States, for Clonmel Monarch was needed at just that time and he filled the place that his owners so confidently predicted for him. When it comes to this question of selling the best, there are always two viewpoints. Messrs. Mills and Buckley certainly had the right to run their own business to please themselves and furthermore, by sending young champions to us, they not only pleased their customers, but aided very materially in popularizing the breed, thus enlarging the market for other English breeders and creating a demand among American fanciers for the best to be had. In Airedales, probably more than in any other breed, it is noticeable that the best invariably came to this country and no doubt it is because of this that American breeders were able to produce specimens good enough to compete with England's best in such a brief space of time. Whatever opinion one may have of the policy adopted by English Airedale breeders, the charge can never be made that they sent over the old, worn-out dogs, or their culls.

Clonmel Monarch was used at stud in England at a very young age which is quite conclusive that he came over to us at just past two years old. Despite his tender years, however, he began siring good ones almost from the very start and among the many excellent sons and daughters which he left over in England were Clonmel Bed Rock (he having been purchased by Foxhall Keene with such other good ones as Clonmel Sensation and Rock Princess, the latter, however, dying aboard the transport). Tone Regent, Clonmel Majesty, Broadlands Royal Descendent, Clonmel Coronation, Strathallan Solace, Claverhouse Enchantress and many others.

Referring to Claverhouse Enchantress, she is probably better remembered as a matron than a winner. By Clonmel Monarch out of Clonmel Winifreda, she soon left the kennels where she was bred and at six months old was owned by a Mrs. Cuthell with the string attached that the Clonmel firm was to select the dog to which she should be bred. Enchantress herself did some winning and she was in every way a nice bitch with the stamp of terrier all over her. As a mother, she produced many good ones, but no doubt her best was Dumbarton Sceptre, which after having first been overlooked at Manchester by J. R. Cooper, who was judging, much to the surprise of all the knowing ones, she was never again really defeated. By some mischance, however, the Clonmel firm, although having the first opportunity to buy her, allowed Theodore Kershaw to get in advance and he purchased what was considered the best bitch in England. It was not long after this that she became the property of Theodore Offerman, of New York, and in this country she did considerable winning. There was a litter brother to Dumbarton Sceptre which came out practically at the same time and it was thought that he would make an equally famous record as his noted sister, but after his early days he seemed to go wrong in skull and shoulders, and while he did some winning after leaving England, he was never in the class with some of the other dogs of his day.

After producing Sceptre, Holland Buckley arranged with Mrs. Cuthell to take Claverhouse Enchantress on a breeding proposition. The dog selected for her this time was Master Briar and from this litter resulted Mistress Royal, a bitch that proved to be almost a marvel such was her great quality. She won everything in England including breed specials, variety specials and in fact best of all breeds. She was purchased by Jos. A. Laurin, of Montreal, and I doubt if he ever made a better purchase than he did when he acquired Mistress Royal. I saw this bitch on various occasions at American shows and always thought her one of the best I ever had the pleasure of going over. There was a dog puppy in this same litter which produced Mistress Royal which, it is said, would have been fully the equal of his sister, but just at that age when he was right to be shown he was taken off by death. It was Buckley and Mills who eventually secured Mistress Royal for export to America.

The later history of Claverhouse Enchantress is brief. She was bred the next time to her son, Claverhouse Sorcerer, the dog previously referred to as the litter brother to Dumbarton Sceptre, but before this litter was born Enchantress picked up poison from the effects of which she died. A brother to her was Strathallan Solace, and a good specimen he was when one judged him for points; coat, color, size, head, everything, were in his favor but he lacked the dash and the fire in the ring and that has beaten many a good terrier. Solace, however, I have it on good authority, was one of the gamest and fieriest terriers that ever lived when given an opportunity in real action and it is a pity that he was not used to greater extent or that he did not get into the hands of such men as C. P. Hubbard who were breeding at that time for Airedales suitable to tackle the big game of the Rockies. He left Strathallan Solitaire and Cheery Royal in England, two dogs of more than average merit.

Clonmel Bed Rock, one of Monarch's earliest sons to come over, did some consistent winning in this country for his owner, Foxhall

Keene. Comparing Bed Rock with his half brother, Broadlands Royal Descendent, the former had some advantage in legs, feet, bone, skull and hindquarters, although Descendent was a free and easy mover. In Bed Rock and Clonmel Coronation, which had gone to Mr. Keene shortly before the dog, the American fancier had a brace which at that period was about as good as the best.

In this country Clonmel Monarch sired even more winners than he did in England, but coming at a period when a really first-class stud was needed, he had the best bitches sent to him, but even this would not have been much assistance had Monarch not possessed the qualities and the prepotent ability to reproduce himself.

Among his sons over here which made their mark on the bench and were also quite successful in reproducing the working qualities, perhaps Champion The Gamecock stands high, although as a bench dog he did not last as well as was excepted. He was royally bred, for his dam was non other than Colne Miracle, the daughter of Clonmel Marvel and Clonmel Sensation. At this day no doubt The Gamecock would be considered coarse, but he was the kind of a dog the hunter would look over again and again. Possessing good size, he had a wealth of bone to go with it. He grew heavy in skull in later years, but he had a punishing jaw and with his powerful frame behind it he was the dog par excellence for the breeder of practical Airedales. During the early part of his career he was owned in Philadelphia, but in later years he became the property of C. P. Hubbard, then of Atlantic, Iowa. Mr. Hubbard was one of the very early pioneers who did more to introduce Airedales to the hunters and trappers of the West than any man at that period. The Game Cock was an excellent cross with the many good bitches that Mr. Hubbard owned and the acquisition of this dog proved a great benefit to him. I have said before, and reiterate here, that when it comes to building up a foundation strain of working dogs, those with an abundance of the Clonmel Monarch blood in their veins have always proved their value. The Gamecock himself was one of the most courageous of Airedales and he imparted this quality to most of his progeny. The Gamecock sired among others, Champion Red Riding Hood out of a Master Briar bitch, and Culbertson Beaver, which sired some good working dogs.

Another good son of Clonmel Monarch which did well to perpetuate these game qualities was Wyndhill Vandal, out of Sweet Briar, a daughter of Master Briar and Vampire, which was by Waterside Ranger out of Floss. Wyndhill Vandal's name is seen in a number of pedigrees of the working stock of the West and South and he usually imparted type and quality also, though his kind would no doubt be considered large and coarse at the present time. Among his daughters was Champion Red Sunlight, which was out of Red Queen, a daughter of Clonmel Monarch and Red Hackle. Among the sons of Wyndhill Vandal was The Rook of Ashborne, a big, powerful dog, which in turn sired The Red Rook of Ashborne when bred to Ashborne Frills, a daughter of Red Raven and Culbertson Lichen which was by Clonmel Monarch out of Colne Black Belle, a daughter of York Masterpiece and Colne Nellie Bly, by Colne Lucky Baldwin, one of the early importations of Jos. A. Laurin. The Red Rook of Ashborne was another of those powerful dogs which were needed to impart size and courage. He was wide in skull and rather short in head, but he was a dog of beautiful coat and color, which he imparted to his progeny. One of his sons is Teddy the Terror, a dog that I owned from a puppy and I can say for him that he is one of the best bodied dogs that one would wish to see. Powerful loins and quarters, short, strong back, excellent spring of ribs, rich tan, beautiful black saddle, good eye and small, well-carrier ear, but like his size, too wide in skull and short in muzzle. He seldom got an off-colored one, however, most of his sons and daughters inheriting through him the good coat and color, no matter what kind of bitches he was bred to. When it comes to the question of gameness and working qualities he never sired a poor one. Teddy the Terror is an intensely line-bred Clonmel Monarch, obtaining this blood through The Gamecock, Wyndhill Vandal, Red Raven and Culbertson Lichen in proportions that balance up well.

Red Raven was another of those powerfully built dogs with marvelous bone and substance. Perhaps he was not as good as one would like to see before the eye, but his jaw was strong and he had the look of the fighter. Red Raven was campaigned fearlessly and was the winner at New York during the early years of the first decade of the present century.

In following out these blood lines we have practically come down to modern times; let us, therefore, revert to those earlier days, the days of Clonmel Monarch's victories in this country. Unquestionably the dog which had the best right to dispute the grand Champion's way was York Masterpiece, known in England as Tone Masterpiece, but after coming to the kennels of Theodore Offerman he was rechristened and given the prefix, York.

It was at Cruft's show just before leaving England, that Clonmel Monarch met Tone Masterpiece, the latter taking second to Monarch, and this is about the way they stood under various judges after both dogs arrived in the States. Masterpiece, which we shall hereafter designate as York Masterpiece, that being his American name, was also a son of Master Briar, that great root from which so many good ones spring, but his dam was Houston Nell. In purchasing this dog, however, his American owner showed his good judgment, for through him he replenished his kennels with the Master Briar blood, which seems no kennel could obtain too much of. The early days of Masterpiece in England did not pressage the later greatness of the dog if we are to judge by his first appearance which was at the Kennel Club show in 1900, where he only received a V. H. C. under Mr. Pendlebury as judge. Master Briar at this same show was also in the same class and received the same mark, hence it was no particular disgrace for the son; it was simply one of those cases where condition was given the priority over quality and type and neither Masterpiece nor Master Briar were in the best of form at this show. When Masterpiece appeared again, some time later, it was an entirely different story. He was put down in the best form and he showed like the real terrier that he was-all fire, dash and nerve. His eye had the true smoldering spark ready to leap into flame at the slightest provocation and he stood as straight on his legs as any one could mold them. From tip to stern he was symmetry. His coat was good in color and of proper texture and yet, while Masterpiece eventually won his championship, it was rather long in coming, but that he was deserving of it, no one seems to doubt. His principal fault was lack of strength in jaw; in this respect he lost both to his sire and to his half brother, Clonmel Monarch. Had Masterpiece been endowed with more power in this one respect, it is doubtful if his half brother could have beaten him. York Masterpiece appears in the pedigrees of quite a few dogs in this country and has been unquestionably a decided stimulus toward the improvement of the breed in America. His American owner had particularly good success with his daughters as brood matrons, but among his sons none stands out more distinctively than Clonmel Floriform, which though bred in England, came to this country also and joined his sire in the Offerman kennels.

Clonmel Floriform had quite a vogue after coming to America where he won consistently, being shown as late as 1907, at which time he came to the New York show with one of his ears badly mutilated, the result of a fight which left him minus the greater part of the right one. I was kennel editor of the Sportsmen's Review during this period and therefore, attended all of the shows, East, West, North and South. I can recall very vividly when Floriform came into the ring. The prestige of a great past record must no doubt have played its part with the judge for he seemed to like Floriform mightily in his class, although he was not given winners; this honor falling to the son of Clonmel Monarch, namely, Red Raven. I confess, seeing the dog at that period he did not impress me like some of the younger American-breds, but looking at a dog which is not "all there" and especially one whose ears are such an important part of his makeup, may have much to do with forming erroneous conclusions. As I was "doing" the bird dogs at this show and as C. P. Hubbard volunteered to write the report of the Airedales for me, I gladly accepted his proffer. This is what he said of Clonmel Floriform in his review of the New York and the Boston shows which he embodied into one:

"Another question which seems to be unsettled is the extent to which accidental mutilation should penalize. The old imported champion, Floriform, was shown at both New York and Boston. He had lost a portion of one ear since coming to America. At New York the judge placed him over two very good Airedales and at Boston the judge dropped him to the bottom, giving as an excuse that he would not judge an incomplete dog. . . . Owing to the extensive use that has been made of Floriform at stud and the numerous good ones sired by him, he was the object of much attention and criticism. He is a dog of good size and medium height, standing on sound legs, with a perfect coat of dark grizzle, the shadings being more the color of buff than tan. In spite of his five-and-a-half-years, he is still a good mover, and has plenty of fire. He has a most peculiarly shaped head, being very flat and wide and slightly dished. He has a short, flat and wide foreface; in fact, his head might be called turtle-shaped. His eyes might be darker in color, but as a whole, his expression is very good."

Coming from a man who knew the breed at that time as well as any one in America, and being wholly disinterested, this estimate of Clonmel Floriform is of particular value to students of present-day Airedale history.

Among Floriform's get, Ingaflora, a very typical bitch of pleasing stamp, was among the best. She did some wining during her hey-day, including winners at New York in 1905. Floriform himself, however, was not the great influence upon the breed as was anticipated at the time of his debut in this country.

Among other dogs of this period when American breeders were going to England for the best that could be bred over there are Hastings Clipper, owned by the Hastings Kennels, of New York, and Colne Lucky Baldwin, owned by Jos. A. Laurin, of Montreal. The latter was also a son of Master Briar and a dog which had the quality to reproduce. Cholmondeley Briar was the sire of Hastings Clipper, the latter being always given credit in this country for siring Clonmel Marvel, but Holland Buckley, who sold Marvel to America, is responsible for the statement that it was not the Hastings Clipper that came to America which sired Marvel, but another Clipper which never left England. During this early period quite a number of good bitches came over also, among them being Mr. Offerman's York Victoria, Mr. Buckley's Boltonwoods Blossom, and we must not overlook the very handsome York Sceptre. In addition to these there were a number of other dogs, some of the lesser lights among the importations, if you will, but these with the more prominent ones, all aided in bringing the breed to perfection in this country. Under the circumstances it is not out of the ordinary that breeders formed the impression that there was no further necessity for going to England for more blood. As a matter of fact, the impression became quite general on both sides of the water that England was depleted of her best and consequently could not breed them up to the same high standard as in the early days. How mistaken this idea proved to be, however, is shown in the next decade when English breeders continued sending over dogs as good, if not better than any that had made their bow at American bench shows during that early influx of England's champions.

CHAPTER V.

Later History-Increasing Popularity of Breed in America.

In 1902 the English Kennel Club suggested that the Airedale terrier be removed from the group of terriers and be known as Airedale, thus placing him on a footing with the St. Bernard and other breeds, but this created a storm of protest. Those who were fostering the breed declared that he was a terrier in every characteristic except going to earth, and to put him in another group would be to stigmatize the dog's sporting instincts. The matter was finally dropped and the Airedale will, no doubt, remain a terrier to the end of doom, even though the word terrier is seldom used in connection with his name at the present time, except in official show classification.

This agitation in 1902 was the last, and after that the breed made very rapid strides. It was in this country, however, where he gained such wide-spread popularity in the space of a few years. This was greatly due to the fact, however, as I have previously pointed out, that he was taken up by the sporting as well as the strictly bench-show element.

During those years from 1904 to 1907 I followed all the shows in all parts of the country and while I continued this for the next ten or twelve years, it was during the period referred to that I began taking particular interest in the breed; an interest that is as keen today as it was in 1904.

I recall the winter of 1906 and 1907 particularly. It was during that period that I made practically the whole of the Eastern as well as the Western circuit, and was in the company of C. P. Hubbard much of the time. At that period he was the leading Airedale breeder of the West, and it was through him that many another fancier of the breed was created. I confess freely that much of my preference for the Airedale came through my acquaintance with C. P. Hubbard.

Attending the New York and Boston shows we had ample opportunity to observe the types in the various localities, and it was already quite noticeable that Boston type varied from New York and Philadelphia was still another matter. But the notion seemed to be general that we could breed our own Airedales in this country and need not go to the other side for new blood, for we had the best of the period. Before going further into this let us see what C. P. Hubbard had to say of the Airedales of the East and of the West. His knowledge of the breed at that period was second to none, consequently his opinions were of value then but they are even more so today. It is especially noteworthy how well he had Airedale matters in hand, and how recent developments have in a great measure borne out his statements of nearly two decades ago.

Relative to the New York and Boston shows I have already quoted his criticism of Clonmel Floriform; following are his observations on the other dogs shown and conditions in general:

"The number of American-bred Airedales entered and the quality of those at the largest shows this season demonstrates the fact that the American Airedale breeders are fast gaining supremacy over the English product.

"It further gives illustration of the popularity which 'the all-round dog' has gained in the brief period that has elapsed since his introduction into this country.

"At New York about ten of the thirty-seven Airedales entered were importations. Of these not over three passed mediocrity when compared with the home product.

"At Boston some seven of the thirty-five entered were imported dogs and of these only two were thought good enough to get into the running. Even with this slight recognition it was generally conceded by fanciers that but for excellence of condition and skill of handlers in showing, the imported ones at New York and Boston would have ranked lower than some of the American-breeds.

"It was suggested by the knowing ones that a certain importer has been looking more to the dollars to be made in buying inferior stock cheaply and selling it at a round advance than he has to improving the breed. Be that as it may, it is certain that the breed has not been improved much by the importations of the past twelve months and some of the imported one have brought long prices, only to bring their owners to grief when they have come into competition with those home bred.

"Excellence of quality and evenness of type were noticeable features at New York and Boston, the latter showing rather the better of it. One feature deserving criticism is the obvious 'faking' which is carried on without protest from judges and exhibitors. A rough-coated terrier requires more or less trimming to put him down to where he will stand comparison with non-trimmers, but when the use of clippers, scissors, razors and the knife become as apparent as it was this season, it is time to call a halt. The old controversy over what constitutes faking and what is legitimate trimming will undoubtedly never be settled, but where cutting is plainly in evidence it would seem that the duty of the judge is obvious. . . . .

"Among stud dogs that have recently come into prominence there were exhibited: The Barrister, a good sound terrier, extra well muscled, whose only weak points are lack of finish in foreface and a bad mixture in color. Wynton Tyke, a good-colored, good-coated dog, with excellent bone and substance, standing well up on capital legs and feet, but a trifle thick in head and prominent in eye. York the Conqueror was absent, having been recently sold by Mr. Offerman. (This dog was known in England as Jergens De Witt. He was brought over by George Thomas who picked him up at one of the English shows where he was considered quite among the first flight. Soon after bringing him to America he went to the kennels of Theodore Offerman, who, however, did not keep him very long, but sold him to another American fancier. The dog never did much in this country in the way of propagating the species.) Bronside Billy a new one just brought out by Mellin E. Stevens, is a right good little dog, lacking only in expression and depth of foreface. Kismet Flashlight is a very stylish dog of true terrier type and but for a long coupling and too much of a pronounced stop, might easily have had winners at New York. Red Raven, the winner at New York, stands rather low on the legs and has not strength enough before the eyes that Airedale men like to see. He is the right size, however, and has a good coat and color and substance."

Before proceeding further, let us quote his article written only a week or two later, on the Airedale at the Chicago show. The two will give one a very fair idea of the progress of the breed from that time to the present and also enlighten the reader on the reasons for various types:

"One thousand miles in distance may be responsible for the vast diversity in type between the Airedale of Boston and that of Chicago. Even the short distance between Philadelphia and Boston results in great divergence of opinion as to correct type, and the winners at one city will hardly do to compete with those of the other.

"Around Philadelphia great stress is laid upon heavy bone. At Boston an equal amount of emphasis is laid upon style and action. At Chicago conditions are in rather a chaotic state, no certain defined quality having been decided upon.

"A study of pedigrees will enlighten us on the reasons for these conditions. It is undoubtedly true that the Philadelphia fanciers hold the key to the situation. The blood of Clonmel Monarch, now retired from stud duties, has proven such a potent factor in bench winnings of the past five years that it becomes almost absolutely necessary to accept him as the foundation of American breeding. At Philadelphia they have Champion The Gamecock, a son of Champion Clonmel Monarch, and Champion Farleigh Mikado, his grandson on the side of both sire and dam.

"Champion Wyndhill Tackle, owned at Bryn Mawr, Pa., is a grandson and Champion York Sceptre, owned at New York, is a granddaughter of this dog, while Champion Prince Hal, owned at Boston, and Champion Master Royal, owned at Montreal, are both grandsons, and Champions Clonmel Bed Rock and Clonmel Coronation, at Jericho, Long Island, are son and daughter, and many other good Airedales well on their way toward championships are descended from the grand old dog.

"Going back one generation, we find Master Briar, the sire of Clonmel Monarch, also the sire of Colne Lucky Baldwin, owned in Montreal, and Champion York Masterpiece, owned in New York. Master Briar is the good, strong root upon which the Airedale in England is planted. Back of him we find Cholmondeley Briar, his grandsire, who is responsible for Champion Hastings Clipper, imported by the Hastings Kennels near New York; Champion Highgate Kitty, owned near Boston; Champion The New King, owned at Boston; Champion Boltonwoods Blossom, imported by Mr. Buckley, of Philadelphia.

"Champion Kismet Rockferry Pounder, owned at White Plains, New York; Champion York Victoria, owned by Mr. Offerman, at New York, and in fact nearly all champions of record in the American Kennel Club Stud Book trace more or less directly to Cholmondeley Briar.

"All this is perhaps astray from what is necessary to describe the Airedales at Chicago, but divergence in type may often be explained by a study of pedigrees. Among the first Airedales owned in Chicago was Briar Thorn. He was sired by Puff's Jerry III, a Philadelphia dog. His dam was Colne Asia, a Montreal bitch. The breeding was entirely indifferent.

Puff's Jerry III never made a record on the bench or as a sire, but he was a descendent through the breeding mentioned, his sire being Broadland's Bunkum, a winner in England, a son of Jerry II, who was sired by Cholmondeley Briar. Briar Thorn is owned by Mr. E. A. Munger, of Chicago, who judged Airedales at the show. He is a big dog as Airedales go, and more especially is he a dog with a big head. The size of his head is emphasized by the huge whisker which he sports. He is a dog of most excellent disposition, and for this reason as well as for the reason that he may be said to be the pioneer Airedale of Chicago, he has been accepted as a criterion and the Airedale fanciers of the West have shaped their breeding accordingly.

"This has given rise to the opinion in the East that the West wants a big dog, and results in Endcliffe Briar, a dog which George S. Thomas imported, that took reserve winners at New York last year, landed winners at St. Louis and was sold to Mr. Sam C. Davis of that city. Mr. Davis, with characteristic pluck, sends Briar through the Eastern circuit of bench shows this year with the result that he takes no honors until he gets back West again, where he lands winners at Cincinnati, Milwaukee and Chicago, and is undoubtedly bound for the green (now purple) ribbon at the coming St. Louis show.

"Endcliffe Briar is a strong, classy Airedale that catches the eye in the ring and shows well, but he is of a type that has been rejected in the older Airedale circles of America and rightly so, because he lacks altogether the essential qualities of a terrier, and while some authorities have been trying to legislate the Airedale out of the Terrier Class, they have not provided another class for him to step into, and terrier he will remain to the end of his days.

"While the Airedale standard of England (none has been adopted in America) calls for a dog weighing from forty to forty-five pounds, Endcliffe Briar weighs fully sixty pounds, and as long as sixty pounds is accepted by judges, why not eighty pounds or one hundred pounds, and so on until the Airedale gets the right to be classed among mastiffs and loses entirely his terrier characteristics?

"The older terrier breeders have begun to recognize the tendency toward overweight and have reverted back to the acceptance standard, as shown by the awards at most of the Eastern shows of this season. According to the opinion of New York and Philadelphia Airedale fanciers, the Boston breeders have gone too far toward the lighter type and the Western breeders too far in the opposite direction.

"New York and Philadelphia are right and it remains for the Airedale Terrier Club of America, the Airedale Terrier Club of New York and the newly-formed Airedale Terrier Club of Chicago to get together and formulate something in the way of a standard to satisfy all breeders of this dog, both East and West.

"The Chicago show brought out twenty-one Airedales. None of them, with the exception of the winner in bitches, could compete with any hopes of success at any Eastern show. Among the dogs there is very little choice between Endcliffe Briar, the winner; Fritz, reserve winners; Culbertson Bristles, second open class, and Bob

Fitzsimmons, second limit class. All of them are coarse. Endcliffe Briar, as before mentioned, is a direct importation. Fritz was sired by Mr. Munger's dog, Thorn Dumbarton Newcoyn, imported from England two years ago by Mr. Munger, and a full brother to Colne Rooley Toff, owned at Montreal, both Newcoyn and Rooley Toff being by Master Briar out of Dumbarton Lass. Culbertson Bristle was sired by Mr. Munger's dog Briar Thorn, before mentioned; is owned by the writer and considered by him as easily the best of Airedale in the show if put down in proper condition. Bob Fitzsimmons is out of Briar Bush, a full sister to Briar Thorn and has all the bad characteristics of the Puff's Jerry II-Colne Asia breeding, viz.: thick head, bad ears, overweight and a generally clumsy appearance.

"The winner in bitches, Miss Roxie, is by Puff's Jerry II out of Colne Asia and is a little sister to Briar Thorn. She is the only real good one that ever came from this breeding. It is doubtful if she would be accepted in the East, but in the opinion of the writer she is the best type of Airedale bitch in America today. She is of the same type as The Gamecock, owned by Messrs. Johnson and Buckley, of Chestnut Hill, Pa., and should be bred to him."

The two articles of Mr. Hubbard's give the present-day student information about Airedale conditions such as no writer of the present day could portray of that period, for it is the contemporaneous authority who gleans his knowledge at first hand who can give us real facts. Perhaps some of the statements made by him are a trifle prejudiced, for where is the man who has not his favorites and also his opinions, but nevertheless it is beyond dispute that type in Airedales at that period was governed entirely by latitude. The Boston type which was small and light of bone, did not please the practical sportsmen any more at that period than it does today, but the exaggerated weights such as Mr. Hubbard alludes to were equally out of place, although even to this day some of the Airedales seen in certain localities where big game is hunted border very closely on this large type. The majority of big game hunters, however, have begun to learn that it is not the large and unwieldly Airedale which does the work, neither is it the small Welsh terrier-like kind, but a dog weighing between forty and fifty pounds, and many breeders have adhered faithfully to this kind obtaining therefrom the best results. It is surprising, however, how soon after that period of which Mr. Hubbard wrote that there came more of a unification of size and type between the East and West. Kennels sprung up everywhere, Chicago alone boasting of a dozen or more, among which were the Abbey Kennels, the Vickerys and others if not quite of equal note at least of sufficient strength to lend some weight in the improvement of the Airedale. The kennels farther West were also rapidly coming in line, but one important feature about the most of these was that they never lost sight of gameness in their breeding operations. They bred principally for Western fanciers and they catered to their wishes in producing dogs for work.

Among those in the West, as I have pointed out, C. P. Hubbard continued along the lines he laid out. He realized among the first that there was no necessity for extreme size and coarseness, but he also steered clear of the shoals so many strictly bench show kennels were nearing-that is, breeding undersized specimens for so-called quality alone-and in keeping away from this extreme he did an incalculable amount of good for the breed not only in preserving type, but particularly in keeping the breed within the realms of the sporting dog and for the all-round hunter. Mr. Hubbard, while he maintained his principal kennels in Atlantic, Iowa, maintained another at Dome Lake, Wyoming, where all the dogs where given ample opportunity for work, not only on big game, but also on upland feathered game, as well as on ducks, geese and other aquatic birds. The Kootenai Kennels were in Montana and they also bred good working dogs and bench winners as well: and at Kansas City were the kennels of C. W. Buttles, which are still very active in bench show realms. Perhaps they did not themselves go in much for big game hunting, or any other class, for that matter, but many good working dogs came from the Elmhurst Kennels, as they are called. Red Raven was an inmate of the kennels for a time and various other noted ones. The dog whose blood I always preferred above all others, however, was that of Elmhurst Apache. This dog at the present time might be considered somewhat coarse and off color, but he was a fine upstanding animal of bone and substance, with a long head, fiery, if rather light eye, and remarkably well proportioned in body, especially when it came to his great strength of rear parts, which in an Airedale is all essential. Elmhurst Apache was a strongly bred Oorang on both sides of his pedigree, which in other words, contains the combination of the Cromptons and the Midlands, two strains that became famous in England and subsequently here in America after that period alluded to in Mr. Hubbard's articles, when it was thought unnecessary to go to England for new blood. But American fanciers did go to the Tight Little Island on numerous subsequent occasions and many good ones continued to come to the States from there, and while we on this side of the water were wrestling with size and type and what should constitute the exact weight of the Airedale, let us see what our English cousins were doing in the way of producing dogs that eventually were to come to this side.

While the danger was still very prevalent-and is to this day-of making the Airedale a toy dog exclusively, by breeding for the bench alone, it is noticeable that some of these show strains that became leaders in their own realm, when crossed with some of the old families in this country, produced the very best kind of all-round working dogs, but this also will be shown as the later history of the breed is evolved.

CHAPTER VI.

Modern History-Later Strains and Types-More Uniformity in the West-New Stars from England.

Several years passed by. American breeders went along smugly secure in the belief that the best of England's stock was now on this continent. The three distinct types which C. P. Hubbard alluded to were more pronounced than ever; New England with its small types of light bone and lack of substance, but teeming with quality, was everywhere in evidence in the East, although the breeders round about Philadelphia and New York remained true to their first ideals and demanded quality as well as substance, together with coat and color. Around Chicago, the Briar Thorn and Endcliffe Briar types were still being bred and continued to win in that locality, but this condition did not last long. The Western breeders came East and the latter reciprocated by invading the Western country. It was not long until more uniformity was to be seen at shows and dogs that formerly were invincible in Chicago and St. Louis could no longer cope with the winners of the day. The various clubs devoted to the breed were doing much toward bringing order out of chaos which eventuated in dogs with type and quality, minus the coarseness, being recognized in the West as well as in the East. It is true, extremes of both were still winning occasionally, but this was the exception rather than the rule. The surpassing feature of it all was that the Western fanciers were beginning to import dogs also and the breed was no longer one of sections; a uniform type was demanded, and that type was a medium-sized dog combining substance with the quality.

This rapid transition from chaos to order was due to several things. First, because a number of large breeders in the West took up the Airedale on a scale that was even more sensational than was ever attempted in the East, and among those were the Abbey's of Francis Porter, the Vickerys, the Briergates, the kennels of Alex Stewart and a number of others in and about Chicago, while all through the West a great many other good kennels were distributed, even as far out as California, and among the latter were the Anoakia Kennels at Santa Anita, and the kennels of H. M. Robertson, of Lamanda Park, Calif., while farther inland the Elmhursts remained active and others were those of the Mountainviews, of Jas. Keefe, though he went in more for working dogs; the Gopher Kennels at Mankato, Minn.; the Pike's Peaks at Colorado City, and the Cragwolds at St. Louis. It was because many of the aforesaid kennels maintained their dogs for actual work, that the West, while emphasizing type, was kept from drifting into the mere bench show evolution.

All these kennels of the East and West and in Canada, however, would not have made such rapid strides towards perfection had they been unable to obtain more dogs from England. Contrary to the prevalent opinion, the foundation stock of that country was far from depleted in the early part of the present century and those fanciers of the Tight Little Island, breeders always, and purveyors secondly, soon built up their strains and were sending over dogs with the same regularity and for the same big prices as the early pioneers did. As a matter of fact, the dogs that began coming over in the later days were even better than the early ones and American breeders never stopped at prices. I have said it before, but it is not out of place to reiterate: Airedale breeders in England were unlike the setter and pointer breeders. They invariably sold their best when the price was forthcoming, while with settlers and pointers it was frequently a case of securing the culls for America only.

While America was passing through this period of smug confidence in its ability to produce dogs as good as any in the world-and in certain quarters there was reason for this feeling of certainty-England continued to breed along brobdingnagian lines, but most of the breeders kept in mind that the primary consideration should be to produce dogs with balance and general symmetrical proportions. They realized that a phenomenal head with no symmetry in other parts was as faulty as an indifferent head with hound expression, light eyes and large ears. They also kept in mind that the coat and color were considerations that should always be a part of the general make-up. It is in this respect that many of our American breeders went wrong; they felt that when they produced a long, lean head with well-carried V-shaped ear, a barrel-shaped muzzle and an alert expression they had accomplished their end, not taking into consideration that weak quarters, light thighs and stifles, and bad feet are an abomination and as a consequence many a dog with head alone, but entirely out in other respects went to the front with the result that more than one strain of weaklings was thus created, only to take Airedale further and further away from the essential considerations, which are soundness in body conformation and sufficient substance to cope with the problems that a sporting dog is called upon to face. It is because of this lack of foresight that many of our strains bred in the kennels of bench show men exclusively, are utterly worthless to the sportsman and why with many, the Airedale has received a bad name. Such a result is but natural for the average sportsman hearing of the many good all-round qualities of the Airedale, after securing specimens of this class has given them up promptly, and codemned the whole race on the limited experience he has had with a few of the wrong kind.

English breeders, however, have done much to counteract this and it is due to many of the later importations that this happy result has been effected. Among the English strains of that period which later figured prominently on this side the "Barkerends" of Herbert Croft, of Bradford, Yorkshire, are more or less conspicuous. Bred in the heart of the Airedale country, his dogs while never obtaining the vogue in America that some of the other strains have are the kind which assisted greatly in maintaining the balance, and blood of this kind is always valuable. It was the Crompton Kennels of Leaver Bros., however, which proved an immense boon. The Chomptons stand to the Airedale of the present decade as Rhoebe does in the foundation blood of the Llewellin, for they were part of the foundation of a strain that at the present time is among the leaders in Airedales, representing type and quality together with all the gameness and the Airedale terrier attributes that the real lover of the breed is seeking. It was the combination of the Crompton and the Midland strain which is the basis upon which the "Tinterns" of W. J. Phillips is founded and perhaps in the past ten years no strain has made a better name for itself in America and England than the latter.

Leaver Brothers, of Blackburn, never went into breeding of Airedales on a large scale, always keeping their kennels down to a few select bitches seldom numbering more than a dozen, but their individuals as well as their blood were select. Their Crompton Marvel was among the first to attract attention. A good dog himself, but for some reason never able to win championships honors in England, he was nevertheless the kind of terrier to stamp the characteristics of the breed upon his progeny and among his get may be mentioned Freeman Terror and Crompton Oorang, both English champions which also made names for themselves in this country. His daughter, Crompton Almeda, is another of the right stamp which went to championship honors. Among the later-day dog was Crompton Theobald which came to this country not so long ago, but with the present plethora of high-class ones, he did not make the expected showing here. Theobald was brought over by Brumley Brothers, of Long Island, and has been shown with somewhat indifferent success. He is a fine, big upstanding dog with nice head and good general balance, but rather light in color of coat and in this day when deep tan and intensely black saddles are sought for, dogs of the Theobald type are frequently overlooked. That he will become a sire, however, seems to be a foregone conclusion, as he has the right blood black of him to perpetuate the desirable qualities even though he, in a slight degree, may be just a degree short in them.

Crompton Oorang changed hands several times; Leaver Bros., whether they failed to recognize the good qualities of the puppy or figured that it was better to sell their promising stock at a good price and thus distribute their wares to their own subsequent gain, is not quite clear, but however that may be , when the puppy was six months old he was purchased by Preston Smith, who, however, did not keep him long. William Proudlove saw the puppy and coveted him and the subsequent development was that he became his owner. He journeyed on to the Birmingham National Show with him, but the judge did not recognize the merit of the youngster and he failed to even get into the money. Nothing daunted, however, he continued in his faith in the dog, for he was terrier man enough to realize that the turning of the tide would come, and some day a judge would spot the dog no matter what company he happened to be in.

Perhaps this is going back over early history, but it is necessary to revert history in order to bring out the later developments. Crompton Oorang came out the next time in the best of form, was promptly given his just dues, and from that period he was never headed, winning his championships in very short order.

While Crompton Oorang was a great dog as an individual, he had the prepotency of his race concentrated within his veins to such a high degree he invariably imparted all those necessary physical and mental attributes to his progeny with even added intensity. He was unquestionably to the Airedale terrier of his period what Master Briar stood for at an earlier epoch. Among his sons and daughters are numbered many sons and daughters which came to this country to carry on the fame of the family and to impart it to later generations. One of his sons was Danny Craig Commander, which I believe was picked up by George Thomas for Theodore Offerman, and though he won championship honors in England before coming over, his name was changed to Prince of York in America, and on the bench in this country he soon landed enough points for championship honors. I believe I saw Prince of York the first time he was shown in this country and I saw him on frequent subsequent occasions. To my way of thinking he was a pleasing type of dog, but like many of the Cromptons, he was just a shade weak in foreface. His coat was of that profuse but rather soft variety which required constant barbering. It was said that on occasion his coat was manipulated to give harshness, but if this is so, it was done my a master hand, for when in the ring it had the color and the texture so much sought after.

Perhaps one should not speak of Prince of York in superlatives as there are many dogs as good as he ever was in his palmiest days, but nevertheless such specimens are always worthy of attention. Prince of York, while he soon became a champion in this country met many ups and downs in doing so. It was Danbury, in 1910, that he met Tintern Royalist, his great rival and frequent opponent, that George Raper put Royalist over him, and in the estimation of most unbiased fanciers this is the relative position he was entitled to although at an earlier show the late James Mortimer put Prince over Royalist. In New York, in 1911, I was at the ringside when King Oorang, Kilearn Oorang, and Prince of York came together and as King Oorang had come over just before this show, imported by Andrew Albright, Jr., ostensibly to beat Prince of York, the interest was very great. W. L. Barclay, of Philadelphia, one of the earliest Airedale fanciers in this country, was judging. The open class, in which these three met, was an unusually large one, but the much talked-of trio was soon spotted and put to one side, although Kilearn Oorang which was only a puppy had appeared before, winning the puppy class with something to spare.

There is no gainsaying the fact that Prince showed to the best advantage on this occasion. His coat looked right; harsh in texture and rich in color; if he had any false aids to put it in this condition, it must be conceded that it was cleverly done. The judge eventually gave him the decision, and at the time in my report of the show for the Sport's Review I commented on the award saying that it was all dependent upon the existing conditions, though had Kind Oorang shown better advantage, it is more than likely that the latter would have won. As a sire, Prince of York was never a great success, although he was greatly sought after by breeders for a short period.

While Crompton Oorang is entitled to more than passing credit as the sire of Prince of York, the latter is not by any means his only claim to notoriety for among his other progeny were Rockley Oorang, Tintern Desire, Clonmel Imperious, Rebound Oorang, and a number of others, nearly all of which came to this country, and therefore their history is interwoven with that of our latter period.

If the Airedale spread rapidly throughout all parts of America, his popularity became equally great in England and there was scarcely a community in that country that did not have its noted kennel, while Wales, Scotland, and Ireland were not very far behind. In the Midlands the Airedale had taken by this time as firm a root as in the Yorkshire counties, and it is to this part of England that breeders owe much, for here the kennels of E. Blunt began to assert themselves. I select this particular kennel because, like the Cromptons, the Midland Kennels of Mr. Blunt aided very materially in the foundation of a family. In other words, the Midlands were the "other side of the house" in forming the "Tintern" strain.

Mr. Blunt came into prominence originally along about 1906 when he brought out a puppy which he called Midland Royal. He was by Master Royal, which came to the Kennels of Jos. Laurin in Montreal some time before, out of Madam Briar, hence his blood lines were the regulation ones, going back to the great towers of the breed.

Midland Royal, even as a puppy attracted the attention of the knowing ones, and W.J. Phillips, afterwards the breeder of so many good Tinterns, confesses in his book that, when he saw the puppy at the Birmingham National show, the idea then struck him of the possibility of forming a strain some day by combining the Crompton and the Midland blood; an idea that proved to be more than a passing fancy, for it eventually came to pass that by this combination came a long line of good Airedales which not only did the breed a great amount of good in England, but subsequently proved to be the bulwarks of present day breeding here in America. Midland Royal came before the public at a period when there were a number of good ones on the benches in England, and among them the most noted was Crompton Oorang, but Royal lived up to the expectations of his admirers and soon annexed championship honors. He was a dog that for allround quality could scarcely be faulted. His cost was close and harsh in texture, his color was good and he possessed another attribute which at that time was particularly desirable, namely - size. England, as well as America, or at least some parts of it, became victims of the quality craze with its accompanying lack of bone, substance, and size. Midland Royal came into the spotlight at a time when size was absolutely essential to prevent the Airedale from degenerating into the undersized Welsh terrier and his appearance in stud was a boon, although perhaps this was not realized by many during the period that he was before the public. To W.J. Phillips, though younger in Airedale breeding than many of his contemporaries, must much of the credit be given for keeping the Airedale ship of state off the shoals, and his decision to combine the two important strains then before the public proved to be a boon which the following years have clearly demonstrated. Midland Royal sired a number of good ones, some of which perhaps made more of a record in the breeding ranks than on the bench, greatly due to the fact that their owners preferred it this way, but among those that came before the public were Midland Marvin, Midland Rollo, Mistress Ida, Miss Killmansegg, Wood Green Squire, and several others of perhaps slightly lesser note.

In a work as limited as this, it is scarcely possible to take up each and every family of Airedales and go into the history with full details, much as I should like to, but the reader will get a good knowledge of the breed by following the main lines as it were; a system I have been endeavoring to follow throughout this book. Before taking up the breeding and the manner in which the Tinterns were originated I may mention that contemporary with these dogs were the Springbanks of the Messrs. Wilson, of Musselburgh, Scotland. These enthusiastic brothers soon put the Springbank prefix to the front. Their dogs were also noted for good color and the quality, though many of them were on the small side, and for that reason I was never personally as much interested in them as some of the other strains. Among the dogs to gain international fame emanating from these kennels are Springbank Diamond, Springbank Sunshine, Springbank Sceptre, and Springbank Radium. The three bitches came to this country and did considerable winning, but Radium, which is a dog, went to South Africa, where his light was hidden under a bushel, as it were, for he had the opportunities in that country, neither in competition nor at stud. In an earlier chapter I have made passing notice of the Danny Craigs, the Caerphillys, and others of this and earlier periods. Of the former, Danny Craig King was quite prominent on the bench and at stud. His name figures prominently in many present-day pedigrees, among them that of Soudan Swiveller the sire of Abbey King Nobler, and in passing I might state that the latter dog though not bred entirely along the lines of the Tintern combination is nevertheless a mixture of the Crompton and the Midland Royal blood with the Danny Craig King blood in addition. This dog was a fiery, well-made terrier which won considerably in England taking reserve to Midland Royal on several occasions. It will be remembered that Prince of York in this country was a "Danny Craig" in England.

Of the Caerphillys it might be observed that this family also had quite a vogue with a fair measure of success in this country and in their native land. Caerphilly Admiral was a splendid terrier in every respect, the outstanding features of these dogs being their sharp, almost crameo-cut neck, so clean under the chin as to remind us of the sculptured images of the breed. Admiral came to America-going to the Canadian side-and had a fair measure of success. Another good one of this line was Caerphilly Performer, a dog, that won the hearts of the quality-seeking element, though I have never learned just how much real punishment any of them could stand in the rough and tumble life of big-game hunting in the South and West. However, Performer was a dog with a magnificent head and front and, like all of the family, had that clean-cut appearance that is so taking. To my mind there is just a shade too much refinement in the family to stand practical usage, although I have no doubt that there were exceptions especially in some of the descendants that were given an opportunity on the big game of America.

There was something about the Crompton-Midland combination, however, that had impressed the practical man. They had size, bone, substance, coat, color, gameness, great power fore and aft, and withal, were teeming with quality, perhaps of a somewhat different stamp than many of the other families, but nevertheless they filled the eye of those who kept the idea uppermost in their minds that the Airedale was created for a working dog. This is the thought that came to mind when I looked over Tintern Royalist shortly after he was imported by Andrew Albright, Jr., and shown in the East.

When W. J. Phillips conceived the idea of combining the families of Crompton Oorang and Midland Royal he may have been guided by the individual qualification of each, rather than by any specific knowledge of the blending qualities of the two lines of blood; both were excellence itself; both were siring winners, and these were dogs of good size and substance, which as I stated previously, was much needed at this particular time. Take Rockley Oorang for instance; the son of Crompton Oorang, he was a dog of not overgrown size but amply large; his legs, feet, bone, and substance together with the appearance of great power was sufficient to attract the attention of any one, not only the man looking for a useful animal, but those who were interested in the show end only. When the late George Raper, famous as an international judge, saw him for the first time he was enamoured of him and promptly purchased him.

Perhaps he had a customer in mind, but be that as it may, when Raper bought a dog it was generally a good one and worth the price.

Later, in this country with Albright as the owner, to which I referred earlier in this chapter, the dog sustained the promise of his early days. It was the same with Midland Royal; he also had a number of good ones to his credit, hence on the theory of "like begets like," Mr. Phillips was not taking chances. His reasoning was at least logical even though it might have been speculative. Subsequent events lead one to the belief that he must have been inspired, for from the very first, results were forthcoming. He had a bitch called Witton Lady, a daughter of Midland Royal and Kitty Briar; a good useful bitch with the points that are necessary; that is, fire, terrier expression, coat to a fair degree, size, and bone sufficient for her sex. Witton Lady was mated with Crompton Oorang, and from this breeding resulted the dog which was eventually called Tintern Desire. This dog became famous in England and America as a winner, but particularly as a sire. After his successes in England he came to America and went eventually to the Gopher Kennels, owned by Dr. R. M. Dodds, of Mankato, Minn. The kennels were among the oldest in the West and few in the East have much priority over them, for they were established in 1898, which is a very early period in Airedale history for America. After Desire made his home in that far away North country he was not so accessible to breeders of the East and perhaps he suffered some of this account, but nevertheless there were many who did take advantage of him. Tintern Desire, however, left numerous progeny in England before he was expatriated and in making good use of him as a stud dog Mr. Phillips was wise, for he proved very promptly that he had the power to transmit the best qualities of the two great families he represented.

It was the success of his son, Tintern Royalist, that drew the attention to this dog as a coming sire. Royalist, as a matter of fact, made a brilliant record in a brief time before coming to American shores, but once over here, the fame of the Tinterns was established. Tintern Royalist was bred, owned and shown by W. J. Phillips, although he left Albion's shores after a short career on the bench. American money-and it came in large packages-proving the magnet which induced his owner to let him go. Royalist was by Tintern Desire out of Tintern Blossom, she a daughter of Midland Royal and as Witton Lady, dam of Tintern Desire, was also a Midland Royal bitch, here were two crosses of this blood, close up in the pedigree of Tintern Royalist. In this new star W. J. Phillips found the consummation of his desires, and this not intended as a pun either.

Tintern Royalist was whelped June 28, 1908, according to our American records, and at the early age of seven months made his first appearance on the bench. This was at the Blackpool show in England where he gave Rockley Oorang, then the leading Airedale before the English public a close run, Chris Houlker, of Accrington, judging. Not long after this he won his first championship at Crufts when he was less than eight months old, beating a field of matured dogs that was truly remarkable. Before leaving England he won four championships and still came to America at a very early age in life. Andrew Albright, Jr., was the purchaser, and though he paid a high figure for the dog, I have no doubt that he felt well repaid for the outlay. Royalist was in every sense a large dog, but he had the head, the neat ear, the strength of jaw, and the fiery eye of the real terrier. He possessed a wealth of bone and there was power to him in his every line and in all his actions. His color was the best, his coat was of proper texture, and to all appearances he was easily kept in condition, though he did have some bad times, not, however, when he came under judges who really knew an Airedale from every angle. Some thought that because he was a large dog his career would be meteoric and that by the time he reached three years his winning days would be over. They based their judgment on the fact that he matured early, and therefore would go fast. In his case, nothing like that happened. Mr. Albright showed him fearlessly and later sold him to Vickery Kennels of Chicago, then in the zenith of their fame and in 1913, when he was five years old he took winners at New York. It was a wonderful show of Airedales that year and every class proved interesting, but when the open class for dogs was called everyone was on tiptoe. The dogs filed into the ring, one after the other, nineteen in all, and a great array it was. John McGough, of Brooklyn, was judging. Prince of York and Abbey King Nobbler were entered, but shown for specials only which left the competition among the seventeen others, but those who were at the ringside soon saw that the real fight lay between Tintern Royalist, now carrying the Vickery colors, and King Oorang, owned and shown by Andrew Albright Jr., the latter having disposed of Royalist to the victory kennels, purchased King Oorang shortly after and thus came into the ring against a dog that was once his standby. Though both dogs had been seen frequently on the benches at various shows, I do not know if they ever came into direct competition as they did here. Royalist never looked better than he did on this occasion. Five years of life had not affected his shoulders in the least, and he was as good in head and cheek as ever, furthermore he showed with even more fire than I had ever seen him show on previous occasions. These two dogs were spotted by McGough and placed in one corner and next came Vickery Emperor, the German-bred dog which the Vickerys had purchased only a short time before, and a very good one he was, too. The fourth one to go to the corner was Soudan Swiveller. In referring to my notes made at the ringside at the time of the judging I find that I made this notation: "Royalist never looked better; King Oorang in good form. A close decision between this two, but Royalist was deserving of the blue." As for the merits of Soudan Swiveller and Vickery Emperor, my choice for third was Swiveller.

Tintern Royalist was used quite extensively by breeders and a number of his puppies were soon seen on the benches. That very year a son of his-Vickery Lodestar-won the American-bred class and did considerable winning at the Western shows. He was not of the same stamp as his sire, being rather light in bone, clean-cut about the head, small in eye, and well finished in muzzle and jaw. His dam was Ch. Larchmere Mistress Magnet. While on the subject of this show, I might mention that this was one of the banner years for the Airedale in America and in point of numbers the breed at Westminster ranked second in the show, being out-numbered only slightly by Boston terriers. The Vickery Kennels were equally successful in bitches, taking winners and Gamecock Sally, one of the G. S. West breeding. Reserve went to Bothwell Scorceress, a daughter of Prince of York, owned and bred by the Kenmare Kennels.

The fame of Tintern Royalist, his winning career, his lasting qualities and his ability to sire winners, naturally brought the Tintern Kennels into greater prominence than ever and several more good ones came over through the activities of their owner, Mr. Phillips, but one of the best that he sold to America was Tintern Tip Top.

The dog at this writing (June 1921) is well up in years, but he seems to be good for several years more in the stud. Tintern Tip Top is a remarkable dog in many ways. First, he is the near approach to the ideal in terriers, considering the question from all sides. In England he went through to championship honors without a skip, and after coming to the United States, going to the Anoakia Kennels of Miss Baldwin, located at Santa Anita, California, the dog continued his successes here in America. He is not what might be called a particularly large dog, but he is one with marvelous bone, possessing a head of unusual length, but unlike many of these extremely long-headed specimens, he has the strength of jaw that is sometimes lacking, and a terrier without strength of underjaw particularly, us an abomination and defeats the purpose for which he was bred. Tip Top, however, has this strength and he is well filled up in foreface, possess a fiery eye, a well-carried ear, a remarkably good expression of that "varminty" kind which we see described so frequently, but which in actual life is not so common. His back is short, his body well muscled, and altogether, he is a terrier of the correct poise and proportion, while his coat and color are good. In the endeavor to get the short, harsh coat we have in many strains sacrificed the pily underjacket which is so essential in a dog, if he is to resist all kinds of weather conditions or if he is to be used in water; and what Airedale would be worthwhile if he could not go to water at any and all seasons of the year? The coat of Tintern Tip Top seems to be of the right quality and texture to suit the practical man. In matter of breeding Tintern Tip Top represents a shinning example of judicious line breeding and is the exemplification of what Mr. Phillips intended to do when he decided to combine the blood of the great families in this strain of his own. With such an intensification of blood lines it is no surprise that this dog is able to stamp the qualities of his family upon his progeny, for we all know that the more a certain family is intensified, the more likely one is to get the desired intensified results of one's breeding operations. In this close combination of the Midland and the Oorang blood, Tip Top represents for his particular family just what Teddy the Terror represents in the intensification of the Clonmel Monarch blood. Tip Top goes back on both sides of his family to his foundation strain in such proportions that the individuals in each generation may almost be figured with scientific precision which is a condition similar to that of Teddy the Terror, the latter representing one of the best working families, while Tip Top represents the modern bench-show type.

Stretton Squire, the sire of Tip Top, was by Midland Rollo out of Manor Princess, she by Havelock Pyppe which was by Tintern Desire out of Stockfield Bluebell. Floss, the dam of Manor Princess, represents lesser known individuals, her sire and dam being Rufus and Nell, but Midland Rollo was by Tintern Desire, by Crompton Oorang, and Witton Lady, while Yellow Princess, the dam of Rollo, was also by Rufus out of Nell. It is self-evident that this combination of blood was not one of mere chance, but on the other hand, that it was so combined with a definite purpose in view.

Mischievous Girl, the dam of Tip Top, was an intelligently bred; she being by Stockfield Revenge out of Bridgit, the latter by Tintern Desire out of Stockfield Lilly, she by Highgate Heather, out of Watland's Marvel. Stockfield Revenge is a son of Midland Royal out of Floral Wreath which is also by Midland Royal. From a study of this breeding it is easy to understand why Tintern Tip Top was more than a mere flash in the pan.

Tip Top is now the property of the Caswell Kennels of Toledo, owned by Chas. Quetshke, and in his Ohio home is still doing well in the stud, although his days as a performer on the bench are over. He is getting good puppies and his daughters are producing. As this is coming down to present-day times we cannot go into details on the progeny of Tintern Tip Top, but it is not out of place to mention that Caswell Ladie Boy, the dog which Mr. Quetschke presented to President Harding on the day he was inaugurated President of the United States, is one of Tip Top's sons; one of his best, however, is Normanion Tipil, bred by Phillips, but soon coming here, where he made a great record.

It must not be supposed that while the success of the Tinterns was transpiring in this country and in England, other families of terriers were not also proving their worth in both realms of endeavor, but I shall leave that for another chapter.

IMPORTED CRAGSMAN DICTATOR.

IMPORTED CHAMPION, DOREDA CRAIGMILLER PRINCE.
Winners, Dogs, New York, 1921.

CHAPTER VII.

Modern History (Continued)-Abbey King Nobbler and His Family-Other Noted Strains-Rex Persaltum and His Get.

If the Airedale made rapid strides toward popularity and improvement in the East, this condition was even more remarkable in the West. For a time after C. P. Hubbard wrote that article on the Airedale of the East and West there was still a distinction between the types, for such dogs as Judge Dexter were winning at the western shows. In 1909 this dog, under the late James Mortimer, took winners in St. Louis. He was a rather large-size animal with broader skull and cheek than the more modern conceptions demanded, but he was a terrier of substance; a son of Red Raven and Gamecock's Lassie, he represented the blood that was the vogue in the West and, for that matter, a line of breeding that at the present time is almost essential to maintain the working qualities of the Airedale. Reserve to Judge Dexter was one that Addyman showed, called Watland's Reginald, a dog which was imported from England and a son of Master Briar and Watland's Queen. In bitches, one of the W. J. Phillips breeding called Endcliffe Victoria in this country won the purple, with George Thomas at the other end of the line. Victoria was the new note in Airedales; splendid in her make-up, showing like a princess and very attractive in general balance. She was out Mr. Phillips' winning bitch Princess Ida, by Wellington King. Strathearn Elizabeth, reserve, was not far behind Victoria, some even thinking that the latter might have won, but Elizabeth did not have the strength of foreface nor the expression that her more successful rival had. The same year, at East St. Louis a son of champion The Gamecock won the winner's distinction. This was Wood Grange Topper. It will be seen from this that Red Raven and the Gamecock were being bred to with regularity in the West. Wood Grange Topper was only a puppy when shown here, having been whelped in February, 1908, (the show took place in January, 1909), a big fellow with immense bone and substance, but coarse and lacking in real quality. In bitches a good daughter of Barkerend Marcus took the high honors. This was Dumbarton May Bloom, a real toppy bitch with an abundance of quality. The Gamecock influence was in evidence here also, for a little sister of the winning dog was Wood Grange Vixen, which took the reserve. Dr. C. A. White was the judge on this occasion.

But all during these years the Chicago fanciers were coming fast. Perhaps the most noted kennel in Chicago was that of Francis G. Porter whose kennel prefix of "Abbey" was one to conjure with, but his career was meteoric and after a great flash on the Airedale firmament of the country, the kennels were dispersed to the four winds as it were, but the dogs he brought over from England did American breeders a world of good. The kennels were operated with Richard Abbot as manager and it was mainly through him that Mr. Porter was enabled to buy the best in England, for hardy Lancashireman that he is, Richard Abbot was first of all an Airedale breeder and was able to spot them in the rough. Abbot was responsible for a number of good ones coming over among them being Clonmel King Nobbler, known in this country as Abbey King Nobbler, Clonmel Isonomy, a son of Rockley Oorang, Freeman Terror, and hosts of others, both dogs and bitches, to which we shall have further occasion to allude.

The nearest competitors of the Abbey Kennels were those of the Vickerys who were not only interested in Airedales, however, but spent time and money on other breeds notably Irish and fox terriers. The Vickerys' career was as brilliant as that of the Abbeys, and it was more lasting; they not only bought some of the best-among them Tintern Royalist-but they were also quite successful in breeding them, though their star began to wane after a few years also and along about 1919 the kennels passed out of existence. Another kennel which gave the two mentioned good competition was that of W. M. Reay, known as the Briergate Kennels at Deefield, near Chicago. In these kennels were such dogs as Briergate Rex Persaltum, Briergate Brightlight, and a host of excellent bitches.

Alex H. Stewart, who later became the owner of Abbey King Nobbler, but who was originally a bulldog fancier, was also coming into notice at about this time, and when he took over some of the best of the Abbeys, his place in Airedale realms were assured. I have only touched lightly on the activities in and about Chicago in order to show the connection between the East and the West, principally to point out two things; first, that the difference in type at this later period indicated no material divergence and, secondly, that the later importations from England were even greater dogs than the earlier ones, and that it is to the progeny of these later ones we are obliged to look for the principal winners and not the the American-bred ones descended from the earlier importations. Naturally, there are exceptions here and there, furthermore this earlier blood is essential at the present time in bringing and maintaining balance to the breed in this country. As a matter of fact, had it not been for these earlier importations and the blending of their blood with the later ones, who knows what might have happened. Perhaps the Airedale of today would be a diminutive show dog, of great quality, but no size and substance, and perhaps those who cherish the breed today for its sporting characteristics, might have discarded it for something else long ago, or adhered entirely to the old-time large types as we found them in the West in the very early days. Whatever conclusion we may arrive at, there is no gainsaying but that later importations proved very useful both to the sporting and the show Airedale.

The dog par excellence, the terrier that will live for all time as the great exponent of the breed is to my mind Abbey King Nobbler. In him was represented everything that the Airedale fancier desires: type, quality, gameness, and the power to transmit his qualities, both physical and temperamental. To my mind, Abbey King Nobbler is the best Airedale I have ever seen or ever expect to see. That statement is made after due deliberation; and in making it, I have in mind the dog's record and what his descendants have done toward perpetuating the working strains. This may sound paradoxical when speaking of a strictly bench-show dog, but nevertheless it is a statement that I am led to make through long years of personal experience with his blood and to do so without reservation.

At least I can make it in the face of actual experiences I have had with his daughters in crossing them with the inbred Clonmel Monarch blood.

In some respects Abbey King Nobbler's early career is similar to that of Clonmel Monarch. Unlike Tintern Royalist and several others, he did not come forth with a flourish of trumpets and take the world by storm. He was one of the type that finishes slowly, but when matured, few could pick faults with him. Personally, I should have preferred seeing him a size larger than he was, but if that would have meant the sacrifice of any of his other qualities,then it would have been a calamity. He was big for his size; that is, he was well proportioned, abundance of bone, good substance, sound-looking, powerful. His coat was of the deep rich black and tan and the texture was excellent. There was something about the pose of Abbey King Nobbler that caught the eye at once. He had the long, lean head, the strong lower jaw, the fiery, small eye, and he was well filled up before it. His neck was lean and joined the head with that classy arch that gives an Airedale poise, especially when the neck goes into the shoulders in clean fashion as was the case with King Nobbler. His legs were absolutely straight, his feet were small and catlike and while I always thought he might have had just a trifle more power in loin and quarters, this fault was so slight as to be almost negligible, but it was because of his absolute perfection in every other way that one noticed this very trifling discrepancy in perfect balance. I looked the dog over carefully on a number of occasions, but this was, of course, after he had come to this country, when he had filled out and was at his best. At New York, in 1917, for instance, in that great class of Airedales, he was easily the best of the lot and, when it comes to class and quality, that year brought out a wonderful lot of dogs. His nearest competitor- or at least this was so according to the official placings-was York Ryburn Swell, a dog which became an international champion also and which at that period was sweeping the country, being shown everywhere. York Ryburn Swell was then the property of the Hillcote Kennels of Rochester, having been "discovered" shortly before this period, by Theo. Offerman on the occasion when he judged in England.

As a puppy King Nobbler made his first appearance at Crufts show in London; he was at that time raw and unfinished but just the kind of material to work on by the expert, if he sees a trace of quality and the essential sound points. Evidently some of the "knowing ones" recognized the latent possibilities, despite the fact that the dog did not do much at this show. The result was that they began making overtures to Nobbler's novice owner, who, however, proved to be less of a novice than was anticipated, for he would not listen to cheap prices. His talk in large figures discouraged most of the would-be buyers, but not so the firm of Clonmel, namely Messrs. Mills and Buckley, who were still as actively engaged in picking up good ones and selling them to America as ever. One thing about this firm, however, when they found that they could not buy at their own price they invariably bought at the seller's, and it is a matter of record that they paid larger prices for Airedales than any person or firm in England. King Nobbler became their property, and for a time was known as Clonmel King Nobbler, which name was changed when the firm of Mills and Buckley sold the dog to Francis G. Porter of the Abbey Kennels of Chicago. No doubt, they made a nice profit on their sale, but they are to be commended upon their insight and their perseverance in buying good ones when they find them and few found more than they.

Abbey King Nobbler did not remain the property of Mr. Porter very long, as we stated earlier in this chapter, but he fell into good hands when Alex H. Stewart became his owner along with several others, including Young King Nobbler which, however, Mr. Porter had the distinction of breeding before he disposed of his kennels. Young King Nobbler is not a dog which can be classed quite up to standard with his famous sire, but he is a good one nevertheless. His dam was the very good Clonmel Mesalliance, a Chicago-owned one, which was not only a high-class matron, but an exceptional show bitch also. To tabulate the high-class sons and daughters of Champion Abbey King Nobbler would require more space than the limits of this book will permit, but it may be said that in late years no other dog has approached him as a successful sire. He is in every sense to the present period what Clonmel Monarch was to an earlier decade. Among a few of his well-known winning sons were the previously mentioned Young King Nobbler, Chesney Monique, Brandwood Imperious, Yankee Girl of Ashborne, Brandwood Yankee Consul, Abercorn Gold Edge, and hosts of others. It is not his winning sons and daughters, however, which appealed to me as the outstanding feature of Abbey King Nobbler's greatness; it is the fact that so many of his daughters were of the type that could produce game, courageous terriers when bred to the right sires. I have had considerable personal experience with his daughters and found them all good. I doubt if King Nobbler was ever used as a sporting dog, but he had the prepotency to transmit this quality to a high degree through his daughters and for that reason his individuality and his blood lines were valuable to the practical man.

Most of his daughters were on the small order, but experience has taught that the fiery, small-eyed, small-eared, and snappy females of a family are the ones to reproduce the characteristics of the breed, and these daughters of King Nobbler seemed to be peculiarly endowed with the qualities that in their progeny brought forth the red badge of courage. Of the eminent success of his daughters when bred to working strains, however, I shall have more to say in a subsequent chapter, so let us in the meantime, take a hasty glance at the breeding of this dog which has done so much for the breed in this country.

Strictly speaking Abbey King Nobbler is a product of the combination of the Midland and the Crompton strains, but coming through sources somewhat different from those which produced the Tinterns. His sire Soudan Swiveller, a dog known in the old country as Gaelic Hussar, but after his debut in America his name was changed, which has been the case with so many dogs of the Airedale family and, therefore, occasionally leads to confusion.

Soudan Swiveller, a dog of good stamp himself, was by Elruge Monarch out of Gaelic Beauty, she by Danny Craing King, out of

Morgan Nell, and Elruge Monarch was one of Master Royal's sons out of Clonmel Reseda, by Clonmel Bed Rock out of Clonmel Philomel. So much for the sire's side of the house; it was through the dam of King Nobbler, however, that the Crompton-Midland combination came into evidence. Gay Flossie, his dam, was by Leyton Mainspring out of Leyton Peggie, she by Midland Royal out of Caissbrock Noreen. Leyton Mainspring was by Crompton Oorang and Mistress, hence as far as the combination of the blood in the male line is concerned it is a union of those desirable lines which have always proved successful, and therefore Abbey King Nobbler was no accident, but the result of intelligent mating. That he has done so well in perpetuating the qualities of his breed both in respect to type and conformation as well as in courage, stamina and the gameness, is not at all surprising. He is a dog that will stand out for many years as one of the beacon lights in the modern history of the breed.

Another English Kennel that begun to attract the attention of American fanciers during this period was that of the Karameas; in other words, the Karamea Kennels, owned by Messrs. Sheaves and Thurlow. They began with high-class matrons and after all, this is the keynote to successful breeding whether it is Airedales or any other variety. These breeders followed very much along the lines of prevailing fashion and successes, for their sires went to the Crompton-Midland Royals through Abbey King Nobbler and Tintern Desire. Karamea Rex, one of their leading dogs, was by King Nobbler and Wordsworth Elite, by Tintern Desire. In these two dogs they had the combination which, together with the high-class bitches they possessed, was the foundation for an excellent family. Success in England means only a matter of time until results are seen in this country, and in 1916 a dog from their kennels made his bow to a New York audience by taking winners at the Westminster show. The dog was Briergate Rex Persaltum, which the kennels of that name, located at Deefield near Chicago, acquired. The prefix being added when the dog became the property of his new owners. He came over with the Clonmel prefix, for it seems that the great majority of good ones find the Clonmel firm their clearing house for entry into this country. At all events, Rex Persaltum did not remain long in England after he once came out, but his debut was not a very portentious one.

It was at the Joint show in London, in 1915, that Rex Persaltum appeared in public the first time, where he won third in the open class. However, while this dog was still unfurnished and it remained for him to improve considerably in certain respects he seemed to have the stamp of quality that warranted the faith that was placed in him. I did not get to the New York show in February, 1916, where he took winners, but I saw the dog at Detroit the following June. I liked his size, his bone, and his substance, also his terrier attributes of life, energy, and general fire. He gave one the impression of gameness, and backed up by his blood lines, the dog seemed to have everything that was desired for perpetuating both the show and the working qualities of the breed. One thing that did not impress me quite so well that his ear bordered on the large and in his coat there are traces of that fluffiness, especially on the back of the neck that might be called soft-coated, but in the show ring, when the dog was put down at his best, these shortcomings in the matter of coat were not so easily detected. I have found also, that this quality of coat is likely to be seen in many of his sons and daughters. The saddle is usually black and harsh enough and the coat is of close texture, hence this shortcoming is not nearly so detrimental as the harsher, but more open coated ones which are still prevalent even among the big winners. At Detroit Rex Persaltum had keen competition and the dog which ran him closest was King Nobbler's Double, Norman MacKenzie's good terrier which won the open class over York Master Key, second, Caerphilly Marvel's Double was third, and Vickery Lodestar, reserve. King Nobbler's Double is not a brother or a son of Abbey King Nobbler as some might suppose, but by Wadsworth Royalist out of Miss Nobbler.

Briergate Rex Persaltum had comparatively short career on the bench and is now the property of the Welty Bros., of Wheeling, W. Va. As he was whelped in July, 1914, he should still have several more years in the stud.

Up to the present time he has sired several very good ones among his sons being First Flight, owned by Enno Meyer, of Cincinnati, and Hockwell's Hobo, out of Ashborne Sister Sue, owned by the Hockwell's Kennels of Dayton, Ohio. Both of these sons of Rex are also siring good ones and as I write I have in mind several by Hobo and one in particular by First Flight which should be a credit to the family.

Reverting again to the breeding of Rex Persaltum and the excellent blood lines that he represents, let us examine further into his family tree. His sire, Karamea Rex, is by Abbey King Nobbler out of Excelsior, this bitch having been to King Nobbler before the latter left England. Karamea Rex as an individual was good and he also had the power to transmit his characters to a high degree, but the combination of blood that he represents does not make this surprising. Excelsior was a daughter of Champion Rockley Oorang, out of Nineveh Nettle, and Rockley Oorang is the son of Crompton Oorang and Rockley Vista, the daughter of Midland Royal. Here is the Crompton-Oorang-Midland Royal combination, and will be remembered in the pedigree of Abbey King Nobbler, we have through Gay Flossie another strong combination of the same blood. Is it any wonder, therefore that Rex Persaltum transmits many of the attributes that come also through other lines, particularly that great courage and gameness, which at least, the practical sportsman considers all-essential. Through Karamea Cerebog we get a double cross of Elruge Monarch once more, and therefore we go back to Master Royal on all sides. The breeding of this dog, like so many good ones of other notable families, represents line matings all the way through, and as the individuals of the family were strong, vigorous animals, possessing the desired attributes of the terrier, if follows that these qualities are thus intensified to a high degree.

While on the question of gameness, I recall a puppy bred by the Hockwell's Kennels by Hockwell's Hobo out of a granddaughter of Abbey King Nobbler. As Hobo is Abbey King Nobbler on his dam's side, he being out of Ashborne Sister Sue, it follows that this was a strongly line-bred youngster. It was the one regret of the owners of this puppy that they ever left him go, but he was sold to a man in the Northwest who wanted an allround dog and evidently he received it, for nothing more was heard of the puppy after his expatriation from his own country. Hockwell's Broom Pedlar was the youngster's registered name. He not only had type and quality, but at six months old was one of the gamest Airedales I have ever seen. The conclusion that may be drawn from this is that, if you intensify the blood of two or more families that possess an unusual amount of grit and gameness, you are sure to increase those qualities, if that is the object in the mating, and the policy of the Hockwell's Kennels has always been to increase the working qualities of their strain. Rex Per Saltum may not be taken advantage of to the extent that his quality warrants, but it will be a pity, indeed, if breeders neglect him, for a dog with so many good qualities and the prepotency to transmit them, should not have his light hidden under a bushel.

INTERNATIONAL CHAMPION, YORK RYBURN SWELL.

Painting by Enno Meyer

TINTERN TIP TOP.

CHAPTER VIII.

Beacon Lights of Well-known Strains-Winners at Latter Day Shows.

In this year of 1921 it might be said with perfect justice that the Airedale strains of England and America are so identical that the best in the British Islands cannot improve our families on this side and that neither can the choicest in America improve the breeding of England's elite but mindful of the many good ones that came to America after the days of Clonmel Monarch and his contemporaries when the entire Airedale world agreed that the best was here, I am going to make the statement with reservations. We need not go to England for new blood if we use care, intelligence and logic in making our breeding selections, but the fact remains that breeders on the other side are so far superior to us in this matter of breeding that it will be nothing surprising to see a new one come over now and then that is able to beat our best American-breeds. Why is this? Principally because most of our American breeders wish to begin at the top instead of adhering to some stead-fast policy in their breeding operations and that before success is attained, they lose interest and take up some other fancy or pastime. That is the principal reason why America has produced such few breeders. I have only to cite a few kennels as an example. Some ten or twelve years ago, no kennel or individual had a brighter opportunity to accomplish great things in the breeding realms than the Abbey Kennels of Francis G. Porter. Some of the best dogs and bitches were quartered here and the opportunity was like fortune knocking at the door. Another great kennel was that of the Vickerys; what a wealth of material in these kennels! Both began with great enthusiasm, bred a few good ones, and then like ships that pass into he night, they went into oblivion. The Anoakia kennels of Santa Anita is another example and C. P. Hubbard, formerly of Atlantic, is still another. What opportunities the latter had to produce the best combination of working and show strains in America! But Mr. Hubbard moved to California, took himself a wife and forgot Airedales. Thus through the whole category one finds numerous kennels whose stars shone brightly for a brief time, only to be dimmed when new interests attracted the attention of their owners. Jos. Laurin, of Montreal, has been one of the most consistent breeders, but the Colnes are no longer in evidence at bench shows these days.

Taking into consideration the brief history of these large kennels, one is naturally forced to the conclusion that it will not be the men with unlimited means who are able to buy the best at sky limit prices that will become the breeders of the Airedale in America, but on the other hand the small owner and breeder who has a bitch or two and who is able to raise a litter now and then in his back yard who will bring forth the best dogs of the future. Furthermore, it will be the small breeder who is more likely to keep up the high standard of the Airedale as an all-round working dog, for unlike the large kennel owner who keeps his dogs housed up in expensive kennels the year round except when they are on the circuit, he uses his dogs for practical purposes and thus, perhaps, there is a future for the working Airedale. As a matter of fact, I stand ready to predict that the Airedale's future will be a parallel case with the pointer and the setter-it will be the small breeder who produces a few dogs for his own pleasure who will bring out the flyers ever so often. The stock is in this country to bring about such results and there are enough fanciers of the breed who love it not only for its ability to win on the bench, but for the sport and general satisfaction he obtains in owning one or more. But in this dissertation on the Airedale's future as a bench and working dog, I have lost sight of my original thesis, which is to briefly consider some of the individual winners which have come from England in recent years and also of our own American-breeds that are winning on the bench these latter days.

Although bred by the same man, Mr. Brown, King Nobbler's Double represents somewhat different blood lines from his Abbey King Nobbler. I referred to King Nobbler's Double as having won reserve to Briergate Rex Persaltum at the Detroit show of 1916. This dog was touted by some as being equal, if not superior to King Nobbler and having made a record in England, he soon found a home in America. The purchaser was Norman MacKenzie, of Humber Bay, Ontario, than whom no keener sportsman or better supporter of the Airedale exists either in America or England. Mr. MacKenzie owned other good ones previous to the time of King Nobbler's Double, and he has owned dogs even superior to him since, a notable example being his son, Polam Maxim, the leading bench-show Airedale before the public at the present time, but of this dog, more anon. King Nobbler's Double may not have been the equal of Abbey King Nobbler, but he was a fine, upstanding specimen and judging from the number of good puppies that he has sired, the dog has been a decided benefit to American breeders. A rather notable feature about King Nobbler's Double was that he deceived his experienced breeder, Mr. Brown, who allowed him to get away from him as a puppy, the purchaser being A. C. Mitchell, from the south of England. The dog was one of the kind that did not show what his future would be while still a weanling, but it is surprising how he came along and when he was shown at Manchester, under that well-known adjudicator, John G. Horrocks, he went to the top, although he was sold to America before he attained his full title for champion. In this country he had his ups and downs, but his record is a most creditable one. The dog's greatest fault was that he did not show to advantage in the ring; in other words, he did not make the most of himself and while he was always said to be a dead game terrier, his appearance in the ring frequently denied this assertion, although I am of the opinion that it all depended upon how the dog felt. When he was at his best physically, he generally showed to advantage, when not, he was listless and apathetic. When I saw him in the ring at Detroit in June, 1916, I do not think the charge of lack of fire could be laid against him. He took reserve winners on that occasion to Briergate Rex Persaltum, but there was such a trifling margin between the two dogs that the award might as well have gone the other way without injustice to either.

Polam Maxim is unquestionable the Airedale of the hour. His career began in England as a very young dog, but he was soon selected for a prominent place in the estimation of Airedale judges. His breeder was none other than James W. Gill, who will be remembered as having produced that great bitch, Polam Milkmaid. Polam Maxim came into the limelight at the very early age of seven and one-half months, and at this date, July, 1921, is a better terrier than ever. Having been whelped in the spring of 1915 the dog is now past six years old and still retains his excellent outline, his good shoulders, straight front, and clean-cut head. This is another instance of an Airedale coming to his own early in life and retaining his good form until well past maturity, that is, as ages are reckoned in canine lives. His first judge was Chris Houlker, who awarded him his first challenge certificate in England at the early age just referred to. Shortly after this, at the Bradford show under Holland Buckley, he received his second certificate and then, as a very young dog, he came to America and into the possession of Norman MacKenzie, who at the present hour is still showing him with unabated success, the dog being under the expert handling of Bert Swann. Only a few weeks ago, that is, early in June, 1921, Polam Maxim had the distinction of winning the special for the best of all breeds at the show of the Ladies Kennel Association which took place as usual, at Mineola, Long Island, New York. This show is not an easy one by any means. Polam Maxim was obliged to beat a number of very high-class toys, also the well-known wire-haired and Irish terriers which are on the circuit this season, not to say anything about a few good greyhounds, Russians and other sporting breeds, but he never looked better than he did on this occasion and no one would have taken him for a six-years-old and past, when they say him pose with all the statuesqueness of the born ring master and the fire and power of the real terrier. Polam is a dog of good size, bone and substance as these characteristics go in modern times. As a matter of fact, he is as large as one really cares to have them when that quality is considered from the real standpoint. Polam Maxim is, in other words, balanced. He has the bone, the substance, and the great strength in jaw. He has the well-sprung ribs, the short back and the powerful loin and quarters. A dog need not be oversized as long as he is balanced and there are no weaknesses anywhere, but so frequently we see Airedales which are all that is to be desired in head and front, but entirely out of proportion, possessing rear parts that are not in keeping with their excellent heads and fronts. It is the dog with such faults that one must eschew if he wishes to breed for that power and solidity that are so essential to the working type of Airedale.

The head of Polam Maxim is long and narrow, with a small, properly placed eye of the right color, a neat, well-carried ear, excellent expression and above all, a harsh coat of the proper texture, quality and color. Polam Maxim is undoubtedly the dog to take the leadership of his period, as Clonmel Monarch was in the early day, as Tintern Royalist was somewhat later and Abbey King Nobbler was during those years just preceding the rise of the present star.

York Ryburn Swell was another terrier which had quite a vogue in this country after first beginning his career on the Tight Little Island. He was bred by R. H. Uttley and was by Powder Plot out of Elba, which on the face it might appear as outer line breeding, but in going back in the pedigree one finds that familiar fountain heads of the breed. York Ryburn Swell was discovered by an American and he was none other than Theodore Offerman. He judged Airedales in England about eight or nine years ago, where, at the Kennel Club championship show, he saw a young terrier which appeared in the Novice class only. Mr. Offerman promptly spotted him as the best of his class and then placed him over the winner of the open class, which gave Swell championship honors the first time out. The dog appealed to Mr. Offerman to such a degree that he promptly arranged for his purchase although he allowed him to remain in England for some time longer where the dog soon completed his wins to make him a champion, and when he left England he did so with an unbeaten record. In America he eventually became the property of the Hillcote Kennels of Rochester who showed him fearlessly East and West. The dog was beaten occasionally, it is true, but his record is one that stamps the dog as one of the stellar attractions of his period. The year 1916 was probably his best, winning at Chicago, St. Louis, and most of the Middle West shows. His kennel companion was a bitch called Grey Mist which was quite good in expression and terrier characteristics generally, but not quite the best in stifles. York Ryburn Swell was a dog which attracted attention at once in the ring. He showed to perfection, carried his ears properly and they were of the small variety; his eyes were very dark and nicely placed; he was short in back, but it always appeared to me that he showed with somewhat of a roach; at least his back never appeared to be quite as level as it might be, and another fault, he was just a bit weak in foreface, which gave him a somewhat effeminate appearance. His color was extremely good, being that glossy black on the saddle and deep, rich tan on the legs and feet that always contrasts so well. His coat was harsh enough, but rather open and it required more or less manipulation to make it appear at its best. Withal, however, York Ryburn Swell was a dog that in his day stood well up with the competitors of the circuit. It was at the Chicago show of 1916 where he beat the promising son of Abbey King Nobbler, the latter being out of the good bitch Clonmel Mesalliance. Some thought Young King Nobbler should have had this decision, and whether rightly or wrongly, the decision was a close one. At St. Louis, shortly after, he had little trouble in beating Pike's Peak Bobs, a powerfully made dog for his inches, but rather large in eye and smutty in face. As a sire, Ryburn Swell has a few moderate winners to his credit, but none of his get ever attained the heights that their father rose to.

I have already referred to the Oorangs and of the foundation of that family coming from the Cromptons. Rockley Oorang, which went to Jos. A. Laurin, of Montreal, did a great amount of good as a sire, after he arrived in Canada, but he was already past his best days as a specimen for the show bench. King Oorang was one among the many of his sons that continued to carry on the blood; Clonmel Isonomy was still another and still another was Flornel Oorang. These are only a few of his numerous sons and daughters that stand out as bright lights in present-day Airedale pedigrees.

Clonmel Isonomy was a powerful built dog with immense bone and substance; perhaps a little wide and full in the skull as he grew older, but he was that type of the dog which always appealed to the man looking for power and solidarity. He stood squarely on his four feet as though his legs were pillars of concrete, his loin was knitted to his body with ligament of splintered steel and his stifles were a mass of muscle and bone. Such strength in an Airedale is what we need for a big game dog, and more's the pity that this dog passed literally out of existence without leaving more issue of his kind. I remember judging him at Cincinnati, Ohio, in 1912. Three dogs stood well up in the open class; they were Clonmel Isonomy, Kootenai Chinook, and Sir Bingo Binks. All three were powerful terriers and all were showing well. Richard Abbott held the lead for Isonomy, for at that time the Abbey Kennels were in their glory and Abbott was their head man. Alf Delmont had Kootenai Chinook, and I do not remember who was showing Sir Bingo Binks, but the latter being a local dog it might have been his owner, Dr. Maeder. Chinook was in his scrappy mood and it was all Delmont could do to keep the dog from rushing at the others in the ring. In fact, he is one of those terriers always going about with a chip on his shoulder, as it were, and ready for what might come. Delmont encouraged this desire for a fight at first, for it puts the fire into a dog, although Chinook had just about enough fire as it was. The dog became so excited in his endeavors to get to Isonomy, his particular rival that he would not remain on his feet. Isonomy's eyes were emitting fire also, but Abbott had him under good command. He allowed him to go the length of his lead, but kept him just out of harm's way. Evidently he knew that it was exciting Chinook and causing him to show at his worst, but Delmont started this method of attack and Abbott seemed to know just how far he could permit his dog to go to show the sparkling verve of the daredevil spirit and still not lose his head. Isonomy never showed better, besides there was just a bit more finish about him than Chinook; it was a close thing; both dogs were my kind. Chinook, a big-boned fiery terrier, all gameness and dash. Isonomy with just as much of these qualities, but somewhat more gentlemanly about it in the ring. The decision went to Isonomy, Kootenai Chinook was second, and Sir Bingo Binks, third. Any of the three would have suited me for size, substance, Airedale expression, and character, but Isonomy was in full bloom of coat, Chinook was not far behind and Sir Bingo Binks, while possessing a nice long head, had a rather large light eye, and his color was not the best, being grizzle on saddle with legs and feet of a shade resembling washed out old chamois leather. The next year, under Mortimer, Sir Bingo Binks won the purple in the finals at Cincinnati, but he did not have the competition that he encountered the previous year. I might observe here, that Bingo Binks also carried the Oorang blood through his sire, Crack Oorang.

Clonmel Isonomy was a frequent winner those years, but when the Abbey kennels were suddenly dispersed and the dog became the property of the Cragwold Kennels of St. Louis, little was heard of him. These kennels are the property of Edwin Lemp and are located at Kirkwood, a few miles out from the city. Mr. Lemp is first of all a sportsman and while he may not use all of his dogs for practical purposes, I know of a number that came from his kennels which proved to be excellent "varmint" hunters; some of those emanating from his kennels going into the pack of J. M. Avent, of Hickory Valley, Tenn. Gustave Pabst, Jr., of Milwaukee, also had some of this strain which found their way into the packs of workings strains. In addition to Isonomy, Mr. Lemp also purchased Abbey Master Magic which was a great winner in England, and various others. Referring to Richard Abbott, it was through him that Freeman Terror became noted. He won the title of Champion in very short order. The dog figures in a number of pedigrees and therefore is of interest to American breeders. While I never had the opportunity to look this dog over carefully, he is described as having been a terrier with excellent body, exceedingly short back, good spring of ribs, with nice depth of chest, very good in hindquarters, legs and feet, and an abundance of bone to give him the power. Somewhat lacking in strength of foreface and possessing an eye that was rather on the large order, but in color of coat and texture, he was as good as the best, and as for gameness and grit, he is described as being all that could be desired.

While Watlands Marvel figures in quite a few present-day pedigrees and was himself a remarkably well-balanced terrier, he did not become the great sire that many anticipated he would. He was by Primrose King out of Primrose Marguerite. He possessed the much coveted black saddle, which in his days was far less common than it is at the present time, hence his blood in a pedigree is worth much, for the influence of a line of breeding that aids in perpetuating the desired qualities should always be given due consideration. Vickery Crack, campaigned in 1920 by the Ashborne Kennels of Burlington, Iowa was one of his sons, out of Lady Minerva, a daughter of Crompton Oorang; and therefore Crack combines two very good families. With his bone and substance, he should do well as a sire. While on the subject of Ashborne Kennels it might be mentioned that their Great Scott, a son of Tintern Desire out of Iowana of Ashborne, she by Abbey King Nobbler, has recently come into the limelight by reason of his son,

Ashborne Buccaneer, a dog which is winning quite regularly at the present time. Great Scott is a dog with a wealth of bone and strength all the way from tip to stern, and it is said that he is a very game dog also. It was on the assumption that his blood would make a good cross with some of the strains with which I had been experimenting that I secured two of his daughters several years ago. They were procured when they were about five months old and from all indications they were going to develop coats of the right texture and color, but a shyer pair of Airedale puppies I never saw. They were absolutely afraid of their shadows and could not be cajoled into approaching a human being. This timidity is frequently seen in Airedale puppies when still under a year old, but I have noticed that some of the most timid, when handled properly, eventually become the boldest and the gamest. On this account when these puppies came we endeavored to make the most of them, thinking that in time they would overcome this abnormal fear of men and moving objects, and thus they were allowed to grow up with several others of about the same age. It was impossible, however, to train them to even come and get their food while a human being was about and after keeping them until they were about eighteen months old during which period everything was tried that modern training methods could devise in an effort to develop their intelligence, they were finally given away to farmers in the hope that running wild and taking to self-hunting might develop their latent instincts, but they disappeared after a short time and nothing more was heard of them. One of them had a litter by one of our gamest dogs, from which a bitch puppy was saved, but she displayed no more intelligence than her mother, and she, too, was given away. I believe this was one instance where there was a total lack of brains. Naturally there are idiots of dogs and, therefore, their shortcoming are not attributed to their sire, for perhaps the dam had as much, if not more to do with the mental qualities of these bitches as the male side of the family. At all events, it was not thought wise to intermingle this blood with a strain that had been bred and developed for gameness, hence it was, in my opinion, the best thing to do to allow them to pass out of existence as far as the Airedale world is concerned. Whether they are alive and roaming about at large I am unprepared to say, but at all events they strayed from the farmers' homes where they were left and nothing further has been seen or heard of them. I am inclined to put down this experience as the exception rather than the rule, for this experience would not in the least destroy my faith in a line of blood that has hitherto always proved to be able to perpetuate the qualities so necessary in an Airedale, although through these two particular bitches such would never have been the case.

Reverting again to the Oorang blood, a son of Rockley Oorang made quite a stir when Flornel Oorang made his appearance at the Derby show some years ago, when J. J. Holgate judged. The dog was picked up for the small sum of fifteen pounds by our American fancier, Mr. O'Connell, who was visiting England at the time. Evidently the Yankee fancier had a keen eye and what is more, he arrived at the show a little ahead of the English regulars who made a business of buying the embryo stars as they appear for the first time. Flornel Oorang did not win at that particular show, but he was recognized shortly after and went right on. He was a large, well-developed puppy, possessing unusual bone, with the best of legs and feet, and his head was one of the long kind with the lean cheeks, well-set ears and properly placed eyes. He was criticized for lack of soundness in rear parts, but age improved him in this respect and he eventually developed into an unusually sound and substantial Airedale. One of his sons was Patrick Oorang which came to this country after winning at the Cheetham Hill show, and another was Studholme Sultan, a dog, which was quite well known at the Middle West shows two or three years ago.

Rhosddu Royalist is another son of Primrose Rebound which has been attracting some attention in this country as a sire. In England he gained his honors quickly; in this country his principal success will evidently be in the stud, for he was already well up in years when he arrived in the United States and having been whelped in November, 1913, he is at this writing, (July 1921) well along in his eighth year. His dam was Maesgwene Trixie, herself a well-known and consistent winner in England, and nicely bred, it is no wonder that her son is able to impart his good qualities to his offspring. Royalist is now the property of the Briar Croft Kennels of Youngstown, Ohio, where he is being well patronized at stud. One of his principal winners which is much before the public at the present day is his daughter, Doreda Warland Strategy, the property of the Doreda Kennels, of Highland Park, Ill.

CHAPTER IX.

Outstanding Bitches of Later Days-A Glance at the Winners of Some Recent Shows-The Airedale Bowl-Winners the New King Bowl.

If America was blessed with the best Airedale dogs, it is equally certain that the number of good bitches were almost equal proportion from the very beginning of American Airedale bench-show history down to the present time. I have no intention of enumerating all the winners in bitches or in dogs, for that matter, this being a general treatise on the breed and not a book of records, hence if the reader be disappointed in not seeing the name of some favorite, let him not attribute it to lack of discernment on the part of the author in failing to mention it, but rather to lack of space and the impossibility of alluding to each and every dog or bitch that has gained some prominence by winning on the bench. History has been made very rapidly in this country during the past ten or a dozen years; so fast, indeed, for the Airedale, that a book of complete records of the winners is almost an essential thing for the fancier who wishes to keep in touch with what is transpiring and I have often wondered why the Airedale clubs of the country do not compile such a record which would be of inestimable value for future generations, just as the field trial records of bird dogs, compiled by the late Major Taylor, has now become a necessity to field-trial followers.

In the absence of such a record, however, most of us remember many of the great bitches that have had their day on the Airedale firmament in recent years. I have already mentioned those earlier favorites, but who cannot recall the typical Kenmare Sorceress? A winner of stellar magnitude in her days. Then there was Vickery Soubrette, Clonmel Messalliance, Aman Gem, Chesney Monique, and the beautiful Bingley Blossom, Briergate Bright Beauty, Almonte Peggy, Spring Bank Scepter, and Sunshine down to present times, where in this year of 1921 a number of great bitches are before the public, including Grey Eagles Rexine, Doreda Warland Strategy, War Bond, Wordsworth, Enchantress, Marathon Lilymore, Boxwoods Bashful, Lucknow Dream, Gamecock Supremacy, Banker's Daughter of Grosse Ile, and hosts upon hosts of others. The significant part of it is that all of the late winners are American-bred.

Going back to some of the importations, however, we call to mind that splendid bitch, Cherry Tree Queen, which came over at the same time Tintern Tip Top crossed the Ocean and went with him to the Anoakia Kennels at Santa Anita, California. This bitch was shown as early as 1914 at which time she did not make much of an impression at the Joint show of London, because of the fact that she failed to show the dash and fire so necessary in an Airedale, but in a few moths it was a different matter. She changed ownership after that show and her new master seemed to be able to get the best out of her. As a consequence, later reports of her say that "never was a more fiery bitch shown," which points a moral that I have often found, could be applied in bird dogs. The fact is Queen's first owner evidently did something to her that soured her and for that reason she was never her best. This often is the case with field-trial dogs. In the hands of one man they are sour and lacking in verve, but change them to a new master who understands their idiosyncrasies, and the best is brought out. Had Queen not changed owners when she did, it is quite likely that she would never have made the great record that she did which ended eventually in coming to America as the wonder of the day. She won seven consecutive championships in England, which is very likely a record for Airedales, and then came to America with Tintern Tip Top in 1915.

Casually picking up some of the bench-show catalogues of the past decade and a few of those of the first year of the present, we find that in 1912 Clonmel Isonomy, then in the heyday of his career won the winners purple at the Cincinnati show, and reserve to him was the big, husky, but typical Kootenai Chinook, the son of Lakeview Chipstone and Kootenai Sweet Lavender. I referred to both of these dogs in the preceding chapter as having judged them at this show, but that year both were very much in the limelight and did considerable winning.

In bitches it was none other than the neatly-turned Spring Bank Scepter which took winners at the same show. She being at this time the property of F. G. Porter of Abbey Kennel fame and was shown by Dick Abbott. Sceptre was one of these rich black and tans like all of the Springbanks of the Wilson brothers, and while the accredited breeder of this bitch is A. H. Rushbrook, it was through the Wilson brothers that she was brought up and probably bred also. She was by Crompton Marvel out of Ellerlie Vesta, very typical and possessed of a coat of harsh texture, but to my mind she did not have that rugged appearance which I like to see in Airedale, whether it be male of female. She showed well, however, and her good expression, her small dark eye, and well-carried ear, together with her excellence of pose, despite the fact that there was little fire (and for a bitch this may easily be overlooked) always brought her well to the front in any kind of competition. At this show here in Cincinnati that year it was simply a walkover for her, for Sporty Girl, the daughter of Marshall Tinner and Oaklawn Vesta, was off in cost and deficient in head properties as compared with the beautiful Sceptre.

The Vickery Kennels, one of the leading Airedale breeders during the past decade, generally showed a second string at some of the Middle West shows and thus gave their dogs which were clearly of a second-degree order as compared with their best, a record also. In 1915 they showed a dog called Vickery Vesuvious which won at a number of shows, including winners at Indianapolis. He was a dog which while good in certain respects never impressed me as a first flighter, being rather light in bone and small, besides lacking in that first-rate quality outlook that we like to see. After this season not much was heard of Vesuvious. He was by Yorkshire Hussar out of Benbow Ket. At this same show, Kippen Desire was given the reserve, but it would not have been out of place had he been placed over the Vickery offering, although I do not mean by this that Kippen Desire was very hardly used even if he did receive only reserve winners. He came from the kennels of W. J. Phillips of Tintern fame, but in this instance it appears as though the dog was sold to this country on the strength of some of the earlier Tinterns that came over.

In bitches at this same show, the Vickerys were again successful; this time with Vickery Rainbow, a nice quality bitch somewhat lacking in size, bone, and substance, however, but Rainbow did very well at some of the smaller Middle West shows. She was one of the kennels' own breeding, being by Vickery King out of Judy.

At the Chicago show this same year the Vickerys took winners and reserve in dogs with Vickery Oorang's Advance, a son of Authority's Double and Vickery Vesuvious mentioned as the Indianapolis winner. There was a vast difference in the type of these two dogs, however. Briergate Bright Light was the winning bitch at the Chicago show, owned by the Briergate Kennels and a beautiful bitch she was. All terrier in expression and action, she also had the bone and substance, and in these qualities easily stood over Vickery Rainbow which took reserve winners.

In 1916 a young dog came out at the early Middle West shows called Crack Shot. He was still less than a year old when he took winners at Columbus, Canton, and several other places and by many of the followers he was hailed as a coming star. Crack Shot was a big husky fellow, the kind to appeal to the Western man, who always kept a dog's utility in mind, but when one considered that he was still but a puppy, his future did not seem to be the most promising. He was owned and bred by J. M. Williams, but Frank Addyman was campaigning him and he made the most of the shows west of Pittsburg. Had Crack Shot remained in the same good form that he was as a ten months old puppy, he would have been a consistent winner, but many of these precautious youngsters, showing at their best when less than a year old grow coarse with more age, and that seemed to be the destiny of Crack Shot. He had a rather large ear and a full eye, but his cheek was clean at that age and his shoulder well set, but he was not seen on the show bench which he grew older and whether he died after this one season's campaign or simply became too coarse for the show bench, I am not prepared to say, but even though he did not possess the finer points of so-called, quality in head, his good bone and substance, together with his well-sprung ribs, and his general sound appearance would have qualified him as a good nick with many of the weedy bitches that were so prevalent at that time. Furthermore, he was nicely bred, being by Champion Illuminator, out of Abbey Trixie. Crack Shot took winners at Canton and Columbus, but at the former place, Studholme Sultan was the reserve dog. While the latter could never be termed a real flyer I never thought that he received all that he was entitled to. One handicap that always stood against him was that he never showed with the dash and the fire that an Airedale should. This was the trouble at Canton and at various other places where I saw him; and he was in good hands, too, for it was the well-known bench-show impresario, Alf Delmont, who had him in charge. Studholme Sultan was not in the best of coat at Canton, but I recall very distinctly that Delmont was considerably disappointed in not winning over the puppy, Crack Shot. Sultan was a son of Flornel Oorang.

Patrick Oorang, a dog that was not bred to to the extent that his quality warranted, was responsible for the winner in bitches; this was Patrick Sensation, a very nice sort, with good expression and terrier character. She won on various occasions during that season. The reserve bitch was Briergate Bryn Maurice.

The Columbus show was a repeat of Canton as far as the winning dogs are concerned, but in bitches the very high quality, Brandwood Imperious, the good daughter of Abbey King Nobbler and Clonmel Imperious, went over Patrick Sensation, and this was not her only win, for she continued right on and made and enviable record. In length of head, elegance of front, shortness of back and texture of coat, Imperious was beyond cavil, but I always thought if she had been filled up just a trifle more before the eye she would have been improved wonderfully. However, she met some of the best bitches of her day and won quite consistently.

The Chicago show of 1916 was among important ones, as far as Airedales are concerned, of the year for even though the Abbey Kennels had been disbanded by this time, kennels devoted to this breed had sprung up like mushrooms and competition in the Illinois metropolis was next to New York. All the classes were well filled and no dogs walked away with ribbons for want of competition. The judge was William H. Mulford, of Chestnut Hill, Pa., and he had his work cut out for him. The puppy class brought out a dozen entries, but the young giant, Crack Shot topped the lot, taking the blue from Vickery Rebound, a different type of dog entirely, being on the small order, with light bone and an unfurnished appearance in body, but the class was a rather mixed lot, and he was easily entitled to second place, for the third-place winner, Soo Flashlight, a son of Kippen Desire and Ashborne Bingo, was a rather long-backed, narrow-waisted specimen, which time would not likely greatly improve. There were fourteen entrants in the Novice class for dogs, the blue going to a nice one shown by Richard Abbott, called Abbey Duke, but which was known previously under the name of Pike's Peak Duke. He was a son of Abbey King Nobbler out of Abbey Mistress Magic. Not a large dog was this and rather lacking in bone and substance, besides his eye was a shade too light and rather full, but he showed with terrier fire and stood well up on his legs. Scotch Swell was another of the small order, and I may say here that during this period the small ones were more in evidence than at any other time. Quality, so-called was, so it seemed, bringing the Airedale down to the size of the Welsh terrier. This dog was a son of York Ryburn Swell, a dog which was described in an earlier chapter. Marathon Handicap, the third-place winner in the novice class, was of a somewhat sturdier type, but he failed to show well, being listless and apathetic in the ring and this, in a terrier, is always an abomination, whether it be fox, Irish, Welsh, or Airedale. In the American-bred class Alex Stewart's good young son of Abbey King Nobbler met the Novice winner and Young King Nobbler rightly won. He showed to perfection and while one might have preferred to see him with just a trifle more strength over the loins, he was a terrier with a front and with a varminty expression that is so characteristic of his family.

Abbey Duke was second, but there was quite a stretch of daylight between the two and for third came Pike's Peak Bobs, which Alf Delmont made the most of in putting him down in the ring to advantage, but he was placed rightly when he received the yellow ribbon. The Limit class was a repeat in that Abbey Duke took first, and Crack shot second, Young King Nobbler was not entered here and a new one by the name of Caswell Knight, belonging to Chas. W. Quetschke, of Toledo, took third. The latter, I recall as a nice up-standing dog, but of a very light washed-out tan in color. In this class a new importation by Alex Stewart was also entered, but failed to get into the money. This Judicious Censor, a dog, which came to this country with a very good name, but he did little here, although his blood lines are such that he should have been used at stud much more than he was. His sire was Landscove Oorang, a son of Rockley Oorang and Landscove Lass, and his dam, Jewel Case, by Primrose Rebound out of Landscove Lass, the latter being by Midland Royal out of Landscove Lady, consequently this dog was line-bred much in the same manner that several other great families were produced. Another dog which was shown in the open class and failed to get a place was Earlwood Hickory Limb, by Gamecock Mixer, out of Miss Millitant. This dog became known principally through his son, Earlwood Warlock, which began winning along about in 1917.

York Ryburn Swell won the open class, leaving second place for Abbey Duke, but Young King Nobbler was not in this class and only met Swell when it came to the finals. The decision went to Ryburn Swell by a close margin, but Young King Nobbler beat out Abbey Duke for reserve. The bitches were a very nice lot also, several unusually high-class ones competing. In the puppy class Yankee Girl of Ashborne was the winner over Chesney Cheerful. The former is a good daughter of Abbey King Nobbler and Silverton Muffet which in later years became the mother of winners. She has the terrier type and the small eyes, good ears, and general expression, which generally denotes the producer of type and in this respect, her owner E. G. Marquardt was not disappointed.

It was at this show that the Chesney Kennels of Otto W. Lehman, of Chicago, then rapidly coming to the front, made a great exhibit of bitches with which the kennels were very well stocked at this time. Chesney Monique was the American-bred winner, a very high-quality bitch, rather small and light in bone, which, as I have previously said, was the prevailing note in those days. But Monique beat out all the others when it came to the finals; her nearest competitor being Vickery Aman Gem. For her size I always thought Vickery Aman Gem a little better in bone and substance than Monique, but it was a close thing between these two bitches and much depended upon their condition on the day they came together in competition and how they deported themselves in the ring. Another good one was Chesney Cherry Circle, somewhat tucked in the loin giving her too light an appearance in this respect, but a bitch with quality. In the Novice class Hillcote Scotch Mist was the winner. I always liked this bitch because of her size and her general substance, the only thing wrong with her being that she did not stand any too well on her back feet and was inclined to throw her hock joints in, a fault that is always very conspicuous in an Airedale. She was a daughter of York Ryburn Swell and belonged to the same owner. Chesney Monique, the winner of the purple, was a home-bred, being by Abbey King Nobbler out of Marlborough Sceptre. I do not know if this bitch is still living, but if she is, she would now be nearly seven years old, having been whelped September 1, 1913. Vickery Aman Gem was by Officials Report out of Maid of Caerwent and was whelped August 14, 1913.

The St. Louis show of 1916 followed the week after Chicago, but the classes were not nearly so good; many of the dogs were absent, among them Chesney Monique, which left the principal competition between Vickery Aman Gem and Chesney Cherry Circle, the former winning with some little margin although Cherry Circle was looking very well here. In dogs it was Ryburn Swell once more, and to the surprise of many, Pike's Peak Bobs was given reserve to him in the finals. Baughfell Briar, a good upstanding dog of the Elmhurst kennels was second to Ryburn Swell in the open class, and there was no reason why Bobs should be placed over Briar for reserve winners. The latter, though light in color of tan and lacking the black saddle, was a dog of considerable type and being a sound one with an abundance of bone, he might have easily had the reserve position, for Bobs really had no license to beat him at any point except color. Scotch Swell, referred to in the review of the Chicago dogs, was easily the winner in the Novice class for dogs, while his litter sister, Hillcote Scotch Mist, won the Novice class for bitches, the second-place winner being Elmhurst Electra, a very nice young one, which won the blue in the puppy class. The latter is by Patrick Oorang out of Elmhurst Ballet. Another of this same breeding is Elmhurst Emperor, which only received V. H. C. at this show, but later on did considerable winning. It is interesting to note that in the American-bred class for dogs which was won by Pike's Peak Bobs, Vickery Lodestar, the sun of Tintern Royalist, which began his career so brilliantly several years before, was second. At the time of this show, Lodestar was nearly five years old, having been whelped July 25, 1911. Third in this class was Crack Shot, the big puppy which did so well a month or so earlier, and the reserve was Scotch Swell, which had just won the Novice class.

Passing over a few months and taking up the catalogue of the Detroit Club, whose show was held in June of 1916, it is seen that Briergate Rex Persaltum was the winner in dogs with King Nobbler's Double to which we have previously referred, a close second, taking as a consequence, reserve winners. By taking the winners purple in bitches with a very nice stamp of terrier, called Sunshine, Norman MacKenzie who owns King Nobbler's Double, had his disappointment in losing in dogs somewhat assuaged, though good loser that he is, he generally knows when he is beaten and even though sometimes he is beaten when he should not be, he has been in the show game long enough to understand its ups and downs.

It was at New York in 1917 that Abbey King Nobbler came back at his best and took winners over York Ryburn Swell and never did this well-known winner look better than he did here, despite his years. But new stars were rising on the firmament; stars that while they did not show their real brightness to the extent of being recognized by the judge on this occasion, were destined, nevertheless to come to the front with persistent regularity within the next few months. York Master Key which had his inning the year before and among other places, winning second in the open class at Detroit the previous June, was unnoticed in the American-bred class. It was an aggregation of strong ones, it is true, but he might have gone over some of the flashes in the pan that were exalted.

The winner of the class, however, was rightly placed. This was Granite Invader, a sturdy dog of magnificent bone and substance. He was criticized for lack of refinement and quality, but he at that time was just the type of a dog needed to offset the tendency to go for the weeds which were becoming so prevalent. Granite Invader was power from every angle that one looked at him. There was something to be desired in head properties, it is true, but those excellent quarters, those strong stifles, thighs and hocks, the excellent couplings denoting superlative strength and withal, a good straight front, he was a dog to be recognized, at least in this class where he won. In the puppy and Novice classes the winners on this occasion never went much farther, but there were others among the recognized ones or among those which only obtained inferior places which proved to be "lasters" as for instance, Geelong Terror, which only received third in the open and H. C. in the puppy class. Granite Invader, while it might be conceded that as a strictly bench dog is not in the actual first flight, is at least much nearer to it than many of the others which received high places. He is by the imported dog, Kindale Crack, out of Brilliant, and was bred by his owners, Messrs. Nichols and Wolf. The dog was handled by Frank H. Addyman and he went out through the Middle West circuit with very fair success. At the time he appeared in New York he was just about a year old. Geelong Terror, which did little at this show, was also destined to shine later. He also was bred by his owner, Robert F. Height, and was by York Oorang's Masterpiece out of Geelong Soubrette, having been whelped July 5, 1916, and therefore just old enough at the time of this show to be eligible to competition. The Limit class was won by Polam Maxim, a dog which was just coming to be recognized, but it must be remembered that he was still less than two years old at the time of this show. Not much was ever heard of the dogs placed back of Maxim in this class except possibly Patrick Oorang, which as a sire has shown himself to be successful.

The open class was a very interesting one. I have already pointed out that the two well-known ones, Abbey King Nobbler and York Ryburn Swell accounted for first and second and eventually winners, but back of them was considerable talent and quality. For instance, third in the class was Normanton Tipit, a dog, which also at this time was still less than two years old, and destined to do considerable winning. He was one of the W. J. Phillips breeding and at the time of this show had not been in this country very long. His sire was Tintern Tip Top and his dam, Tintern Vixenish. King Nobbler looked so well here that I do not think he could very well have had his colors lowered, but whether or not Ryburn Swell was in his right place by winning second over such a lot behind him has always been questionable in my mind.

Besides these three already mentioned came Polam Maxim, reserve, and Briergate Rex Persaltum, V. H. C., while Young King Nobbler had to be content with H. C. although under the circumstances it was no disgrace, for trailing still farther behind without a letter were several others of lesser note, but of very fair merit.

In bitches, Chesney Cherry Circle, looking much improved since I saw her the previous year, was the winning bitch, but here also there seemed to be an abundance of room for doubt, for in this class was the hitherto unbeaten English winner, Cherry Tree Queen, which as I stated in a previous chapter had won seven consecutive championships in England and then became the property of the

Anoakia Kennels of California. This, however, does not signify much for conditions all enter into the equation. However, it did seem like there was some question as to whether or not Elms Primus should not have beaten Cheney Cherry Circle for top honors. Elms Primus is, or rather was at that time a grand bitch, all fire and action possessing size and also coat, color, and general balance. She was owned at the time by Messrs. W. F. Patterson and Chas. D. Platt, of New York, and was also a recent importation having been bred by W. D. Jenkins and was by Dargle Declare out of Paint Pot. Her date of birth is January 27, 1915.

The week following the 1917 New York show, came that of Philadelphia, and we journeyed over to the city of Brotherly Love on the Sunday preceding the show which opened at Horticultural Hall on Monday morning, February 26. Kaleidoscopic changes in awards from one week to another with various judges officiating are likely to occur in any breed and Airedales are no exception. W. F. Patterson adjudicated here and he proceeded at once to turn the New York awards of the week before topsy turvy, Volcano, and Charter Oak Advance Guard, winner of First and second respectively in the puppy class at New York, were not shown at Philadelphia, but Nattahnam Headline, the winner of third was there. Here, however, he was beaten by Geelong Terror, unnoticed at New York, and the award at Philadelphia was unquestionably right as subsequent events proved. In the Novice, Teatline was first in view of the fact that Terror was not entered in this class, and second to him was Brandwood Yankee Consul also an unnoticed one at New York. In the American-bred class, however, the judge again put Geelong Terror to the front with Nattahnam Headline second, and Granite Invader, third. The two placed on top are of the smaller type, but Invader, as I have previously said, is one of the sturdy kind. Naturally, one may have his preferences in type, but it was a rather vacillating way of placing types here, for the judge wavered from one to the other kind. Polam Maxim was placed first in the Limit with the puppy, Geelong Terror, second, but in the open, Normanton Tipit was placed over him. In this there was also a difference of opinion. Personally I thought Maxim should have had this decision, but Tipit was given winners and Maxim reserve. Tipit shows well, or did on this occasion although he did not have the fiery expression of Maxim, besides his ear is larger and in expression Maxim had some advantage. Briergate Rex Persaltum was third. There was nothing new in bitches that would have set the grass afire. In puppy bitches, Julia, a daughter of York Ryburn Swell, was beaten out for first by Ridgeton Fire Queen, mainly because the latter was better finished in muzzle. In the

American-bred class, Bingley Barmaid was first, and in the Limit, Briergate Bright Beauty, beat Sunshine, Norman MacKenzie's bitch which won the purple at the Detroit show preceding June, and Bright Beauty rightly won the purple, while it was a question between Sunshine and Marshfield Milkmaid for reserve, the former, despite her head which is a trifle short for real symmetry, won out for this place.

The Philadelphia show closed on Tuesday evening, and on Thursday morning the Central Ohio Kennel Club opened a three-day show at Columbus, Ohio. Not many of the Eastern exhibitors journeyed out to the Ohio City, and the Airedale entry was made up mostly of Middle West offerings, among them being several exhibits from the Oorang Kennels at La Rue, Ohio. This kennel has not been showing to any extent, but they put down several good ones. Their King Nobbler Oorang, a rather cobby dog by Abbey King Nobbler, still less than a year old at the time of this show, took winners over Studholme Sultan, the son of Fornell Oorang. It was a matter of taking one's choice between these two, Sultan, which I had not seen for a year, had evidently grown somewhat coarse in head and thickened in the shoulder, while the puppy stood too low on the leg for his sturdy body. The winner in bitches was Elmhurst Sweet Briar, a daughter of Baughfell Briar and Elmhurst Miss Oorang. The reserve winner was another of the Oorang Kennel's offerings, Promise Oorang by name, she was a daughter of Rex Oorang and Lois Oorang.

Cincinnati was next on the program and be it remembered this was a busy circuit that spring of 1917, hence one had little breathing space between shows. Cincinnati was judged by Dr. J. E. De Mund, but in Airedales he had no new precedents to set. All of the dogs were well known by this time and with the exception of a local or two occasionally, nothing new was to be seen. Like Columbus, there were no Eastern exhibitors and with the exception of the dogs in charge of the regular handlers who made the whole circuit, the entry was principally from the home city. Granite Invader, looking as well, if not better, than he did in the early part of the season, took winners over Brandwood Yankee Consul, while Bingley Barmaid beat Ridgeton Fire Queen in the finals for bitches.

At Cleveland, however, the Airedale entry took on a decided spurt. Dr. De Mund was slated to judge here also, but owing to illness was compelled to go home. The breeds allotted to him were, therefore, parceled out to judges who could be picked up at the show. Thus, our breed was assigned to E. F. Watson, who handled himself with the confidence and good judgment that long experience in breeding and showing gives one. There were only four puppies, but the judge promptly spotted Geelong Terror for first honors, and Caswell Warrior, a new face, and a promising one, for second. This is a son Soudan Swiveller and Elruge Rival, and at the time he was a promising youngster which the later years justified, for he became a sire of several noted ones, among them the 1921 winners, War Bond and War Chief of Davishill. Elmhurst Briar was the third dog on this class. For first in the Novice, Duquesne, a son of Cricketer and Queen Mac, was selected. A rather attractive dog was this at that time, though he had been shown with little success at some of the earlier events of the season. He is just one of those kind which is short of that real quality which attracts one, and yet he has no glaring faults. Personally I preferred Caswell Warrior for first here; he was placed second, Elmhurst Briar third, and fourth went to a sturdy son of The Red Rook of Ashborne called Ashborne King. In the American-bred, Granite Invader was promptly recognized for first honors while Briergate Bruiser, a nice little dog rather on, the small side and lacking in bone and substance, was second. This is the little dog which Messrs. Welty and Frazier, of Wheeling, W. Va., campaigned with varying success for a season or two. He is a son of Abbey King Nobbler and Briergate Bumptious. Herbert M. Straus' Middletown Sandy was third and Brandwood Yankee Consul, reserve. As a matter of fact, Yankee Consul could well have gone to second place in this class. In the Limit, Duquesne, also a Straus offering as previously alluded to, was first over Granite Invader, a decision that few could coincide with from any standpoint and in one respect alone Invader had a wide margin over the little Louisville dog and that was in strength of stifles and quarters. Say what one might about coarseness in head, which criticism was often heard against Invader, but the outstanding fact remains that he had a head to suit the balance of his sturdy body. Briergate Bruiser was third, which decision was clearly a dividing of type, for if Duquesne deserved first then to follow type, Bruiser should have beaten Invader and the latter gone down to last place. It was clearly a case of either first or last for Invader and not an intermediate place. King Nobbler Oorang, the puppy from the Oorang Kennels, at La Rue, which took winners at Columbus, was reserve in the Limit class. Then came the open with a variety. Polam Maxim took the honors and King Nobbler Oorang was second. Rex Persaltum was entered but absent; third was a rather ordinary one called Tintern Flyer, bred by W. J. Phillips and, therefore, imported being Tintern Tip Top out of Tintern Victory. The Red Rook of Ashborne, now seven years old and one of the big sturdy types with excellent color and texture of coat, but with a wide skull and rather short, but powerful muzzle, was reserve. No doubt, the average big-game hunter, one who has been accustomed to hunting with dogs, would have selected the Red Rook out of the entire lot as the kind for his uses and he would not have been far wrong. Polam Maxim was a rather easy winner of the purple and Duquesne was the reserve; no doubt, this was the best win he ever made in such company.

In bitches Marshfield Milkmaid won the purple and Bingley Barmaid was reserve.

There is little to say of Canton which followed Cleveland. Polam Maxim was first and Granite Invader reserve in winners dogs, and in bitches it was Marshfield Milkmaid and Bingley Barmaid.

Chicago was my next show after Canton; here matters went mostly to locals, principally because many of the circuit chasers remained away and, secondly, because there are or were at this time a number of very excellent kennels of Airedales in and about Chicago. The judge on this occasion was George F. Downer, a Chicago man, and it might be said in passing, that the Chicago Kennel Club of those days was as diligent in bringing out home talent in judges as it was in exalting locally-owned dogs, six out of the nine judges who served on this occasion being from Chicago or its suburbs and these six had the important breeds of the show. Local dogs had it all their own way in Airedales, Vickery Kennels winning the purple in dogs and with Vickery Boomerang, a son of Pike's Peak Swiveller and Pike's Peak Prim. Reserve went to Chesney Cordite, owned by the Chesney Kennels. The former, while a fair dog of mediocre stamp, was not one to become excited over while Cordite, a rather pleasing dog by York Ryburn Swell out of Trebor Miss Ginger soon passed out of the limelight after this season. In bitches the Vickerys won both places:first, with the very good Vickery Aman Gem and reserve with Vickery Happy Thought, a good-headed one, but weedy and light in bone. Granite Invader, the dog that looked like a giant among these light-boned specimens, was reserve in the American-bred class and Rex Persaltum, looking quite well on this occasion, shown for specials only, won for best of the breed. Thus it will be seen that the local element accounted for all the important places which in some instances was right, but in others entirely wrong. In glancing over the list of entries on this occasion, however, it will be seen that the exhibitors from places other than Chicago and suburbs were scarcely represented, and those that were, got little for their pains as for instance, taking the open class Vickery Boomerang was first, Vickery Crack, the Burlington, Iowa, dog, by

Watlands Marvel, and Lady Minnie was second, and Polam Maxim, easily the best dog in the lot, was third. the entry shows Normanton Tipit in the class also, but I do not recall whether he was present or not; at all events the officially marked catalogue does not show him marked absent. Another local dog which afterward made more history than the winners, was Warlwood Warlock, owned by Earle J. Woodward. A nice-headed dog with good coat and more substance than most of those which were placed over him, but on this occasion he was absolutely apathetic in the ring and in placing him second in the American-bred class and reserve in the open, the judge was taking more for granted that was consistent in the proper placing of dogs as they appeared on this occasion. One of the notable features about the Airedale classes on this occasion was the exhibition by the Chesney Kennels of a splendid trio of bitches and in this respect these well-known kennels were particularly strong. The bitches they had entered for specials only being Chesney Cherry Circle, Chesney Monique, and King Nobbler's Victory.

Taking up a catalogue of the Ladies' kennel Association of America, whose show took place at Westbury, L. I., in June, 1918, it is found that Normanton Tipit, now just past three years old, is still holding his own. As a matter of fact, he was in good shape at this show. I did not have the opportunity of going over all these dogs at this show, for being busy in one ring at these summer shows where everything moves rapidly, precluded the possibility of "seeing everything." I did notice, however, that several new ones among the crop of youngsters were making themselves known, one of these being Geelong Gladiator, a son of Geelong Cadet and Geelong Sceptre, owned by Jas. W. Ball, of New York City. The dog won the puppy class here and second in the American-bred to Boxwood Benbow, a good son of York Oorang Masterpiece and Ch. Polam Milkmaid, to which I have already alluded. Benbow was the reserve winner in the finals to Polam Maxim. Geelong Terror, a half-brother to Benbow, was entered here also. Boxwood Blue Bird won in bitches and a nice one show is, though rather on the small order, but she has sufficient bone, for her size to give her the proper stamp of substance and balance. Marbald Aranda was reserve, but I failed to get a good look at this bitch, and therefore I am not prepared to give an opinion as to the respective merits of her and Elms Primus which was second to her in the Limit class. The Airedale terrier entry at this show was somewhat light, but June is already becoming late for shows and this was more or less of an off year, for we were in the throes of war and almost within sight of the show grounds was the camp of our own soldier boys who were about to embark for France. In fact, boat after boat was leaving the docks with the brave lads aboard to take part in the affray which was at its height during the eventful summer of 1918.

A week following this show came that of the Ladies' Kennel Association of Massachusetts, at Auburndale, Mass. At Westbury, W. E. Baker judged, while at Auburndale it was James W. Spring. Evidently these two judges did not see things alike but in dogs Mr. Spring did not have the same classes to pass on. Neither Polam Maxim nor Boxwood Benbow were shown and so Boxwood Burgomater, which only went fourth in American-bred dogs at Westbury, was given winners and Abrecorn Chief by Abrecorn Gold Edge out of Empost Briar Sweet was reserve. It was in bitches, however, where the reversals came. Here Elms Primus, which could not even get reserve in the finals at Westbury was placed over Boxwood Bluebird, the winner at the latter place, and when it comes to a personal choice I preferred Primus to Bluebird; the latter was unquestionably a sweet little thing, but rather small; and another thing against her was her age, for she was still less than a year old and therefore not matured, while the daughter of Dargle Deputy and Paint Pot-that is, Elms Primus-was a finished bitch of good character and quality.

In February, 1919, came the great doggy event of the year in bench-show realms-the Westminster Kennel Club show in New York-and naturally this fixture is the one that places the seal of approval upon all that has gone before. Here Polam Maxim, the great young terrier which was stamped as a third rater in Chicago, again came to the front, winning the purple in a good class, and next to him came the puppy of the summer shows of the year before, Geelong Gladiator taking reserve. This dog came right along and sustained the promise of his youth and as for Polam Maxim, it seemed that he looked better every time out. In bitches it was Briergate Bright Beauty for the purple and Boxwood Denlock Duchess reserve, the latter a daughter of Tintern Tip Top and Cintra.

The years 1920 and 1921 marked continued activities among bench-show breeders of Airedales, with specialty clubs springing up in various parts of the country, which is evidence that the terrier that has taken such a popular hold upon the American fancy, is still as well thought of as ever. Polam Maxim, is undeniably one of the leading dogs before the public as his recent wins including the best of all breeds at the Mineola show in June, 1921, testified. A splendid record is this for a dog which has been before a dog which has been before the public as long as he.

Another dog, which during the years of 1920 and 1921 created quite a bit of attention is Brookhaven Laddie, bred by A. C. Fiske and owned by Wilford Wood. Brookhaven Laddie was whelped May 9, 1917, and is by Geelong Cadet out of Brookhaven Folly. He has been shown fearlessly and frequently during the past two seasons and his consistent success with the dogs of the East is some indication that the judges on the Atlantic Seaboard are beginning to recognize size when it is combined with quality and soundness. Brookhaven Laddie it a large and powerfully built terrier, standing on legs that are constructed of a wealth of bone and muscle, and possessing shoulders, ribs, loin, and quarters that denote power. Some have criticized him for lack of fineness, but after all, had we better not sacrifice some of this fineness when we secure all the real essentials of the Airedale? At all events, he is the type of dog that fills the eye of the terrier man, having utility always in mind as the first of the breed's requisites.

In the Middle West activities were never better sustained than during the seasons of 1920 and 1921. At the Airedale Specialty show of Cleveland in March, 1920, with W. E. Baker, of New York, judging, the classes were good and the quality far above the average. The winning puppy was Aberfoyle Warland, by Cragsman Dictator out of Warland Strategy and in the Novice, Brierfield Tipit, a son of Normanton Tipit and Marvelous Girl took the blue, while Richmond Invader , a son of Granite Invader and Richmond Pollyanna, was second, which is some indication that the winners of yesterday are siring the winners of today and that American breeders are well on the road toward producing the right kind of dogs, for bench shows at least. At this same show Vickery Crack won the Limit class, with Briarcroft Fountain Test, a close second, but in the open, Earlwood Warlock was the winner and eventually took the purple in the finals were Vickery Crack, reserve, while Briarcroft Double Decision was third in the open; the latter, a son of Hatties Double and Theaker Judy. In bitch puppies another daughter of Tintern Tip Top, Maplewood Mylady, took first in a very fair class and in the open, The Banker's Daughter of Grosse Ile, made her debut by taking the blue. The latter figured quite extensively in the Middle West shows from that time forward, sometimes securing more than she deserved, at others, not all she was entitled to. I saw this bitch the first time in Detroit in May of 1920, at which time I noted on my catalogue that she was a bitch with a quality look, a keen expression, good skull and ear, light in loin and quarters and exceedingly light in second thighs. In other words, from the front view she looked well, from the rear, there seemed to be a decided lack of substance. I have not seen her since then, however, and it is said that she has improved in this respect quite materially, but there was considerable room for improvement. Marathon Lilymore is another bitch which has been shown extensively up to the present time. She is a daughter of Earlwood Warlock out of Marathon Althea. Briarcroft Lady Bachelor was not quite in the same class with the two bitches just described, but one that could win in very fair company when at her best. Another very attractive bitch shown at the Cleveland specialty show was Clonmel Rhos Royal, a daughter of Rhosddu Royalist. At this show it was The Banker's Daughter of Grosse Ile and Marathon Lilymore for the final honors.

The show of the Mahoning Valley Kennel Club took place at Akron, Ohio, September 24 and 25, 1920, with Enno Meyer, of Cincinnati, judging the Airedales. The classes were not so large, but the quality good. In the Limit, the imported Crompton Theobald was a rather easy first, and likewise Braircroft Fountain Test won well in the open. The two coming together in the finals, the judge gave the purple to Fountain Test. Briarcroft Double Decision, taking second in the open, was not looking as fit as he does at times. Many picked Crompton Theobald for the winner in the finals, but according to the judge's own explanation, in his estimation, Fountain Test beat Theobald in ability to show and in color for according to his report, Fountain Test was at his best on this occasion and was full of fire Theobald is a big, strong terrier with exceptionally good quarters and stifles which are qualities that are always important ones to many of us.

The puppy winner was that good youngster, War Chief of Davis Hill, a full brother of a later litter to War Bond, being by Caswell Warrior out of Peggy-the Rough-Neck, she by Teddy the Terrier, out of Hockwell's Tess. Both are owned by R. L. Davis of the Davishill Kennels of Ft. Thomas, Ky. War Chief, at the time of this show was still sapling puppy, scarcely passed the limit puppy age for showing, but he appealed to those who can detect a good one in the making. I saw this dog the last time the latter part of May, 1921, and he has filled out, attained finish in head and is in all essentials a real terrier with excellent dense, harsh coat, wonderful terrier expression, perfect ear carriage, and what is more, built for substance and power. War Bond, his elder sister, won here in the Novice class and many picked her as an easy winner in the finals, but according to the statement of the judge, she did not show to suit him, being very listless and apathetic in the ring. She accordingly was awarded reserve winners to Briarcroft Lady

Bachelor, a bitch which she can easily beat when both at their best. Another good bitch at this show was Parlston Sweet Olive, which, however, is not as good now as she was, having thickened up in shoulder and cheek.

In San Antonio, Texas, the Club of that name held a show in November, 1920, where the Airedale interests were much in evidence, this perhaps is due greatly to the fact that the Mountainview Kennels, formerly of Butte, Montana, are now located there, and these kennels were formerly devoted to the breeding of working dogs, although they had the individuals to win on the bench on the bench, also. In these kennels at various times were such dogs as Champion Illuminator, Champion Bolton Woods Rush, and Champion Kootenia Radiance. In their new home in the Lone Star State, the kennels seem to be thriving well. At this show in November, 1920, Mountain View Sedan, by Mountain View Rush Light, out of Mountainview Reseda, took winners while one of the Ashborne breeding, namely Yankee Boy of Ashborne, now owned by Hillsview Kennels, was reserve. In bitches Hillsview Mistress won the purple while Frowzy Peggy was reserve. The interests in Airedales in this part of Texas, I may say en passant, are exceedingly on the increase, perhaps greatly due to the fact that Arthur Ward, now the owner of the Mountain View Kennels, is the secretary of this enterprising club.

The Mid-West Circuit of 1921 was one of the ups and downs for the various winners, especially among the bitches that were going the circuit. Once it was the War Bond, again it was The Banker's Daughter of Grosse Ile, then Grey Eagles Rexine, then Doreda Warland Strategy, and much the same applied in dogs. There seemed to be no consistency among the various judges on this circuit. One exalted bone, substance, and soundness when judging the dog classes, and when he came to the bitches, did just the reverse. A case in point is the series of shows in Northern Ohio. The Specialty show of the Cleveland Airedale and Fox Terrier Club had Enno Meyer for its judge. In winners dogs he placed Fern Top Rocket, the son of Ridgewood Rocket and Winsome Lassie over Ashborne Buccaneer. One of the strong features about Buccaneer is his unusual strength in rear parts, particularly in quarters and stifles. In this respect the dog placed over him fails. In bitches War Bond was placed over The Banker's Daughter of Grosse Ile. The latter loses greatly to War Bond in the same essentials that Fern Top Rocket lose to Buccaneer; at least this is the view of those who want absolute strength and soundness in rear parts. That same week under Breese, The Banker's Daughter of Grosse Ile was placed over War Bond, while Buccaneer took the honors of Fern Top Rocket. Thus it will be seen that both judges were inconsistent. The next week at Akron, Clyde Schaffert judging followed Meyer in placing the winners, proving that he thought this was the correct manner in which they should be placed, regardless of the apparent inconsistency, or perhaps only having the one idea in view, and that was to follow precedents. While on that subject I might add that there is too much stress laid on this feature in judging at bench shows; in any event many judges seem to prefer falling into the groove as made by their predecessor, rather than establish grooves of their own. This is particularly the case with novice judging, many of them placing dogs, not because they have any defined ideas, but because it has been done before. I do not intend to infer by this, however, that the judges just cited come under this category. Reverting again to those four bitches referred to, namely War Bond, Grey Eagles Rexine, Doreda Warland Strategy, and The Banker's Daughter of Grosse Ile, all have their little faults, it is true, but this is a quartette of bitches that will likely go down the circuit for several seasons to come and eventually take their place in Airedale history as four outstanding Airedales of the third decade of this century.

Thus I might go on indefinitely naming all the great and near Airedales of the day, or I might attempt to enumerate each and every kennel that is figuring at the present time in the production if the Airedale. At best this is an evanescent situation. The kennel that is prominent today may be out of business tomorrow; furthermore it is such an easy matter to inadvertently leave out just the particular one that I should like to mention, and for this reason I shall content myself with leaving matters as they stand, for in the course of unfolding this history of the bench-show Airedale I have practically touched upon all the stellar lights.

Before closing this rather lengthy chapter, however, I want to allude to several historical episodes that have done much toward creating competition and stimulating interest in breeding. One of these is the competition for the "Airedale Bowl" offered by the Airedale Club of America, competition open to all. The bowl has been in competition since 1910 and will remain the perpetual property of the Club, but a gold medal is awarded to the successful contestant to commemorate the win and the names of the winners are engraved upon the bowl. The trophy may be offered at the discretion of the committee at any show, not less than five times every year. This bowl having been in competition now nearly eleven years is in a measure the bench-show history of the Airedale in America. It has been won one or more times by the following dogs or bitches, all of which are champions: Prince of York, Kenmare Sorceress, King Oorang, Soudan Stamboul, Vickery Soubrette, Bingley Blossom, York Ryburn Swell, Vickery Aman Gem, Briergate Bright Beauty, Polam Maxim, Normanton Tipit, Almont Peggy, O. C. of York, and Doreda Warland Strategy.

Almost as important is the "Champion The New King Bowl," offered by the Airedale Terrier Club of New England, the bowl having been donated by Arthur Marritt in memory of his dog, Champion The New King. Like the "Airedale Bowl" this special goes to the best Airedale in the show: in the case of the New King Bowl, however, a replica of it is given to the owner of the winner. Among the dogs which have won this are: Soudan Stamboul, Kenmare Sorceress, Vickery Soubrette, Bingley Blossom, York Ryburn Swell, Kenmare Conjurer, Polam Maxim. It is curious to note that Vickery Soubrette won the trophy five times. No doubt, there were and are still as many good dogs and bitches whose names do not appear on these trophies, but that does not signify that they lacked the ability to do so. Circumstances in their case might have been the deciding factor.

The third notable event in Airedale circles which should be of special interest to all breeders is the Futurity show which has been established by the Louisville Airedale Club of Louisville, Ky. To qualify in this event it is necessary to nominate the dam at the time she is bred, the progeny of the union being thereby made eligible to compete, provided, of course, the owner of the dam complies with the stipulated rules as laid down by the club. This Futurity show takes place every year at Louisville, Ky., in September; the prizes are large enough to make it worth while to enter all dams and in time, if breeders support this event as it should be supported it will rank in importance with the same class of stakes that are offered in field trials.

HILLCOTE SCOTCH MIST.

THE AIREDALE TERRIER, VICKERY CRACK.

CULBERTSON BEAVER,
One of the last of Ch. The Game Cock's sons.

CHAPTER X.

The Working Airedale-His Many-Sideness-As a Big Game Hunter-As a Farmer's Dog-as an All-round Dog.

"**O**PPORTUNITY makes the man" is a trite, but very true saying and by the same token it applies to the Airedale. The human pupil in the early grades of his school life could not be expected to solve an intricate geometrical problem and neither can the Airedale, despite his reputation for intelligence, be expected to be taken from a kennel of bench-show ancestors and with no experience, give a satisfactory account of himself in the hunting field, whether it be on big game, the smaller "varmints" of the woods, wild fowl retrieving, or any other of the many accomplishments in which this many-sided dog has shown himself to be a master.

As I am writing these lines on this hot July morning, Teddy the Terror and his daughter, Hockwell's Patsey, are excitedly barking up one of the huge hackberry trees on the rear of my premises. They have a squirrel treed and they are telling the master about it. The squirrel is safely ensconced among the leaves of its nest in the crotch of the tree, out of harm's way, and is evidently enjoying the discomfiture of the dogs. Shortly before this climax the dogs were hunting in the field just north of the house and chased the squirrel out of the young corn. His squirrelship immediately took the adjoining fence and made for the tree. It is a regular morning's pastime for the dogs, for squirrels are protected here the year round and they are very plentiful, several families living in the adjacent trees while still a greater number make their homes in the oak woods across the way, but come over to the field for their early morning and evening meals-and perhaps for the sport of aggravating the dogs. It is good practice for the latter, however, and they are adept in the art of treeing. They will remain at the tree until they are called off, for it is a certainty that the squirrel will not come down, neither will he be molested by human foes, and evidently the squirrels of this locality know it.

In like manner the dogs have such experiences on the rabbits which are as plentiful as the squirrels, and thus the Airedales on my place obtain abundant practice. It is such experiences and such opportunities that make the all-round Airedale and I have no doubt that many a strictly bench-show strain, if given similar opportunities as fall to the lot of these dogs, would soon develop all the instincts that are latent in many families simply through lack of usage.

There are some strains, unquestionably, that are better qualified to make working dogs than others, but it is surprising how many strains are in existence today whose ancestors have had no work for generations, and yet puppies from such strains, if started properly, will come to their own. As I have stated on various occasions, so many breeders prefer the honors of bench show to making working dogs out of their dogs, because of the very natural fear that this rough-and tumble work of hunting may mar their chances for showing, and particularly do they hesitate in placing their dogs in packs that are used on big game as there is a likelihood that they may be killed or if not that, at least maimed to such an extent that their usefulness as show specimens might be forever ruined. One cannot cavil at this, however, for if an owner obtains more pleasure in showing than working his dogs, then by all means let him bring up his terriers for the purpose he intends to use them, but it is because so many families have not been worked for generations, that the distinction arose between the working and the show Airedale.

Another concomitant feature is that many of the show strains have been bred for show points to such an extent, that while certain improvements in so-called quality have been made, these were secured through loss of stamina, size, bone, substance, and above all, gameness That has much to do with the bad name some Airedales have received.

Not long ago a man told me that he, with a party of friends, was going on a big-game hunt in the far Northwest and that he was taking with him four Airedales that he had recently purchased. "Fine specimens," he assured me, "all of their ancestors are winners." "But have these dogs you are taking with you had any experience?" I inquired. The man looked at me in blank amazement. "I thought," he said, "That all Airedales would fight and that they take to big-game hunting as a natural thing." "I fear you will be disappointed in your dogs," I replied, "but perhaps if you go slowly, they may learn through sheer necessity." Months afterward this same man assured me that as a big-game dog the Airedale was a decided failure, that he left his dogs in the Northwest as he did not think them worth the price of carfare to bring home. Such experiences are to be expected, but they are frequently encountered.

The Airedale has won a reputation for being an all-round dog, game to the death and suitable to be used anywhere. Because of this impression, many sportsmen are thus misled by thinking that as long as a dog is an Airedale he should be ready to fill his requirements wherever he is used, experience or no experience. One would not expect the bird dog to perform his natural mission in life without training, nor would one expect the beagle or the foxhound to prove satisfactory when taken out of a kennel the first time and put into the field; nevertheless there are numerous people who imagine the Airedale should do everything any other dog can do without a day's experience or training.

While, as I have said, there are many dogs of the breed which will make good, even if descended from stock which has had no practical work for generations, I would advise the sportsman looking for a really useful dog to select one from a family known to be practical dogs, which does not necessarily mean that he must be an ungainly brute. There are any number of Airedales with show points which are also good working dogs, even though perhaps some of these strains lack the "quality appearance" that is the shibboleth of present-day bench-show breeders. Rather sacrifice some of this so-called quality for other essentials which, as previously pointed out, consists of size, substance, bone, gameness, and above all, intelligence.

For a working Airedale size should always be given consideration. I do not mean that it is necessary to select great, massive animals weighing eighty pounds or more, for such specimens are not only ungainly, but they lack in shiftiness, which, in bear or mountain lion fighting is sometimes as essential as extraordinary size. Many of the Western Airedale breeders who use their dogs in the Rockies have some large specimens, but they are gradually coming to the point where they realize that a dog weighing between fifty and sixty pounds will answer all purposes provided they have the heart, the courage, and the alertness that are so necessary. Personally for an all-round dog I prefer the males to run from forty-five to fifty pounds and the females slightly less. One bitch that I saw in one of the Southern packs recently, weighed about forty pounds, but she was the gamest of the game and would attack so fearlessly that sometimes it was her undoing.

While on this question of gameness, it is not out of place to digress here for a moment. Gameness and courage are decidedly different qualities from reckless impetuosity. Frequently one finds that when an Airedale is game, he is game to a fault, and when he is timid, he is so to exaggeration, and yet it has often been noted that many Airedales are very timid as puppies, but which with time and experience become the best kind of dogs. They discover their own powers, and while they lack the ferocious, daredevil recklessness they will eventually make the best kind of big-game fighters, for they are more cautious.

Er. Shelley has had considerable experience with Airedales in handling the Paul Rainey Pack in Africa. Perhaps no man alive today has had more varied adventures with dogs in Africa than Shelley, and as this extended over a period of several years, his opinion is above reproach. When one hunts lions, leopards, and other African big game with a pack of dogs ranging from hounds to mongrels and does this day after day for such a length of time, he is qualified to know. In the Rainey pack of dogs were two divisions: the hounds, or trailing dogs, used for following the scent of a lion or other animal and trailing them to their lair or where they came to bay, and the fighting does, which were released after the quarry made its stand. In this pack of fighting dogs were retrievers, hounds, mongrels, Airedales, and, in fact, any kind of a dog that would fight a lion. In a previous work, "The Working Dog and His Education," I quoted Shelley's opinion of the Airedale as a fighting dog and it will bear repetition here. "Some Airedales," says Shelley, "are more careful fighters than others, and a careful fighting Airedale is the most valuable of all fighting dogs when it comes to lions or the other big game of Africa. They never know when to quit and they can deal out dastardly punishment. On the other hand, a reckless Airedale can never be taught to be careful. He may rush into the thick of the fight and make a straight lunge for the lion's throat only to receive a serious blow from one of the huge paws of the infuriated animal which, if it does not kill him, makes it necessary to take him home on a stretcher, and the dog is of no use until he recovers. If this experience would teach him to be more careful the next time, it would be worth while, but it does not; for on the very next occasion he will do the same thing. I admire the Airedale for his extreme gameness, but when I get one that is game and careful, too, I think I have a treasure."

Some years ago, J. M. Avent, who at that time was one of the most indefatigable bear hunters of the South, had an Airedale bitch in his pack which was of the type that Shelley describes. She was a medium-sized bitch, powerfully built and as game and fearless as she was good in make-up. This bitch was introduced into the heterogeneous pack composed of all breeds from fighting hounds, setters, pointers, collies to common mongrels and through the spirit of emulation soon took to the business of fighting bears. In a short time she was the leader of the pack when it came to a bear fight. On one occasion Mr. Avent had a party of hunters down in the Mississippi cane bottoms not far from Memphis where bear were unusually plentiful. The cane was so dense that the dogs could not be seen more than ten feet ahead, but shortly after entering this place, pandemonium broke loose only a short distance away. The hunters with their corn knives hacked their way through the tangle as fast as possible, and as they came to a little opening they beheld a sight. A large she-bear of the black variety was standing there on her hind feet with the dogs baying around her, taking nips from this side or the other; once in the flank, again from the rear and again in the front. The old bear was kept busy turning from one side to the other; occasionally she succeeded in dealing a blow with her powerful front ways to some more daring mongrel that came too close and sent him howling away, and again she turned on the dogs as they nipped her from behind, causing her to spin about like a top. Just as Avent came upon the scene with gun cocked and ready to fire, the Airedale bitch made a lunge for the bear's throat and succeeded in fastening her sharp teeth in the soft flesh under the lower jaw. She gave a howl of rage and closed her powerful arms around the bitch. The other dogs were after her from all sides; she was a much-harried bear, but she cold hold her own in that howling pack; there was no opportunity to shoot and nothing could be done but await developments, everyone expecting momentarily to see the life crushed out of the Airedale's body by that terrific embrace and see her fall lifeless at the bear's feet. Such noise, such a medley of voices, such bellowings from the bear. It was a fight unto death for some in that party, and the first victim at that stage seemed destined to be the Airedale bitch. Meanwhile there came other cries and whimperings from a short distance, and some one in the party presently discovered that there were two cubs of the she-bear in one of the adjacent trees. One of them was shot, but as the real fight became more exciting, the attention of those present was attracted to the old bear which still held the Airedale hugged closely up against her body. However, it was evident that the dog was getting in some deadly work. The snarls of the bear became more vociferous, but the Airedale kept her hold. At last the opportunity came; that was a moment's lull, and as the dogs had momentarily cleared from the front leaving only the Airedale bitch clinging to the bear's throat, Avent took aim at her head and fired. The ball went crashing through her brain and she came down in a heap, taking the Airedale bitch with her, tightly gripped in her arms. In the confusion of the attack and the subsequent rapid maneuvers of bear and dogs, it was impossible to determine just what was happening, but when the bear fell, everyone expected to see the Airedale crushed in the terrible death grip of the bear. The latter was dead as she fell, but the dog? The arms of the bear were literally pried apart; blood was streaming down the sides of the bitch, but she still had her hold on the bear's throat where a great series of gashes gave evidence that her work had been deadly. She was actually pulled away from the bear, in the expectation of at least discovering that her back was broken, but such was not the case. Other than a few deep gashes made by the bear's large claws, she was unhurt and eager to go back to her work. Fortunately for her, in making her leap at the bear's throat she got directly under her head, which prevented the usual result of such encounters. Had she been farther down, there is no question, but her fate would have been sealed then and there. She soon recovered from this fight and became the mother of a number of puppies, all of which proved to be good fighters, but eventually after age and the strenuous life that she was leading began to tell she went into another such an encounter and met her end fighting gamely. That bitch, though her owner cared little for pedigree, carried in her veins the blood of Clonmel Monarch and his son. The Gamecock, and she held up the honors of her strain most royally.

It was the blood of this strain that really proved to be the foundation of many of the families that became big-game heroes in the West. C.P. Hubbard, to whom I have alluded on various occasions, bred dogs that went directly to the big-game hunters of the West and his establishment of kennels, in addition to those he operated in Atlantic, Iowa, at Dome Lake, Wyoming, in the heart of the big-game country, furnished quite a number of them. From these kennels many of the dogs of the present day are descended in more or less close relationship.

Steve Elkins, one of the well-known hunters of the Rocky Mountains has from ten to a dozen Airedales in his pack at all times and considers them a necessary part of his equipment. I met Mr. Elkins at Spokane in 1919, at which time he spoke very highly of the Airedale as a big game fighter, provided one adhered to the kind that had the proper qualities. For undersized bench-show specimens he had little use. James Keefe, who for a number of years operated the Mountain View Kennels at Butte, Montana, began his experiences with a son of Champion The Gamecock and has always used the breed since, for all of his hunting adventures, and he has had a world of experience hunting in all parts of the Northwest, particularly in the Blackfoot and Swan River country.

I might go on ad finitum relating experiences of hunters of big game to prove the gameness or almost daredevil recklessness of the Airedale, but let us take the other side. In all breeds of dogs one finds extreme gameness, courage, and sagacity in some specimens of the breed and on the other hand he finds some, even from the same litter, that are very timid, and still others that are rank and arrant cowards and, therefore, of no use in a practical way. What applies to other breeds fits the Airedale equally well. As a matter of fact, it is nothing unusual to find a majority of puppies more or less timid. This, however, is not a bad fault; the average Airedale is cautious by instinct until, as I have pointed out previously, he finds himself. A timid puppy should be brought up in an environment where he will see and hear strange sights and sounds. Frequently a puppy is shy of human beings. In such instance I have found it beneficial to place this youngster in a kennel or yard where many people pass, and if one can place him where children and especially boys go to and from school he will soon learn to take care of himself. Care, however, should be taken that he is not frightened by some animal or object to the extent of causing him to have a fear for it all through life. In the same manner firearms should not be introduced suddenly. Accustom him to strange sounds and sights gradually and he will soon overcome his timidity. Some strains are naturally lacking in intelligence, however, and this in addition to timidity in the most difficult to cope with. Usually it is a family characteristics and under such circumstances the better plan is to get rid of puppies of that strain and seek for others. That is another reason why the puppy descended from a strain that has actual working, rather than merely and solely bench-show experience are the most practical to acquire, if the object is to make all-round working dogs of them.

That the Airedale will fit into any sphere, provided he is properly trained, is unquestionable. I have often wondered why more farmers do not adopt the Airedale as the breed for stock purposes. He can not only be trained to make an excellent sheep and cattle dog, but when not used for this he will answer for a sporting dog whether it is for hunting rabbits, squirrels, 'possums, 'coons, or as the wild waterfowl retriever, or even for the hunting of upland game. Furthermore, the farmer owning a good Airedale bitch will find that as an investment she will bring him greater profits than any live stock on the place. The puppies are always in demand at good prices, and the mother can be used to do the ordinary work of a sheep dog in addition to being a good watch dog, and a sporting companion. Some time ago a farmer brought a bitch to breed to Teddy the Terror. He stated that the bitch was the best sheep and cattle dog that he ever owned and that in addition, she was an excellent watch dog, and when the season for squirrels and rabbits was on, she filled the capacity of a shooting companion. He bred this bitch as he desired and now has several puppies coming on which he is training to drive his cattle and sheep. The surplus puppies of the litter were sold at a good figure. The Airedale is an emulative dog to a much greater extent than most breeds. Leave him follow his master to the pastures a few times, and he will soon learn how to drive the stock in the most approved fashion of the professional sheep dog. He may not be greatly interested at first, but leave him alone; allow him to play about at your heels, but all this while he is watching every move and before long he will grasp the situation and help with the work. I have heard of many other instances where the Airedale was used on the farm in like manner as the bitch this gentleman just alluded to had, and when once the general merits of the breed becomes known among farmers, I look forward to seeing one or more Airedales on every farm where dogs are kept for actual utility. In selecting a dog for the farm it is advisable to obtain a bitch for the reasons already pointed out, but aside from this, bitches are less given to roaming and they are more susceptible to training, but again I must add the caution to select a puppy from strain that is noted for its intelligence. One need not be so particular about the bench qualities, but at the same time in making a selection type need not be disregarded entirely. One or two bitches on the farm will bring greater financial returns in the sale of puppies than the same number of pigs.

Another niche in which the Airedale fits in very well is as an all-around dog for the city dweller, who loves a bit of outdoor sport in woods and fields, but who cannot keep more than one dog. Here the Airedales is the Jack of all trades. He can be broken to guard the house, to act as a companion for the automobile and as a pet for children, for introduced into the home as a puppy, he makes a perfect companion for the little ones. They may maul him and pull him about, and even do him bodily injury and yet the faithful animal will not resent it, for he seems to understand the pranks of his youthful human companions.

He loves to ride in an automobile and in a few lessons he can be taught to remain in the machine and watch it when perchance the master finds occasion to park it somewhere in the city as he goes about his business and woe to the thief who would dare steal the machine while the faithful tyke is on duty.

Many professional men, doctors especially, secure an Airedale as a companion to ride with them while making professional visits. But sometimes there comes a half day of recreation when the busy doctor would hie to the woods and fields for a short hunt among the rabbits in one of his patient's briar patches. Here again Tyke is the companion; or it may be a half day with squirrels, or a try for the ducks, which are flying well over at the pond. The busy Medico may take a half hour morning and evening to give his dogs the necessary education and while he is watching his Airedale puppy develop, incidentally obtains much necessary relaxation from his duties. I personally know of a number of medical doctors who have thus trained their own Airedales for all-round companions at home, in the city or in the field.

Some years ago Dr. H. T. Ortman, of Buffalo, procured a puppy by Teddy the Terror out of Lady Bismarck, a daughter of Elmhurst Apache, for the purpose of making an all-round dog of him. The puppy, at the time he received him, was about ten weeks old. He was named and registered Chicko the Jester, and the name fitted him very well in more ways than one. The Doctor and Chicko soon became well acquainted and before he was many weeks older became quite companionable. The Doctor used his spare time in teaching the puppy the various little things about the house and yard that a well-behaved puppy should know, and by the time Chicko was five months old he was following his master out to the fields and woods where he met new sights and objects and obtained many experiences that stood him in good stead in later life. His owner was enthusiastic over the way the youngster learned his lessons. Long before he was a year old he was killing rats and mice, and before his first birthday was reached Chicko was an adept in routing out and killing wood chucks. The Doctor began his training by getting the puppy accustomed to the sound of firearms, using at first a small calibre pistol which he discharged while Chicko was interested digging about for moles or wood chucks, and thus he soon learned to understand that the report of a gun carried with it nothing to harm him. Chicko became a retriever from land and water in a very short time and would bring anything out of the deepest, swiftest, and coldest water. As a duck retriever, Chicko eventually became the mainstay of a little party of duck shooters with which the Doctor spent his vacations; and on pheasants, Chicko learned to work like a well-behaved bird dog, pointing them when the occasion required and holding his points until the bird was flushed or killed, and he was just adept in spotting them in trees, when with a sharp and quick bark he indicated to the master that the bird was in a certain tree remaining there until his master came. For several years, Doctor Ortman used Chicko solely as his shooting companion during the short seasons for pheasants in New York State, and as previously stated, as his duck retriever. In the water, Chicko was particularly expert and would dive any distance after objects. On more than one occasion Chicko's master surprised his friends by the exhibitions of water retrieving that Chicko gave for their benefit. In short, during the brief life of Chicko the Jester, he was conceded to be the best all-round dog in those parts and the training was all given him by his master during the little half hours between office duties. Incidentally, the owner as well as the dog were benefited by these lessons for it was recreation for the one and great sport for the other. Chicko the Jester was born in September, 1915, and was from the first litter Teddy the Terror sired. Teddy, at the time he was bred to Lady Bismarck, being but a year old. Unfortunately for the Doctor, Chicko was poisoned when he was four years old, and thus passed out of existence a real exemplification of the all-round Airedale, for Chicko was good at everything except big-game hunting, on which he had no opportunity to display his ability in the state of New York. After Chicko's death Dr. Ortman secured another puppy, this one by Hockwell's Hobo out of a daughter of Teddy the Terror. This puppy was registered as Hockwell's Chicko. At last account the youngster is coming along very nicely, his owner having adopted the same plan for education as he did with the first Chicko.

I could enumerate dozens of cases to Dr. Ortman's to indicated that an Airedale puppy of ordinary intelligence in the hands of a man who takes enough interest in a dog to educate him, what can be done in the way of training, even though only those remnants of days which usually go into the discard are utilized for the purpose. However, I might add that these Airedales with which the Buffalo Doctor experimented were from a strain of dogs that had been educated for practical uses from generation to generation, thus the high intelligence and the sagacity which are the natural heritage of the Airedale had never been allowed to become latent.

TEACHING TO TRAIL IN SNOW.

TEACHING TO CLIMB.

CHAPTER XI.

Personal Experiences with Various Strains.

The trend of one's life is shaped very much according to the result of circumstances or environment, also by the shades and influences of other lives that are cast upon it. I do not mean to go into a philosophical treatise on the "destiny which shapes our ends," but the thought came to me as I sat contemplating the manner in which I became interested in Airedales.

Had it not been for C. P. Hubbard, who was one of the early pioneers of the breed in the West, perhaps the Airedale would never have appealed to me; and had it not been for his dog, Culberston Bristles, in all probability my interest would have been confined to the bench show, instead of the real working lines of the breed. C. P. Hubbard, however, was an enthusiast, and his knowledge of the Airedale was second to none. In the first decade of this century few were his equal in general Airedale knowledge and no one I have ever met before or since was a more thorough student of Airedale pedigrees and blood lines.

Through the natural process of association at bench shows, I became acquainted with him and subsequently we traveled much together from show to show, during which time I absorbed considerable Airedale lore, but along with that, the desire to own some of the breed and especially was I enamored of Culberston Bristles. No, Bristles was not winning against the Airedales of the East; as a matter of fact he was holding his own in the West, but for all that, Bristles at the time he made his show campaign was not trimmed and doctored like most of the dogs that were shown-and at that period the barbering bordered very nearly on the verge of faking, for the use of he knife, scissors, and razor was clearly noticeable on some of the specimens that were winning. Bristles was simply all dog and a real man's dog. Bold, fiery, upstanding, plenty of size, bone and muscle, he represented all that one would desire in the all-round dog, and especially in one that could be used on big game. As Mr. Hubbard at that time maintained two kennels, one at Atlantic, Iowa, the other at Dome Lake, Wyoming-it was an easy matter for him to have his dogs educated along any line that was desired. The

Hubbard Airedales were in use everywhere in the West for they represented the sporting division of the Airedale family. Thus, the association with the owner of these kennels and the first-hand knowledge I had of Culberston Bristles, caused me to become interested in Airedales and particularly in the kind that could be used for practical purposes.

The principal requisites in the working Airedale are, as I have frequently pointed out in the pages of this book and elsewhere, first of all, courage and gameness; secondly, powerful loin, quarters and stifles. Without the latter no Airedale can stand the pace of the big-game dog, if he is to be used on bear, lion, or even the smaller "varmints," such as lynx, cougar, bobcat, raccoon, etc. In addition to these qualities coat was another consideration. Culberston Bristles in those days represented all the qualities of the working Airedales, and in my mind he became the ideal to work up to. With such a tutor as C. P. Hubbard, it did not require a long time to become familiar with the various families of the day and observe what strains were producing the dogs. No doubt there were any number of strains that were successful on the bench, which also proved good working dogs when given the opportunity, but I am only speaking here of those I had personal experience with. Some of the bench-show strains-and among these the very best-proved all that was desired, others I considered worthless at that period, and their descendants up to the present some are not any better. With these I am not concerned; it is the strains that did prove up that I shall dwell upon. And here let me impress upon the reader that because he does not see certain strains mentioned here that they are considered useless as working dogs; no such thing is implied; but simply the fact that I know nothing of them in the way of first-hand knowledge.

In a previous chapter I have dwelt somewhat upon the blood lines that produced the strains from which emanated many of the dogs to which I allude, but again I must beg indulgence of the reader for the apparent repetition, as it is necessary in order to demonstrate what I mean by the building up of working strains, which in my own experience have been successful.

Culberston Bristles, the dog of early days which, as I have said, formed the foundation of my love for the breed, was by Briarthorn out of Marshland Flo. Briarthorn was a big, sturdy dog, rather too large for present-day dogs, even for sporting purposes. His sire was Puff's Jerry III, which was by Broadlands Bunkum, by Jerry II. Colne Asia was the dam of Briar Thorn. According to Mr. Hubbard's own statement, he considered this dog rather indifferently bred, but when one runs out the pedigree it will be found that it goes to the fountain head, furthermore it is upon the blood lines of Culberston Bristles, that dogs, which became famous in the Hubbard kennels in later days, rest. He was bred to Colne Briaress Nut, a daughter of Willow Nut out of Colne Princess Briar, and from this union came Culberston Fin de Siecle, an excellent bitch, rightly named. In the meantime Mr. Hubbard made his famous trip East looking over all the kennels in and about New York, Philadelphia, and Boston. The Clonmel Monarch blood was making a name for itself and the Culberston prefix already had behind it much of the blood of this famous sire, for Monarch, though the leading show dog of his day, transmitted all the qualities that one wished for in the matter of essentials for a working dog. The Gamecock had made reputation by this time and the title of champion had come to him rapidly; he was a son of Clonmel Monarch out of Colne Miracle which was by Clonmel Marvel out of Clonmel Sensation. Bred right for quality, courage, and gameness, and possessing an immense wealth of bone and substance, even though as some of the Eastern critics said he was not a "laster" for bench purposes, he was just the type of a dog needed by the western fancier, for he could impart the necessary requisites in the way of working qualities, as well as give the necessary finish. The Gamecock became the sire of a number of winners of his day, and practically every one was a good dog in the field also. One of his sons was Culberston Beaver, out of the grand bitch, Fin de Siecle. Beaver became the property of Mr. and Mrs. R. D. Lampson, of Jefferson, Ohio, when he was a very young puppy, and in due time did considerable winning on the bench, for the few times he was shown, winning among other places, the special cup for the best Airedale in the show at Akron, Ohio, in 1910. He was never used for big-game hunting, but for the ordinary purposes on an Ohio farm, a more sagacious dog of any breed never lived. As a watch dog and household companion he was invaluable in the Lampson home and only lacked in the human attribute of the power of speech to make himself understood. As a sire he was also a great success, and though he was never placed in the public stud, he invariably sired good puppies to the few matrons with which he was mated; Culberston Beaver was whelped July 6, 1908, and died in June, 1921, hence at the time of his death he lacked only a few days of being thirteen years old.

Among his daughters was one bitch named Judy. Her dam was Waterside Romp, by Ch. Waterside Wizard out of Waterside Ripple. Judy, through her sire, obtained one cross of Clonmel Monarch, but her owner, W. V. Sked, whether he recognized the good qualities for this blood or whether it was through accident, decided upon breeding her to Red Rook of Ashborne, a powerful, well-knit dog of size and substance, possessing an excellent coat of the proper color and texture. In many respects, Red Rook of Ashborne was of the old type, particularly in head, but he was an excellent all-round dog, and he possessed and quarters that denoted power. If it is one quality that I always look to in an Airedale that is intended for work, it is strength in rear parts and this is what Rook of Ashborne possessed to a degree that was almost an exaggeration. Several litters came from Judy by this mating.

With the strong predilection I formed for the Clonmel Monarch blood, this breeding appealed to me very forcibly. In the third generation were five sons and daughters of either Clonmel Monarch or his son, The Gamecock. Nothing that I knew of carried the line breeding of Monarch, and through him the old Master Briar, to a closer combination. Having observed how the offspring of this breeding developed for practical dogs, this Red Rook of Ashborne-Judy combination carried in addition to this, the blood of another good working strain in the female tail line. This came through Waterside Wizard and Waterside Ripple. From one of the litters I obtained several puppies for others who were interested in Airedales and noting how rapidly these youngsters displayed all the intelligence and rare gameness of the race, I obtained a dog puppy from a later litter which was named Teddy the Tramp. This puppy developed rapidly, although in the matter of type, there were some things to be desired. For learning rapidly, however, I have seen few Airedales or any other breed that proved so amendable to training. Unfortunately, Teddy the Tramp was killed by an automobile when he was about fifteen months old and did not leave any progeny. A week after his fatality I secured another puppy of the same breeding from a litter whelped in July, 1914, the puppy being about three months old when he was received. This young scion of the Clonmel Monarch intensified blood was a better type than the first Teddy, with perfect color and the best of coat as it afterwards developed, for at the time he was received not much could determine in this respect. This puppy was registered as Teddy the Terror. As a puppy he was rather timid, but he was far from being a coward. He simply kept away from the things that he did not understand, but in time he acquired an investigative turn of mind and soon acquired more boldness. At much less than a year of age he was killing rats like a past master and that following summer after his birth he was placed on a farm for about six months. Here he learned to drive cattle, to herd sheep, and particularly to hunt night and day. Little training was needed; he simply acquired his knowledge by experience, and when a little past a year old he could tackle any "varmint" of the woods, night and day. Thus he became an adept night hunter. Squirrels and rabbits were his daytime delight and next to this was the driving of cattle, and in this respect he had considerable experience. On the farm there was a herd of cattle, at the head of which was a vicious bull which was feared by man and beast alike. On one occasion this bull broke pasture and got into adjoining fields. The farm hands, as well as the owner, were afraid to go after the animal and there was a debate as to how he to be brought from those fields. Teddy had acquired the knack of driving cows to the barn previous to this and he took great delight in the pastime. The men started for the field where the bull was grazing, and incidentally throwing up his head and waving his tail challenging any one, by his demeanor, as plainly as words could put it, that he defied them to come and put him out. Teddy followed along an interested spectator, and when he arrived at the gap in the fence, one of the party said: "Get him out, Teddy!" never dreaming that the dog would go after the bull. But Teddy was spoiling for an adventure himself that afternoon and went promptly into the field and straight at the bull. The latter lowered his head and charged. Teddy watched him come, evidently surprised at the action, for hitherto he had been driving cows and not bulls; they did not approach him in this menacing attitude. The bull came on and Teddy waited, and when at the moment everyone thought the bull was about to gore him, he dodged to one side and again faced him. Once more the bull employed the same tactics, and again Teddy dodged and turned about to face his antagonist. By this time the dog's ire was up; hitherto he did not seem to understand the situation, but it began to dawn upon him that it was a case of defending himself. The third time when the bull made the dash, Teddy met him half way, and just as the bull lowered his head, the dog made one lunge, caught him by the nose and hung on like grim death. the now thoroughly infuriated bovine gave one loud and long bellow, began shaking his head and prancing about, evidently with the surprise on his side. He did succeed in shaking Teddy off, but the latter made the attack the next time and again secured a nose hold. There was another series of rapid movements on the part of the bull, and once more he freed himself of his tormentor, but he turned tail, made for the gap with the dog after him nipping at his heels and thus driving him straight for the barn yard and into the barn, where the bull promptly made for his stall. He was now thoroughly subdued, for the men had no trouble in securing him after he reached the stall. After that, when the bull was turned out in pasture he made no further trouble, for as soon as he saw Teddy coming for him he started in the direction he was to go without putting up any kind of a protest. The farmer who kept Teddy the Terror on his promises that summer was loath to see him go, for he assured me that there was never another dog on the place that could handle this bull, although at this writing he has a son Teddy which is learning to do practically the same work that sire did.

The first matron bred to Teddy the Terror was Lady Bismarck referred to in the preceding chapter as being the dam of Chicko the Jester, Dr. Ortman's good dog, and it is significant to note that, when Teddy was bred to this bitch which resulted in such a good liter, he was only a few weeks past a year old. Naturally, I do not advocate breeding dogs to any extent so young, but his was done more in nature of an experiment than with any idea of allowing the dog to serve matrons indiscriminately at that age.

At that time we were more or less at a loss as to what policy to follow in the selection of blood lines to breed to this intensified Clonmel Monarch blood and the early breeding operations were all more or less tentative. Lady Bismarck's breeding on her sire's side was strongly permeated with the Oorang blood, Elmhurst Apache being by Ch. Rockley Oorang, by Crompton Oorang, while his dam was Solid Comfort, a daughter of Tintern Desire, also a son of Crompton Oorang, as was also Solid Comfort's dam, she being by this dog out of a daughter of Midland Royal, hence it was going back to the combination of the Crompton and the Midland blood which founded the Tintern strain, Further experiments with the Oorang blood, through various lines, all proved good crosses which produced type and also working qualities.

The cross par excellence, however, proved to be with the daughters or granddaughter of Champion Abbey King Nobbler, and when this blood was to be had in an intensified degree, it seemed to be all better. Most of the daughters of this dog were on the small order, but they had an abundance of bone and substance for their size; withal they were courage and gameness personified, possessing that small, fiery eye, that extreme varminty expression, with the excellently carried ears that mark the real terrier. In breeding, select your bitches with these physical and mental qualities and the chances are good for the best of results. The dam must have the terrier characteristics to a high degree, even if at the sacrifice of size, for the sire will impart that if he has it as an individual, and the dogs that go to make up his pedigree are of that stamp. The mating with this King Nobbler blood which was found so excellent in producing game offspring together with type, coat, and show points was, I must confess more or less an accident; that is, it was not a carefully thought out plan of campaign, but reason that King Nobbler was himself a fiery terrier, which perhaps would have made good as a working dog had he been given the chance, his daughters bred to a working line of blood should bring forth the desired results.

When my son, who really owned the dogs, formed a partnership with Claud Wells, and thus instituted the Hockwell Kennels, Mr. Wells owned a bitch, called Lady Brilliant Briar. She was by Abbey King Nobbler out of Cherryhill Megs which was herself by Abbey King Nobbler out of Krestly Kleo, she by Tintern Royalist out of Krestly Betsey. Lady Brilliant was bred to Teddy the Terror and produced a wonderful liter of working dogs, all of which proved all-round workers, and furthermore, they had the deep, rich tan, and the black and the black saddles together with the dense coats so essential to the Airedale which is to be used in any kind of cover, in any kind of weather, and many times in any kind of water. A gamer lot than this first litter never existed. There were two sisters of Lady Brilliant Briar owned in Dayton, the home town of the boys, and they lost no time in securing these. One of them was called Ted Bear, the other, Smith's Mayflower. All three bitches produced good puppies to Teddy the Terror; as a matter of fact, not one of them ever threw a badly marked one, or one that proved inferior in intelligence. From these three bitches a number of puppies were bred and they are now to be found in all parts of the country. Lady Brilliant Briar died after producing her second litter; in the meantime, Smith's mayflower after producing three litters for the boys, was sold to Dr. Horton, of Columbus, Ohio, and is now in his kennels a valuable producer. Ted Bear also died early in life, but left a number of her progeny, among them being Hockwell's Za-Za, one of the best all-round bitches I know of and a producer of winners on the bench, but particularly good ones for the field.

Cherryhill Peggie, by a brother to the bitches referred to, called Cherryhill Jack, was another of those fiery bitches, all verve and courage, and she also became a producer although she was bred to the other dog of the Hockwells, namely Hockwell's Hobo, but in advance of my narrative.

Finding that such good results were obtained by this crossing of the King Nobbler blood with the inbred Clonmel Monarchs, another bitch was secured representing this line with some other crosses intermingled. This was Hockwell's Tess, a line bred King Nobbler, being by Pete Fuller, of Ashborne, a son, out of Iowana of Ashborne a daughter, from a different dam.

Unfortunately only two litters were produced from this union of Teddy the Terror and Hockwell's Tess, the bitch dying at a very early age. She left several sons and daughters, but the sons have passed out of the kennels, having been disposed of when young, for it was the intention of the owners to save only the daughters for breeding stock. Of these two, have shown to advantage. One is Hockwell's Chloroform, now owned in Dayton, and a great all-round bitch for work as well as show; the other Peggy the Rough Neck, now owned by the Davishill Kennels of Ft. Thomas, Ky. The latter was given to the late George Morlidge, of Ft. Thomas, Ky., when she was a puppy, but at his death she passed out of knowledge of her breeders, until she made her name famous as the dam of War Bond and War Chief of Davishill, bred and owned by the Davishill Kennels. R. L. Davis is the proprietor of these kennels and will undoubtedly make the most of these two dogs, which already have done some exceptional winning, at all the principal shows of the country. Their sire is Caswell Warrior, as was stated in a previous chapter. Peggy the Rough Neck bids fair to produce still many more good ones, for she is still a comparatively young bitch. As for Hockwell's Chloroform, this bitch is unquestionably a remarkable one in coat, color and conformation, and a natural-born hunter. Unfortunately it has been impossible to secure any litters from her up to this time, but she will be tried again.

Reasoning along the lines that if the daughters of Abbey King Nobbler produced good dogs in the way of courage and gameness when bred to the Clonmel Monarch blood on the sire's side, why should not the daughters of Teddy the Terror prove good producers of the same type, if bred to a dog with the Nobbler blood? Acting upon this thought, the kennels secured a dog from the kennels of E. G. Marquardt, of Ashborne fame, where Hockwell's Tess came from. This dog was registered as Hockwell's Hobo and is by champion Briergate Rex Persaltum, out of Ashborne Sister Sue, the latter by Abbey King Nobbler out of Silverton Muffet, a sister to Iowana of Ashborne, the dam of Hockwell's Tess. Rex Persaltum, as I pointed out in earlier chapter, is a descendent of Abbey King Nobbler through his sire Karamea Rex, the latter being a son of Nobbler, Karamea Cerebos, the dam of Rex Persaltum, is also a descendent of the Elruge Monarch blood through

Clonmel Rough and Ready.

Hockwell's Hobo came to the kennels when he was about one year old. What I liked about him was his short back, his flat skull, his strong jaw, well-filled up foreface, small eye, clean shoulders, and strong quarters. What I did not like, was his color which shaded a little too light on the neck, and the tan was more washy on the legs than we were accustomed to seeing in the other lines of breeding. He was also just a trifle too small for a real working dog, weighing about forty-four pounds, which for the bench-show man is not all out of the way, but for the breeder of working dogs, is a serious matter.

The dog, however, was marvelously bold and courageous and would tackle anything, no matter what its size. In fact, he was what might call a rather quarrelsome dog which trait is not common with the Airedale. He had one mix-up with Teddy the Terror which crippled them both, and it was all that Teddy could do to defend himself. Several years later he mixed it with one of his sons-a very game one by the way-and again both were torn up. Courage he had to a fault and he soon made a good all-round dog, though he never received the training that fell to the lot of Teddy the Terror. Bred to the latter's daughters he more than made good. All of his progeny proved to be game to the core. To Hockwell's Za Za he produced exceptional litters every time and bred to Cherryhill Peggie, the bitch previously referred to as a granddaughter of Abbey King Nobbler, he sired some of the best puppies of all, both in the matter of type as well as gameness. The blending of this blood and that of the inbred Clonmel Monarch combination of Teddy the Terror proved and is continuing to prove a happy one, and it may safely be said that the cross has been established and that this strain will uphold the traditions concerning the courage and the gameness of the Airedale terrier. That is one of the principal reasons why I became interested in the Airedale, and these experiments with various lines of blood have been interesting studies in the reproduction of the species with a view to enhancing the characters in the progeny that were most desired. Hockwell's Hobo was lost some months ago, and at his writing not the slightest trace has been heard of him; the probabilities are that he was killed somewhere while on a self-hunting expedition, a trait that he was in the habit of showing. He would manage to get out of is kennel yard in some manner, and away he went to the hills east of the city where he could hunt the river bottoms to his heart's delight. On one occasion he failed to return. It was a decided loss to the kennels, for Hobo was less than five years old at the time, but he has left some sons and daughters through which the experiments, which were begun years ago, may be continued. One of his daughters, Larkin's Bridgit, out of a strongly-bred Oorang bitch, is a remarkable producer when bred to Teddy the Terror. By remarkable, I do not mean in the sense of the bench-show breeder. She produces type and conformation to a high degree, but it is the boldness, the grit and the courage of her progeny that are the principal features and cause them to be in demand by big-game hunters, though all the bitches of this breeding that could be produced for home use were never sent away.

From this breeding the kennels have one daughter, Hockwell's Patsey, and it will be an interesting problem to decide how to continue the strain with her. Shall it be through sons of Rex Persaltum or through the sons of Teddy's daughters? The kennels have the opportunity to try both ways, but as this litter is to be for home use, a cross will be made, whereby the daughters of such a union will have the blood of all the strains with which the earlier experiments have been carried on, and it is needless to say that the principal aim will be the perpetuation of the working qualities. Accordingly the daughters of such a union with Hockwell's Patsey to whatever dog might be decided upon, will be kept for the future reproduction of the strain.

I have no doubt that there are many other strains just as game and just as good in every way as those with which I have been experimenting, but as I said in the beginning of this chapter, this is one personal experiences only. After all, when it comes to the breeding of intelligent Airedales it is through the selection of the most intelligent and the most courageous, that one attains what is desired, but it must always be borne in mind that no matter how good a strain, if its members are not regularly hunted or given the opportunity to learn the ways of the woods, they are not going to develop into the all-round dog the Airedale is expected to be. After all, the owner is the deciding element whether he is going to have working Airedales or dogs that are simply good to look at.

CHAPTER XII.

Breeding-Choosing the Sire and Dam-Rearing and Selecting Puppies-Profit in Airedales for the Small Breeder and Farmer.

While there are a great many people who are not so situated that they can breed Airedales because of limited quarters and the want of time, still there are a number who can do so, but simply lack the knowledge of the fundamentals in dog breeding, and with many this is the sole deterrent. The Airedale is one of the hardiest among the canine races. He will thrive where many of the more tender breeds would be the source of worry. He is not so susceptible to the diseases many of the breeds are heir to and even though there come times when he may contract some of the common ills, he is constructed of such a well-balanced organism that he will come through them with ordinary care and attention, and seldom it is necessary to call for the services of the skilled practitioner in veterinary medicine. The novice beginner, however, must possess at least a general knowledge of dogs, for even Airedale breeding cannot be left to blind chance, and, therefore, it is well, if he knows absolutely nothing about dogs, to make himself familiar with the general laws and principals. The first of these is good care, which covers feeding, exercise, grooming, and proper quarters. The second is fully as important and may be summed up in two words: good judgment and common sense.

In selecting the stud dog the breeder must have in mind the characteristics that he wishes to produce. If his leading desire is to produce progeny which will eventuate into working dogs he must select his sire accordingly. Let him look for a strong, vigorous animal with blood lines that are known to produce these qualities. If this stud dog is broken as an all-round working dog, all the better. He must further study the pedigree to see how it will nick with the blood lines of the bitch which he owns or has an idea of buying or leasing. The stud dog should have good Airedale type and character along with his working qualities, and there are many good dogs which have these desired attributes. A dog need not be a useless ornament simply because he is good looking, but along with these qualities that come under the head of type and character the color and texture of coat should be a consideration. Still another is size, bone, and substance. One seldom produces good working dogs from small sires, unless the bitch so mated with him has this quality to an exaggerated degree, and while I have seen and have bred to dogs which were small in size, the mating was made for a purpose. For instance, if the dog, although small, is a well-balanced one, possessing a wealth of bone and substance, and furthermore, if he possess extraordinary courage, and intelligence, then such a dog, bred to a bitch of good stature should produce very satisfactory puppies, provided the general average among the ancestors of both, sire and dam, measures up to fair size. Another thing that should be taken into consideration is the health of the dog. A strong, vigorous sire without any constitutional diseases or weaknesses is far more desirable than one coming from a family that is known to transmit such undesirable characters, and occasionally one will encounter this kind, although this is far less common among Airedales than it is with any other breed. If the object of the breeder is to endeavor to produce show dogs, then of course, he must look for such qualities in sire and dam. Let him select a dog which is strong in the points where his bitch is weak, but by this it is not meant that the progeny will thus be perfect, for many a time the sire may be a good individual inheriting his quality from some individual ancestor who possessed them to a high degree, but the general average of the family might have been just the opposite and therefore, it is not at all likely that this single individual from the family is going to transmit all the good qualities and not the family characteristics. Breeding is very much a law of averages and one must take this into account. However, blood lines being satisfactory, it is safe to breed with this idea in view; that is, to select the sire and dam so that one will offset the weaknesses of the other. However, the novice should ever bear in mind that he is breeding a dog which was primarily intended for a worker and, therefore, even though show specimens be his aim, he should eschew the coward and the weakling, no matter how good he might be in show points.

As for the matron. If the beginner is buying a bitch for the purpose of breeding, let him select one of those fiery kind, full of snap and dash, with small dark eye, a well-carried ear, and the oft quoted "varminty expression." Let her be a bitch that is game to the core, and at the same time see that she possess the Airedale instincts to even a greater degree than the sire to which he intends to breed her. Size is not so much consequence, although if a bitch of goodly proportions, possessing all the qualifications enumerated, can be secured, it will be an advantage, but I should sacrifice size for terrier qualities, if it came to a choice between the two unless the bitch was an undersized weed with no bone and substance whatever. Coat is also a consideration. Select the short-coated ones of harsh texture; discard the sheep coats. It is also well to have your bitch broken for an all-round dog, and the more intelligent she is, the more likely she is to have puppies of that order. It should also be borne in mind that a bitch possessing the Airedale characteristics is more like to bring forth good-show specimens. Never breed to a bitch showing no intelligence, for her puppies are likely to be idiots. The offspring usually inherits the temperamental qualities of the dam, hence one cannot be too careful in his selection of the matron.

The beginner, who has an idea of breeding, would do well to buy a bitch as a puppy, one from a good strain, all dependent upon what kind of stock he wishes to raise; whether for show or work. The chances are, if he buys a good specimen from the proper line, he will be able to raise dogs which will make good in either sphere.

Assuming that he secures a bitch puppy at twelve weeks old. Let him educate her himself and he will find that it is not an unpleasant pastime. A half hour night and morning will do wonders, and if he is do situated that he can give her practical work on rabbits, squirrels, coons, etc., or in retrieving wild water fowl, he will soon have a very valuable companion.

The period of oestrum or coming in season varies much according to breed. Usually in Airedales they will come in season the first time between nine and fourteen months, but sometimes it is earlier, sometimes later. The first thing notice-able is that is a change, sometimes very slight, in the bitch's demeanor, and careful watching will disclose a slight swelling of her genitals. In a few days there is a white mucous discharge which soon changes to pinkish-white and finally pure blood. She is now in full season and immediately after the flow has ceased, is the best time to breed her. The entire period of oestrum usually extends over a period of twenty-one days, and it is needless to say that during this time she should be closely confined, in an upstairs room in loft or barn, if one is available, for it is surprising how bitches contrive to escape during this period or how the dogs of the neighborhood learn of one being in season.

It is well, if the bitch is to be sent some distance to a stud, to have all arrangements made and send her when in about the middle of her season-that is, from the time the swelling first appeared. One service is all that is necessary. In fact, most large breeders of the present day prefer the one service plan and consider if the safer and the surer. After her first season a normal female should come in every six months, although this time varies slightly occasionally.

The bitch, having been returned after the service, she should be confined for a period, in order to make absolutely sure of no mesalliance. The average period of gestation is nine weeks or sixty-three days. Some times more or less. During the period she should be treated much like dogs in normal condition, but her feed should be nourishing and wholesome. It is well to feed at least twice a day during this time. When her time is near have a box prepared in a dark out of the way corner, large enough so that she can move around freely, in a stable, barn or out-building, where she can be to herself. When she whelps leave her alone. Too much attention at this critical hour worries the mother and does no good. It might be advisable to look in occasionally to see that all is going well, and this being the case, do not disturb her. If she is very nervous and excitable a slight pat on the head with a few words, and sometimes the offering of a little water are acceptable. In cold weather it might be well to take the puppies away from her as they are born, wrap them in flannel, place them in a basket in a warm place. Never have the whelping room under seventy degrees Fahrenheit. The mother looks after the puppies as they are born, removing them from the sac, cleaning them, and disposing of the placenta or afterbirth. When the whelping is all over, sponge the mother off with luke-warm water, but only where her coat is soiled. Give her a feed consisting of milk or gruel or milk with dry bread broken into it. Vary this for a few days with broth and biscuits and a little meat, and in two or three days she will be ready to eat in normal fashion, but having a large family to take care of, it must be borne in mind that she must be fed accordingly. The nearer one adheres to the nature method the more likely it is that the mother as well as the puppies are apt to thrive, and the nature method is to allow the mother to do very much as she pleases, for her instincts teach her better than any well-meaning human being could, how to care for her young.

I have only touched on these topics in a general way in this book, but the novice wishing for all the information on breeding and care of dogs is advised to secure my two previous books: "Practical Dog Keeping for the Amateur," and "Dogcraft." In these they will find complete chapters on the care of dogs in health and in disease.

Airedales usually have large litters. We had three bitches, each of which had from ten to twelve puppies in three succeeding litters. Sometimes it is advisable to remove some of these on the grounds that they are too great a care on the mother, and, no doubt, there is truth in this, but it happened that we had no foster mother at hand on either occasion and the puppies being valuable, we did not care to destroy any of them. The remarkable thing is that two of these bitches raised all of their puppies in three litters while the third lost two in one of her litters the first night, but raised all the others. The mother was assisted, however, by hand feeding the puppies, but this is an indication of how hardy Airedales are. I never had such an experience with any other breed.

The novice must not be alarmed when he sees the newly-born puppies for the first time. At birth and during their early puppyhood days they are black. On more than one occasion I have had new fanciers call up at birth of a litter and ask, if there was a possibility of the puppies being mongrels, because all were black! I assured them that all was well and they were much relieved. In time the youngsters attain their natural coat and color. The first care that thing falls to human hands in the raising of a litter of Airedales, unless as just stated, hand feeding is necessary with large litters, is the docking of the tails. This should be done between the fourth and seventh day, and by all means before the ninth. At this tender age the candal appendage of the puppy is but a soft but of unformed bone and tissue, and the operation is a very simple one. The better way is to have an assistant hold the puppy while the operator takes hold of the tail pushing the skin back toward the body and with a scissors, snipping of a little less than one half. If the scissors is held at a trifling angle it will be all better. Nothing should be put on the wound which is only a slight one that will heal in a very few days under the mother's care. The operation may be done with a sharp knife also, by placing the puppy's tail on a block, but the scissors method is really the easier. In four or five days after the operation there will be scarcely a scar left where the tail was cut off. Airedales, like most other breeds, are occasionally born with dew claws. These are extra toes on the inside of the legs just above the front or the rear patterns as the case may be. In the event that any of the puppies are born with these, it is a good time to remove them at the same time the tails are docked, and they be snipped off close to the leg with the same scissors, provide it is sharp, and it should be in either case.

Choosing a puppy out of a litter is always more or less of a hazard. That is, at the age of eight or ten weeks, when the puppies are usually sent away, no one can tell to a certainty what they will develop into. The coat is still black, or nearly so, and it is the soft fluff of babyhood, the head is undeveloped, but some idea can be had of the size of the ears and the eyes. Of course, much of this is conjecture also, but it is generally a safe plan to pick the blackest puppies with the smallest eyes and ears, and if one is taking character into consideration, then let him take the liveliest and the boldest one, for in an Airedale these qualities have much to do with the future career of the puppy, no matter if it is on the show bench or in hunting field. The novice after breeding a litter or two will soon know how to be governed in these cases, but if he wishes further details on all these matters, I would suggest the two books previously referred to, namely, "Dogcraft," and Practical Dog Keeping for the Amateur."

The Airedale being one of the easiest breeds to raise and the litters all being large ones, I know of no breed in which there is more profit than in this one. I have already pointed out that an Airedale bitch is more profitable on the farm than the raising of swine, for there is always a quick market for Airedale puppies. He is a dog popular, with the masses and wherever one goes, one generally finds where but a single dog is kept on a place or in a home it is an Airedale, and the breed is becoming better known from year to year. One bitch, well kept, will raise two litters of puppies a year. The puppies will sell at any price from fifteen to one hundred dollars each according to the breeding, the individuality, and the reputation of the sire and dam, but it is not beyond the bounds of truth to say that one can figure the average price of each puppy to the litter at $35.00 in normal times; that is, counting dogs and bitches together. During the period of general high prices, it was no trouble to obtain one hundred dollars each for all the dogs in a litter, at eight weeks old and seventy-five dollars for the bitches. These prices were inflated along with everything else, it is true, but the great demand for the Airedale, and his constant increase in popularity in all quarters of the globe will be the means of maintaining the prices at the average given previously, and that is a very low estimate. For the purpose of calculation, however, assuming that there are eight puppies in the litter and there are two litters per year. This would mean sixteen puppies at thirty-five dollars each, this would total a gross receipt per year of $560.00. The cost of feeding puppies on a farm is very slight, hence it will be readily seen that the profits are more than worth the trouble. The city man would find his cost of feeding somewhat higher, but he, too, would find an Airedale bitch one of the best investments he ever made. It is true, this is a high estimate in the number of puppies, but not at all out of the ordinary.

Naturally one cannot continue to breed a matron season after season, which must also be taken into consideration. There must be a period of rest occasionally, especially if she begins to show the wear and tear of too frequent maternity. The owner must be able to determine this, but it is a safe plan to allow at least one season to pass by in two years; sometimes, more. Say, for instance, she is bred in December and has a litter the following February. Normally she would be due again in June. It is a good idea to skip this season and breed her the next time, but the owner must be governed entirely by circumstances. I know of a bitch which had four large litters of puppies in two years and did not show the least sign of breakdown, although this was an exception, and even though bitches will go through this strenuous period twice each year, they are likely to become prematurely old, although the bitch in question is now in her sixth year and has a litter of nine puppies at the present time.

A KENNEL OF FAMOUS AIREDALES AND SOME CUPS WON.
Left to Right: War Bond of Davishill, War Spirit of Davishill, War Chief of Davishill, Man o' War of Davishill and War Lady of Davishill.

CHAPTER XIII.

Conditioning and Care of the Coat-Plucking.

The welfare of any dog depends upon good condition, and this is the result of proper care, sanitary surroundings, pure water, wholesome food, and sufficient exercise. Add to this daily grooming and an occasional bath, and the average-highly-bred dog will thrive.

The Airedale is one of the hardiest of breeds and seldom suffers from the ordinary inconveniences that mean disaster to many varieties. He will do well with an old box or barrel in the backyard, winter and summer, for sleeping quarters, and if allowed sufficient exercise, food and water, he can shift for himself. Indeed, many people owning an Airedale imagine that this is all that is necessary, basing their ideas on the assumption that anything is good enough for a dog, and yet this faithful guardian of the household returns such precarious attention with love and affection, is honest and devoted to those of the household and makes the interests of his master and mistress his own. The majority of people owning one dog, those who are not real fanciers, of course, imagine their duty to their dog is ended when he is given these few attentions, and thus the dog is allowed to thrive as best he may. He is unkept and shaggy, for seldom, if ever, is a brush applied to him, and thus the Airedale has gained for himself the name of being the homeliest of dogs. But what a difference can be made in the appearance of the dog by a few minutes' attention every day!

Personally, I should not care to have an Airedale about, if I could not keep him looking like the well-groomed canine gentleman that he should be, and if the average one dog owner would feel likewise, he would find that his dog would improve in efficiency and good looks in proportion to the extra time spent on him.

To keep an Airedale at his best he should be groomed every day. This should be done by combing out the loose hairs with a terrier comb which should be followed by ten minutes' brushing with a hound glove or other stiff-bristled brush. The dirt and filth should be thoroughly brushed out of the coat, and if the owner is inclined to give him still more care, then ten minutes of hard rubbing after the brush will have its compensations.

I always like to see an Airedale well barbered, whether he is to be gotten ready for the show or whether he is to be taken on a hunting trip. It is surprising how these few minutes every day make for improvement in coat and color. The loose hair and the grime taken out of the coat not only makes the dog feel better, but look better, and enjoy better health, for it prevents skin diseases and stimulates a healthy growth of hair. Besides, there is no need of the shaggy outer coat even for the dog that is to be used for all-round hunting purposes. The grooming will put the outer as well as the under coat into condition and make it even more impervious to water or to withstand the wear and tear of thorns and briers than the heavy coat. The latter at best, is but a catch all for burrs when the dog is working in cover, while if he takes to water, it is more like a mop. When the coat is brushed down closely, the outer coat is flat and bristly, and withstands these annoyances of the longer-coated dog.

My plan is to brush every dog once a day, winter and summer, as outlined above. This is done in the morning after they have been allowed to run and exercise in an adjoining field, and it is surprising how they seem to understand that this is a regular routine. In the summer they are taken to the river three or four times a week where they are given a swim in the cooling waters. They are then allowed to run and roll on the greensward of the banks and the grooming follows. At this season of the year I always use a one-in-fifty solution of any of the creosote preparations, which is put on the hound glove after their coats have been well groomed out. This is rubbed well into the hair and allowed to dry in the coat after which they are rubbed for another ten minutes. It is surprising how the flies and the fleas keep away from them, and furthermore, the solution tends to keep the skin in good condition. As a matter of fact the dog feels better in every way after this treatment. Perhaps I devote an hour each day on the two dogs I usually keep on the place, but it is an hour well spent, for it means health to the dogs and exercise for me. Any professional or business man, who loves dogs, can easily follow this method of mine before business hours and will be the better for this early-morning exercise, while it goes without saying that it will benefit the dogs.

As for plucking, I believe, as I said previously, in keeping an Airedale's coat in the right form at all times. In fact, it is an easy matter. All this air of mystery surrounding the conditioning of an Airedale's coat is sheer nonsense, unless it approaches the border line of faking, then perhaps there are some tricks that are not known to everybody, but perhaps it is as well that this is so. Legitimate barbering of an Airedale makes for improvement in the animal's appearance and as long as that can be done without violating any rules, there is no reason why it should not.

The professionals have a system of plucking some parts of the body one day, then waiting a few weeks, when another part is plucked and so on. This may be necessary, but I never could see any reason for it. Personally I like to begin on a puppy when he is about eight or nine months old, take off his entire coat and then keep him in condition, by the daily grooming, naturally allowing for a trifle more growth in winter than in summer. I begin at the head, strip his cheeks, skull, and neck, then continue on, working back to his tail. After the stripping he is gone over with the terrier comb with which the linty loose hair is taken off. The whiskers, if unusually profuse, or if there is much dead hair, are also gone over, but his muzzle is not stripped closely like the other parts of the head and neck. Little is taken off the legs, but sufficient hair should be taken off so as to make the dog look balanced. After the first stripping it might be well to wash the dog with a good mild soap and luke-warm water, drying thoroughly with drying cloths.

To stimulate a healthy growth apply a dressing to the entire body rubbing it well into the skin, consisting of equal parts vaseline and coconut oil melted together. This dressing may be applied to the coat as often as desirable during the ten or twelve days after the stripping, and it is well to blanket the dog, to prevent his taking into the coat a lot of useless grime and dirt. The dog may be washed again after this treatment, but during all this time he should be brushed daily. It is surprising what a difference will be noted in your dog in a short time. The idea is to keep the hair very close on the skull cheeks, and neck, while on the body it may be allowed to grow to the length for a working, and even a show dog is preferable. Sometimes it is advisable to use a small amount of the dressing referred to, to add luster to the coat. In this event take an ordinary comb with blunt teeth, dip it into the mixture and run it through the hair. After this is thus applied, rub well with the hound glove or by hand. Dogs treated in this manner may be kept in excellent condition the year round, and it is needless to say that they always present an attractive, gentlemanly appearance.

Preparing for shows requires a few more details, and the way, it is generally done, is to begin the stripping process about three months before the dog is to go on the show circuit. The plucking in all instances is done with finger and thumb pulling the hair in the direction that it lies. The stripping comb or a dull knife blade may be used whenever it is necessary to remove tufts of hair that are particularly tight or tough. Usually the professional begins the stripping operation by taking down all the coat from the shoulders, back down the hind legs to the hocks, including the tail. The entire top coat on this part of the body is thus taken off, and if there is much undercoat, or a particularly soft nature, this is also taken off. This as I previously said, is done three months before the show. About six or eight weeks before the show the shoulders and neck are stripped in like manner, and if the dog is a thick, shouldered specimen, some experts wait until just a few weeks before the show, but the handler must know his dog, for is he is one whose coat is naturally slow of growth, it is sometimes impossible to grow enough coat to suit show-ring requirements. At four weeks before the show, the skull and ears are stripped and two weeks before, the cheeks are trimmed down closely, which includes the neck, for it is particularly essential to have a clean-cut appearance under the jaws and all the hair is taken off here which gives the dog an appearance of having a much longer neck than he really possesses. The feet must also have attention. The long and ragged hair must be removed from the toes, the top of them being trimmed down particularly fine and the toe nails must also be trimmed closely. This feature, in a working dog is to be tabooed, however, for any tampering with a working Airedale's feet is likely to result in making him unfit for best work. Here, in my opinion, it is best to leave nature alone, although for show purposes it is quite essential to have the dog appear at his best and a cat-like foot which this trimming gives it, is one of the great essentials of the show dog. The cocoa-nut oil and Vaseline preparation is used in like manner as described previously. Many professionals wash their dogs the night before they are shown and after the drying rub a quantity of magnesia into the coats allowing this to remain on them over night, but blanketing them until just before the classes are called. The blanket is then taken off, the chalk brushed out of the coat and the dog well rubbed down. His coat now has a harsh feel and there is a sheen on him that is almost mirror-like. The other little tricks that are sometimes resorted to, to make the eye appear darker, etc., clearly come under the category of faking and have no place here.

Further particulars regarding the care of coats are given in my previous book, "Practical Dog Keeping for the Amateur."

TEDDY THE TERROR.

TEACHING TO TREE.

TRAINING LESSONS.

TEDDY THE TERROR.

CHAPTER XIV.

General Remarks on Training.

This is primarily a book on the history of the Airedale and, therefore, it would be out of my province to add exhaustive chapters on training. That is a subject for a book in itself and accordingly I refer the amateur trainer to my recent work entitled, "The Working Dog and His Education," for further information on the training of the Airedale. The former work having been written to aid the novice in the training of all breeds, special chapters are devoted to the Airedale.

It is not amiss, however, to give a few general instructions by which the owner may be guided and in the last analysis, it is the intelligence and the understanding of the teacher that goes the farthest toward success, after all.

An article of mine on the training of the Airedale appeared in the November, 1920, issue of *Outer's-Recreation* from which I am taking the liberty to quote excerpts here. A careful perusal of these instructions will, I think, give the novice a clear idea how to begin with his puppy:

"No bird-dog fancier would think of taking an unbroken animal out and expect him to handle birds like the seasonal veteran, and by the same token the Airedale is not a super-dog, and therefore cannot perform all sorts of work without training. To the man or the woman who is looking for a general-utility dog I would say, select from a working strain of Airedale, or one known to possess a reputation for gameness and intelligence, a puppy from two to six months of age and train him yourself for those particular duties in which you wish to use him. Obtain the right kind of material to work upon and the training of your Airedale will be a pleasure, if for no other reason than to observe how his mentality develops and how he gains in sagacity and intelligence from day to day.

"Personally, if I were to keep but one dog, I would select a female. Females are more cleanly about the house and yard, more docile, less inclined to take to roaming and, with the exception of two periods each year, need not to be housed up closely. Furthermore, taking them collectively, they are easier to train, while at the same time they are fully as courageous as the males and in many cases more so.

My experience has been that in most of the bear packs of the South and West Kipling's famous line, "The female of the species is more deadly than the male," has invariably been substantiated as far as the Airedale family is concerned.

"My experience is no different than that of others who cater to working Airedales. At the present time in the Hockwell's Kennels, which I founded several years ago, but in which I have no pecuniary interest now, are several bitches as game as any dog that ever stood up to the most pugnacious "varmint of the woods." The policy of these kennels has always been to select from each litter what females were wanted to develop for breeding stock and begin their training as early in life as possible; starting them on rats-later on, in the art of treeing squirrels, and still later, in running rabbits; finally, on every species of furred game. Retrieving is also usually begun at an early age and the puppies are taught not only to fetch objects on land but from water as well. Fortunately the kennels are so located that the puppies can easily be given experience on squirrels; as a matter of fact the latter abound in number so close to where the dogs are quartered that there is not a morning on which they do not have the opportunity to tree these frisky little quadrupeds. As for water experience, the river is only a block away and it is well known that all Airedales take to the latter as readily as a duck, and they soon become adepts in bringing objects out of the water, no matter how cold or in what condition it is. In this manner, Hockwell's Chloroform, Hockwell's Peggie, and Smith's May Flower were educated, and a gamer trio of Airedale bitches never lived. What is more, their puppies are fully as game as the mothers, for after all the offspring inherit the temperamental qualities from their dams and a matron that is courageous and full of fire and terrier character will invariably produce game sons and daughters. Hockwell's Peggie at six months of age was a perfect rat killer, and at nine would try conclusions with anything that wore fur, sometimes to her own discomfiture. Larkin's Bridget, a daughter of Hockwell's Hobo, was another which began very young and her puppies have all proved good. She has raised two litters by Teddy the Terror up to this time, and before this article appears will have another. It is not beyond the bounds of absolute truth to say that there was not a mediocre puppy in either litter.

"It is impossible within the narrow limits of a magazine article to expound a full set of working instructions whereby the novice can break his dog and make him the all-round utility companion that his ideals call for, but with ordinary intelligence and common sense methods, the average person can make a dog out of his Airedale puppy to suit his purposes, provided, of course, that has been secured the right kind of puppy. Assuming that he has purchased a puppy from an intelligent working strain, say about ten weeks of age, the first thing in order is to teach him his name. This is not a difficult matter. Call the puppy by the name that has been chosen, repeating it frequently, interlarding it with the usual "puppy talk." The young of all dogs that have not encountered the rebuffs of the hard outside world are confiding and long for human companionship and affection. The puppy will readily come when his attention is attracted, and when he is within reach of you, pat him gently using his name as frequently as possible and offer him a choice morsel to eat. Anything that he likes will do, small scraps of meat, crackers, or such. The puppy will soon learn to associate the mention of his name with a dainty tid-bit and after a few days of this, when his name is called he will come bounding to his teacher with alacrity.

"When but one dog is kept it is more than likely that he will frequently have access to the house at times and should therefore be housebroken, which is not such a difficult thing as one might imagine. Dogs are generally clean in their habits, but a very young puppy must be watched carefully; if he is caught in the act and promptly put out of doors, with a few sharp words of reprimand, he will soon learn that he is being punished for the offense and come to understand what is expected of him.

"All dogs are inquisitive youngsters and a terrier particularly so. If one wishes to have any satisfaction with them on the street they should be taught to remain at heel until they are given permission to run ahead at will and do as they please. Teach them first to lead; this is done by placing the lead about his neck and calling him to you, giving him a bite to eat if he comes willingly, as was done when teaching him his name. Very likely he will pitch and toss at the restraint of the lead, but he will soon learn to follow, if the judicious use of kindness and not harshness is adopted. Puppies at eight or ten weeks can be taught to lead perfectly. Take him out in the open and on the street to accustom him to strange sights and sounds, but always keep him under control. Remaining at heel can be taught to an old dog a readily as a young one, but the latter must not be cowed by harshness. The puppy will naturally want to run in front and all about you, but by using the lead a few times and pulling him back, giving the command the 'Heel!' he will soon learn to remain there until allowed to go at will, but by this time it is assumed that he knows his name and will come promptly to one at command.

"Retrieving is taught by two methods: the force system and the natural system. The first should not be attempted until the puppy is at least nine months of age, and personally I prefer to use the natural system entirely with Airedales. This breed, and a few others, take to retrieving and delight in chasing after a ball or stick that is thrown for them. These lessons may begin as soon as the puppy knows his name and obey the command to come. He will very likely pick up the object and run away with it, but by calling him in to you and giving the command 'Fetch!' he will gradually learn what is excepted of him, especially if he is rewarded with a piece of meat, or other dainty, when he does what is expected of him. Do not make these lessons too long, but a few minutes of this exercise several times a day will do wonders and before long he will fetch any object and consider it a pleasure to do so. Severity, however, must not be used, but the teacher must be firm and make the puppy do what is expected of him. As soon as he loses interest in the lesson, the teacher should desist at once and wait until some other time.

"In the same manner the puppy can be taught to go into the water. After he once retrieves from land and does it well, take him to shallow water, throw the ball or other object into the water just far enough so it is necessary for the puppy to wet the feet, and after he once begins to retrieve at this distance, it is well to throw the object out farther and farther until he is finally obliged to swim in order to retrieve it. Airedales, as a rule, are naturally water dogs and soon learn to this form of diversion. I have seen some of the most perfect retrievers finished in the natural manner, and they were tender-mouthed also. The puppy will very likely wish to hold on to the object even after he comes to you with it, but this must be discouraged. When he comes to you, use the word 'Give!' and gently take the object out of his mouth, If he is inclined to come down sharply on it with his teeth, press his lips over the teeth and repeat the word 'Give!' until he opens his mouth. The pain of the pressure of the lips on the teeth will induce him to open his mouth after a few attempts. Always praise and pet the puppy when he does well and reward him with a bite to eat on frequent occasions.

"There is no particular age at which a puppy should be entered on rats. Some, especially if they are associated with older dogs, will take to killing them at five and six months, others are slower to learn, but never allow the puppy to get the worst of it. Mice or young rats are good to begin on. Allow them to mouth and shake the rat at will and they will soon learn to kill. Teddy the Terror took to it very young and nearly all of his sons and daughters have developed very early in this respect.

"At six months of age or even younger the puppy can be taken to the woods. Airedales are very inquisitive and will run about in much glee, nosing into every hole and stump and cranny they come to, thus their instincts will develop according to the amount of experience they receive. They will take to chasing rabbits or spotting their burrows naturally, and while they are not the equal of the beagle or harrier on a cold trail, they will soon learn to pick up the fresh trails and to enjoy a sight chase, if a bunny happens to start in front of them. To teach them to tree squirrels it is wise to take them to a locality where these rodents are plentiful, and if they can surprise a few on the ground and chase them to a tree, they will soon learn how to make this part of the sport a fine art and also remain at the tree giving tongue until the master finds them. There is no finer sport on small game than killing squirrels which your Airedale has treed for you; Teddy the Terror has given my friends many a good morning's excitement, and the sport is still more fascinating when a small bore rifle is used which is the only way to hunt squirrels.

"The puppy should never be entered into a fight with an animal that is likely to give it the worst of an argument, and therefore I do not think it is wise to allow a puppy to attack a 'coon badger, or such animal alone, or at least not until he is well matured, but once he gets into such a scrap and knows his powers, he will generally come out the victor. The teacher's principal rule should be to use discrimination in all of his lessons. He must under no circumstances lose his temper and he should be circumspect in all that he does. Frequently a very good puppy is ruined by lack of discretion on part of the teacher. While very few Airedale puppies, descended from sires and dams that are working dogs, are gunshy still they must be introduced to the sound of these weapons gradually. To fire a full charge of powder and lead directly over a puppy the first time he is out would very likely make him a gunshy dog for life. Rather accustom him to the sounds of a cap pistol at feeding time at first and then, when he is taken out into the woods the gun may be fired when he is some distance away, until he learns to associated the gun with part of the sport of hunting. If, after he is once well accustomed to the sound of firearms, and a rabbit is bowled over while he is in full chase, or a squirrel is knocked down when he is treed, he will learn to love this part of the sport and become an indefatigable hunter of this class of game.

"The Airedale may also be taught to hunt and point pheasants, quail, and other upland game by practice and persistence, and as a duck retriever there are few dogs which are superior to him, but as I have already pointed out, the novice must not expect to buy a dog that has not had any experience and look for him to do the things that the well-trained Airedale, descended from a long line of working ancestors, will do."

CHAPTER XV.

Common Ailments.

This is not a book on the treatment of canine diseases and again I am constrained to refer the reader to one of my previous works. This is "Dogcraft" which devotes considerable space to the ills that dog flesh is heir to. Before writing "Finis," however, I cannot refrain from referring to some of the commoner ailments of the Airedale.

I have repeatedly said that this breed is peculiarly hardy and is not so susceptible to the many diseases that average highly-bred dogs are, but there come times, when even the Airedale requires some medical attention. In puppyhood all dogs should be treated with some kind of a vermifuge for expelling the worms which are sure to infest them, for I have yet to see the puppy, no matter what the precautions, that did not at some period of its early life, have worms and the earlier these are eradicated, the better it will be for the puppy. He will grow more rapidly, he will be sprightlier, and he will in all respects prove superior to those which are not so treated. My plan is to give a vermifuge at three weeks and another at about seven, which is the period when they should be safely weaned. Naturally one cannot give strong and dangerous drugs at this age, but there are several good vermifuges on the market, one of which I have particularly good success with and I have no doubt there are others just as good with which I have had no experience. At all events, do not experiment with areca nut or other expellers that some resort to. As many puppies are killed with vermifuges that are given to expel internal parasites as by the worms themselves, hence I would advise the owner not to experiment with remedies unknown to him. Rather accept one of the proprietary products and rely upon its guarantees. The chapter on internal parasites contained in "Dogcraft" will be well worth reading and studying, by all who own dogs, whether the dogs are young or old.

Distemper is another disease that is common to all of the canine family. In some breeds it is highly fatal, in others passably so, while in still others it is more easily combated. Among all breeds with which I have had experience, I would rather treat the Airedale than any other. As a matter of fact, I never had any casualties resulting from distemper during the period of twenty years I have been owning specimens of this breed, but in making this statement I do so with trepidation and as the saying goes, tap on wood, for there is no telling when the attack may come in fatal form. However, there is no question but the Airedale can stand the attacks of this disease much better than most breeds. I never treated any of this breed with serum and still they came through. Usually when the first symptoms of the disease made themselves apparent-and these consist of a rising temperature, a dry, husky cough and, in more advanced stages, matterated eyes-we promptly gave the victim a cathartic in the shape of a dose of salts or castor oil. The latter is better when there is the slightest trace if bowel disorder as will likely be in some cases. To combat the fever we then gave two grains each of hyposulphite of soda and quinine three times daily for about a week. Other symptoms were combated as they arose, such as bad eyes, diarrhea, etc. Pneumonia is another complication that must be guarded against and is fully explained in "Dogcraft," though as a matter of fact I only saw one real case of pneumonia in an Airedale, and this one recovered by treating the febrile symptoms and using turpentine and lard on his chest. That is, melting the lard and heating the two together, then soaking a strip of flannel in this and wrapping it around the chest, after which the patient is wrapped in another piece of flannel. This was repeated every three hours for about twelve hours and the dog recovered fully, leaving no after effects. I have no doubt that the serum treatment would be as successful if not more so with the Airedale than with any other breed, but I never tried this.

Mange and other skin diseases are also occasionally encountered in the Airedale, though when he is cared for as was indicated in one of the preceding chapters, this is not likely to occur, skin troubles are generally due to various causes. Mange to a parasite, while eczema may be a constitutional disease, although it is kept under subjection by proper diet and sanitary kennel surroundings.

For the latter disease when this breaks out it is well to change the diet entirely, see that the kennels are dry and airy, give the animal sufficient exercise, but not too much, and cool the blood by administering doses of old fashioned Epsom salts three times a week. As an external application there are a number which will cure mange and dry up eczema. One of them is the following:

Oil of Tar................................4 ounces.
Sulfur.....................................4 ounces.
Carbolic acid...........................1 teaspoonful.

Add these to one pound of melted lard, stir until cool and it is ready to apply. Care must be taken, however, that the sulfur is not added when the lard is too hot. Allow it to cool until it is almost ready to harden, then stir the sulfur well into the mixture. This applied a few times, generally has the desired results.

Another good formula is that of Er. Shelley's which he gives in his book, "Twentieth Century Bird Dog Training." Those who have used it recommend it highly, and its author claims for it that it will cure any case of skin trouble to which the dog is heir. It is as follows:

Boil together one lb. lard, one lb. vaseline, and one half pint castor oil. Remove from the fire and add one pint kerosene. Return to the fire again and boil. When nearly cool, stir in enough sulfur to make a thin paste. Rub well all over the dog even between his toes; do not miss a hair, the first application. If, according to Shelley's statement, "it is only an ordinary case of mange this one application will cure completely, new hair will come out and the dog with be as smooth as silk. Dogs which have had a bad case should have the worst places touched over in about four or five days. In real bad cases, a second or possibly third application may be necessary, but I have never seen a case that two applications would not cure completely."

Canker or affections of the middle ear are also prevalent with Airedales. Usually the common name of canker covers a multitude of affections, but I find that occasionally one encounters real cases of Otitis media, which is an affection of the middle ear, as the name implies. What the cause is I am at a loss to say, but I have an idea that it is due to damp, unsanitary kennels, and sometimes to blows or others injuries, sometimes to an extension of ordinary canker, but whatever the cause, it is generally treated like other ear affections, that is, by using strong lotions which are poured into the ear.

I find that far the better way to treat all these ear affections is to irrigate the ear thoroughly and this is done by the use of a hot-water bag with a two-yard rubber-tube attachment. Take one quart of lukewarm water to which add one teaspoonful of ordinary table salt. Hang the bag high enough so the water flows with some force, then insert the nozzle well down into the ear while the patient's head is held to one side. Allow the full amount of water to run into the ear, for only a certain amount can be retained at a time, but the idea is to continue the flow until the entire amount has been run through the ear, thus irrigating it thoroughly. After this, take a bobbin or any other needle or stick, wrap cotton around the end and dry the ear out perfectly; then fill the ear with powdered boracic acid. This treatment should be repeated every morning for at least ten days unless signs of improvements are apparent before this. I had a bitch brought in from the country not many weeks ago with a very severe case of Otitis media, which yielded to this treatment in about two weeks. Some object to using water in the ear, but it will be found that this irrigation treatment will bring results more promptly than any other method.

Canker or ulceration of the ear flap or broken and torn edges, are also quite common with Airedales as with all dogs with side ear carriage. Some recommend pasting the ears to the sides of the head with shoemaker's wax to prevent shaking. This will, no doubt, have the desired results as far as the actual shaking is concerned and further, it will keep the ears in position, but fastening them down in this manner is likely to interfere with the free circulation of air which is always so essential; furthermore, the wax may also be the source of trouble. I personally prefer taping the ears over the head, but allowing them to remaining in this position for several days at a time only, then retaping after a lapse of a half day. A canker cap made of some soft material through which the air can freely circulate, may also be used, but this also must be removed every half day or so. I used a canker cap on the bitch previously referred to as having Otitis media, but this was put on for a short time only directly after treatment while she was more prone to shake her head. After the lapse of several hours it was removed. In addition to the trouble in the middle ear, this bitch also had ulcers on the inside of the flaps and a severe, bleeding cut on the edge of the left ear. These were healed with Zinc Oxide, which is astringent, yet mildly so and one of the most rapid healing agents with which I have ever had any experience for sores or for any cutaneous affections arising from any cause whatever.

There are times when a dog may become listless and apathetic, lacking his usual vim and snap. Generally this is due to his bowels. Sometimes a dose of Epsom salts will correct this, but a good laxative to have on hand at all times is a combination of Cascara Sagrada, olive and castor oil in equal parts. Shake up this mixture well before giving. The dose for puppies under months is a teaspoonful, over that a tablespoonful. Full grown may be given two tablespoonfuls if a more powerful purgative is desired.

The foregoing category of ills covers the principal ones to which the Airedale is liable. Others may occur at times, but keep your dog well and the chances of disease are small.

Lawrence Wertan's
THE LOST CHAMPION

If you loved *Old Yeller* and *The Incredible Journey*, then you are going to love **The Lost Champion.** It is the story of a high-powered show dog who is the lone survivor of a small plane crash in the Rocky Mountain wilderness of Idaho, and twelve year old Anna Mary McCracken who was born to be his best friend. In the background looms the menace of Heavy Metal - a giant killer wild boar who was the result of a genetics experiment gone bad. **The Lost Champion** is an action packed story that explodes with spirit, heart, love, and a stand-up, cheering, crying finish. **The Lost Champion** is a new American classic about a girl and her dog.

"**The Lost Champion**...is rich with character and ...exciting."
Jeff Cross, Editor, Viking Books

"Hold on to your hats, fasten your seat belts...**The Lost Champion**... is a fast moving adventure story that I guarantee you'll read in one sitting." Lynne Hart Madison, *California ATC*

"You will never look at dogs the same way again."
Henry S. Johnson, Jr., *Full Cry Magazine*

"**The Lost Champion** combines the loyalty and courage of Old Yeller, and the sense of spirituality and destiny of Watership Down."
Mary Reeves, *The Tullahoma Sunday News*

"**The Lost Champion** has a driving narrative and strong prose. It takes the reader into the dog's consciousness as only a handful of animal classics have done."
Richard Gercken, Librarian, Ohio Public Library

The Lost Champion has replaced Old Yeller in my reading curriculum. My students pushing each other to hurry up and finish work so that they could get back to **The Lost Champion**. My kids loved it. It made us laugh, and it made us cry."
Jean Jakob, Teacher, Gifted and Talented Program,
Tampa, Fla.

"A splendid read in the tradition of Jack London, Fred Gibson, and Albert Payson Terhune."
William I. Hampton, CBS Newsman

ISBN 0-9653624-0-X

INTERNATIONAL GRAND CROWN

BY:

Lawrence Wertan

BoXer Books proudly announces **International Grand Crown** by Lawrence Wertan, author of **The Lost Champion. International Grand Crown** is the story of a boy, a champion Airedale Terrier, and a tough old Army Sergeant. Their quest for the International Grand Crown, the national championship of dog showing, renews the old man's faith in life and teaches the boy courage.

The story is set in Charleston, South Carolina but moves around the country as the quest for International Grand Crown heats-up. Breathing down their neck is an adversary so determined to win that he is even willing to kill. Flynn is also in a race with death as he tries to teach Mugsey a life-time of knowledge about Airedales in just a few short months.

Flynn tells Mugsey that the secret to life is to become like an Airedale by having the eye of an eagle, the heart of a lion, and the personality of Emmett Kelly. Mugsey, with Flynn's coaching, discovers his own inner strength when he stands up to the class bully. In typical Wertan fashion there are thrills, spills, laughter, tears, and a finish that will have you standing and cheering .

If you liked **The Lost Champion,** you are going to love International Grand Crown.

"Sheer pleasure. This undeniably good book comes to a rousingly warm conclusion of unity, family, community, and values..."

Scott Meredith, New York Literary Agent

"Vividly illustrates the energy, effort, determination, and courage demanded of all great champions. Personifies the American, Can Do Spirit!."

Henry S. Johnson, Jr., SandHill Airedale Terriers

"A splendid read in the tradition of Jack London, Fred Gibson, and Albert Payson Terhune."

Bill Hampton, CBS Newsman, Ret.

ISBN 0-9653624-1-8

INTERNATIONAL
GRAND
CROWN
MFD

Printed in the United States
15566LVS00001B/217-240

Woman

God's Plan
not
Man's Tradition

by Joanne Krupp

DESTINY IMAGE® PUBLISHERS, INC.
P.O. Box 310, Shippensburg, PA 17257-0310
"Promoting Inspired Lives."

This book and all other Destiny Image and Destiny Image Fiction books are available at Christian bookstores and distributors worldwide.

For more information on foreign distributors, call 717-532-3040.

Or reach us on the Internet: www.destinyimage.com

ISBN 13 TP: 978-0- 7684-4337-0
ISBN 13 EBook: 978-0-7684-4338-7

For Worldwide Distribution, Printed in the U.S.A.
1 2 3 4 5 6 7 8 9 10 11 / 23 22 21 20 19 18

Dedication

To my girls
Beth, Wenda, Jamie, Kelly, Alyssa, Allison, Audra,
and Lennox

It is my prayer that this book will contribute to your being able to enjoy womanhood as God planned it.

Acknowledgments

First of all, I am so grateful to the Lord for opening this whole subject to me in His Word and for the clear leading He gave me to put it into a book. I am also very grateful to the late Mary Riordan who sent us the first book on this subject.

Next, I wish to express my deep gratitude to my dear husband Nate for his unfailing encouragement which served to spur me on to the completion of this task. He also spent many hours going over the manuscript editorially and coordinated the production. Without him this assignment would have been almost beyond my reach.

I also wish to express my thanks to our son Gerry and daughter Beth for the confidence they showed in their Mom to complete such a task. Their "sure you can do it" attitude was of immeasurable encouragement.

I am deeply grateful for those who showed early and continued enthusiasm for the book as they read through the manuscript at its different stages of development and for all the constructive criticism and suggestions they gave me: Evelyn Allen, Sandy Allen, Beth Bachran, Pete and Bev Caruso, Sidney Dosh, Jr., Irene Faver, Jay Ferris, Victoria Fink, Arlene Hughes, Bob Iddings, Charleen Knoch, Gerry Krupp, Tony Mader, Ken Morse, Robbie and Jean Moule, Georgia Penniman, Carol Preston, the late Hans Schnabel, and Sylvia Zook.

I'm especially grateful to the late Treena Kerr who went far beyond the call of duty in preparing to write the Foreword. Her encouragement included sharing with me some of her own unpublished work on the subject. Her diligent reading of the manuscript was, indeed, a labor of love.

Heartfelt thanks to George Moser and his late wife JoAnne for the new computer they provided while I was working on this book. What a blessing! I also wish to thank Dave Hooten who helped transfer the manuscript from the old computer discs to the new. And special blessings to my son-in-law Greg Bachran and Lane Witt who both helped me keep my sanity while learning the new computer. They spent literally hours at my side or over the phone giving me instructions.

I am truly indebted to those scholars who have blazed the trail in study and writing on the whole women's issue from a non-traditional vantage point (see Bibliography). They made my task so much easier.

Foreword

Graham and I have known Joanne and her husband Nate as a couple since 1978. In our opinion, Joanne is one of the most feminine women we have known, for in all that time she has never been anything but honoring to Nate. She may have strong opinions, which she will always voice, yet she combines her words with both humility and submissiveness.

Woman is strong in opinions, but the writer has ample support from nothing less than the Word of God. To honor Joanne's request for input, I have read this book twice. This committment has been both a joy and a learning curve for me. The obvious care to biblical correctness and the desire to be understood and non-judgmental has been accomplished by much sweat and tears. The grace with which she has received creative criticism has been an example to me of true humility. Joanne has shown herself approved and has given birth to a life-changing labor of love, for those who heed her words.

If your ministry involves relationships or marriage, whether you be male or female, this book is an essential tool. As most peoples' lives revolve around relationships of some kind, it makes for a great study book. I would also recommend it as a "couples" book, to be read and discussed together. You will no doubt go through emotional testings as "man-made" traditions are threatened, and maybe the challenges will hurt, but read on. Give this woman of God the honor of hearing her out to the end. If you will, I believe you will receive fresh revelation and bring joy to your lives and to those that love you.

We are both enthusiastic, for Graham and I, in our early walk with the Lord, went through most of the misconceptions and the traditional attitudes toward Christian women and marriage. Man — the head, the boss, the priest, and the decider. We became involved with a well-intentioned group that built up the male by putting the wife in a sub-servient position. The male was supreme; the female his obedient chattel.

Through much study of the Word, Graham and I began to understand this was not God's original intent for His children. We discovered through many tears, prayers, and frustrations this very message that Joanne has written in her book. We have made this subject our own lifestyle, living it for the past fifteen years. The outcome? A happy and deeply-in-love married couple, with mutual respect. We both believe this book is long overdue.

May your marriage and relationships be as God intended, and mercy, peace, and love be yours as you read.

Treena J. Kerr
International Bible Teacher
Producer of The Galloping Gourmet *and*
The Graham Kerr Show

Word of Endorsement

I can heartily endorse the conclusions of Joanne's book. She has done an excellent job. Her book is biblically and theologically sound. It is easy to read and understand. She has included insights on Genesis, chapters 1-3; 1 Corinthians 11 and 14; and 1 Timothy 2, which I have not seen in a number of other books I have read on the subject. Specifically, her book is the only one I know of which shows that Eve was taken from a whole side of Adam, not just a rib. And that the pain in Genesis 3:16 refers to more than just childbirth. Her book is not just on the theology of gender. She shows how God used women throughout the Bible and throughout Church history.

Although I don't know specifically where they came from, my early convictions were that the husband was the boss in the home, and women had a limited role in the church. In 1976 I found myself having problems receiving from women in leadership in Youth with a Mission, the mission agency with which we were affiliated. Loren and Darlene Cunningham, leaders of YWAM, counseled with me and prayed for me regarding this. Their prayer included that God would use me to release women.

In 1981, while pastoring in Oregon, we were again confronted with this whole subject. As I continued to study and pray, God continued to change my views and open my heart to women. And He allowed me to begin releasing women into ministry. The years since then have been challenging years as I have had to come to grips with the various conclusions which Joanne has been reaching in her study and writing. It has not been easy to turn my back on a tradition which I had been led to believe was so biblical.

I can honestly say, however, understanding who women are in God's sight and His plan for them has greatly enhanced my regard for women in general, and my love and respect for my wife in particular. It has brought a dimension of mutual respect and trust to our marriage that was not present before. I no longer see Joanne as someone given to me by God to help me in my ministry, but that we have been given to each other in order that together we might exalt His Name (Psalm 34:3).

I trust that God will use this book to influence millions of men and women around the world. I pray that husbands and church leaders will release women to become all that God wants to make them as godly partners in the home, church, and society.

Nate Krupp

Henceforth it is also war by Satan upon the womanhood of the world, in malignant revenge for the verdict of the garden. War by the trampling down of women in all lands where the deceiver reigns. War upon women in Christian lands, by the continuance of his Eden method of misinterpreting the Word of God; insinuating into men's minds throughout all succeeding ages, that God pronounced a "curse" upon the woman, when in truth she was pardoned and blessed; and instigating men of the fallen race to carry out the supposed curse, which was in truth a curse upon the deceiver, and not the deceived one (Genesis 3:14).

"I will put enmity between thee and the woman," said God, as well as between "thy seed and her seed," and this vindictive enmity of the hierarchy of evil to woman, and to believers, has not lessened in its intensity from that day.

— Jesse Penn-Lewis

Contents

Introduction

In 1988 my husband Nate and I found ourselves in a church situation where, we soon learned, women were not free to teach or even participate in the discussion of the Scriptures in any church meetings. Having been in a similar situation nearly twenty years earlier, my first reaction was, "Lord, not again! Please!" In the earlier situation, Nate had had reservations about women in ministry, but in the ensuing years, God had worked in his heart and understanding regarding woman's role in the Church. He had brought him to the place where, as a spiritual leader, he was able to release women (including me) into whatever God called them to do. But, here we were again. How were we to respond to this situation?

Right at that time, Katherine Bushnell's book *God's Word to Women* came into Nate's possession. This book deals in-depth with the whole subject of the role of women from a biblical perspective. As he began reading it, the Holy Spirit prompted him that I, not he, should be reading the book. He gave it to me and as I began reading, I realized that I really did not know, in fact, had never studied the Scriptures for myself in order to learn what exactly God's plan for woman was. It was then that the Lord ignited within me an insatiable desire to delve into the subject and find the truth from God's Word.

I, like most of us, had been brought up with the traditional teaching regarding women that goes something like this: Eve, because she partook of the fruit of the forbidden tree first, was the cause of sin coming into the world. Because of her sin, a curse was placed upon her by God that was to include physical pain as her body would be involved in the reproductive process. She was also told by God that man was to rule over her. Although it had

not been part of my early understanding, as I moved into adulthood, I learned that there were those who understood that, furthermore, the Scriptures teach that women are not to be involved in teaching the Word of God to men or hold any position of spiritual leadership.

As I studied, there was a question that loomed in my mind: "Was the premise for that traditional teaching found in the Bible, or brought to it by interpretation?"

I experienced many emotions as I studied. I experienced excitement as I came to understand who I am, as a woman, in God's sight. I experienced anger as I was faced with the way Scripture has been twisted to serve the purposes of male authoritarianism. I experienced grief as I pondered the degradation, oppression, and humiliation my sisters have needlessly suffered for centuries. But I also experienced joy as I came to see that God is in the process of restoring woman to her rightful position in society in general, and particularly in her relationship to her husband (and he to her), and her rightful place in the Church.

It is my desire to lead you on a pilgrimage through the Bible that will open the window of truth as it relates to God's plan for women. It is my prayer that this truth, when breathed in by the reader, will aid in healing the tremendous breach that exists between men and women in the Body of Christ.

This is by no means an exhaustive study on this subject. However, I hope I have included enough exegesis to show forth truth, but not so much that the reader might become "bogged down" with details.

"Let me say at this point, I am not a feminist. Contrary to the "feminist" movement of a century ago, everything "feminism" is pushing today I find contrary to Biblical truth.

I know that many women who love and serve God call themselves feminists. I honor they're intent. I have no doubt that in many cases these women have been wounded by leaders in the church who have been unwilling to release or in any way encourage them to exercise their leadership giftings within the church or in the home. They feel they have been "heard" and "honored" more within the framework of the world's idea of the value of women.

I believe, however, that the Biblical vision of the role and status of woman is much deeper and more encompassing than what the Feminist Movement is looking to accomplish and is willing to settle for.

God's plan is not proudly reactionary, demanding, and cold. His plan is a freedom founded in peace, honor, respect, humility, and fulfillment that He has ordained and that brings honor to His Name.

God's plan is not even one of championing for "women's rights." A truly broken Christian who has been crucified with Christ has no rights. Nor am I joining the ranks of those females who are fighting for recognition and superiority of lordship or rulership.

Rather, I am pressing for the God-given equality of mutual submission and servanthood. I simply desire to see God's plan, as outlined in Scripture, lived out in the lives of believers. I long to see men and women, in the home, in the Church, and in all of society, functioning and relating to one another in the way God had in mind from the very beginning of time.

It is my prayer that this book will be used by God to hasten the day when that will be a reality.

ONE

In the Beginning

In order to get an accurate understanding of the kind of relationship God had in mind between man and woman, we must go back to the beginning, as recorded in Genesis. Genesis 1:26-28 gives a clear picture of the relationship that existed in the Garden of Eden; and therefore, gives a clear picture of what God's plan was for the type of relationship that should exist between a husband and wife.

The New American Standard translation says it this way:

> "Let Us make man in Our image, according to Our likeness; and let them rule over the fish of the sea and over the birds of the sky and over the cattle and over all the earth, and over every creeping thing that creeps on the earth." And God created man in His own image, in the image of God He created him; male and female He created them. And God blessed them; and

> God said to them, "Be fruitful and multiply, and fill the earth and subdue it; and rule over the fish of the sea and over the birds of the sky, and over every living thing that moves on the earth."

Together they were created in the image of God. Together they were to rule over the fish in the sea, over the birds in the sky, over the cattle, and over all the earth. God blessed them and told them to be fruitful, multiply, fill the earth, and subdue it. Both were to move through life on an equal status. Not one word is mentioned in this Scripture about man ruling over woman, or any other hierarchical authority arrangement, other than God Himself being over both of them.

Adam and Eve had a mutual, loving relationship in which they moved through that beautiful Garden as one flesh, according to Genesis 2:24:

> For this cause a man shall leave his father and his mother, and shall cleave to his wife; and they shall become one flesh.

Because sin had not yet entered the world, there was no vying for leadership, no competition, no claiming of rights, no jealousy, no shirking of responsibility (with one possible exception, i.e., when Adam didn't protect the Garden as God had instructed him, which we'll touch on later). They were just "one flesh" moving in unity.

Helper, Helpmeet, or What?

Now we know they each had their own unique contribution to make to their relationship. The Bible says God saw that it was not good for man to be alone, therefore He provided *"a helper suitable for him"* (Genesis 2:18). Apparently, Eve contributed something to Adam that he was lacking.

Let's look at the word "helper." *Ezer*, the Hebrew word for "help" in the Old Testament usage does not imply an inferior or subordinate help, but means "to help one in trouble." For example, Psalm 121:2 says, *"My help comes from the Lord."* Exodus 18:4 says, *"The God of my father was my help and delivered me from the sword of Pharoah."* Psalm 20:2 says, *"May He send you help from the sanctuary."* So it appears that the kind of help God saw that Adam needed, and that He created in the form of Eve, was a surrounding, defending, and undergirding help. This was a spiritual and emotional kind of help, not a "bring me my pipe and slippers" subordinate.

The King James Version (hereafter referred to as KJV) says "help meet;" NASB says "helper suitable." The Hebrew word *kenegdo*, translated "suitable," means "as his counterpart, those things which are like one another as a mirror reflection, corresponding to him." Therefore God was saying He was going to create someone for Adam who would be just like him. She would, however, add a dimension which Adam alone lacked; as a couple, then, they would be more complete. She was not to be considered his inferior or his subordinate; she would be just like him. Together they were created in God's image.

R. David Freedman defines *ezer* as more accurately meaning "power" (or strength) rather than "helper," since it is thus used elsewhere in the Hebrew Bible. Furthermore, based on Mishnaic Hebrew, he puts forth that *kenegdo,* usually rendered "suitable for him," actually means "equal to him." Therefore, when God said He would make a "helper suitable for him," He was saying that this woman would be a "power" equal to man, his match, corresponding to him in every way.[1]

Imagine the beautiful union — the smooth flowing together, the give-and-take, the oneness, because they were one flesh — that took place there in the Garden.

The sad part of that beautiful story is that it came to an end with the Fall. The intimate relationship Adam and Eve had with God and each other was broken and destroyed, altering the course of life for both man and woman ever since.

However, Jesus, with His death on the Cross and resurrection, has made possible the restoration of all things (Acts 3:21). Jesus' death and resurrection, as commonly understood, made possible: our being made new in Christ, a relationship with Him, a walk through life with knowledge of sins forgiven, and the hope of heaven. Beyond this, it also made possible the full restoration of all relationships on every level in this life (Ephesians 2:11-22).

Most importantly, it made possible the restoration of the kind of relationship between a husband and wife that existed before the Fall. Therefore, it is possible, under the Lordship of Jesus Christ and the power and anointing of the Holy Spirit, for a husband and wife to walk together through life with total unity, love, and equality. To say that this restoration does not include the restoration of that equal relationship between husband and wife, as experienced in the garden, is selling the Cross of Jesus Christ short and denying the power of His shed blood. Who are we to so restrict the complete work of Christ on the Cross?!

The Rib Origin

Let's take a look at the word "rib" as spoken of in Genesis 2:21, 22. The Hebrew word *tsela* is used fifty-two times in the Old Testament. These two verses are the **only** two verses where this word is translated "rib." In every other case it is translated either "side," "side-chamber," "chamber," or "corner." Had Eve been formed simply of Adam's rib, Adam would not have said, *"Bone of my bone*

and flesh of my flesh" (Genesis 2:23), only "Bone of my bone."

The rib origin came from rabbinical lore which supports woman's low estate. Katherine Bushnell, in her book *God's Word to Women,* writes of a certain Rabbi Joshua who included this piece of lore in his commentaries, and it has been picked up by a number of Christian commentators on the Bible. Here is one rendition:

> God deliberated from what member He would create woman, and He reasoned with Himself thus: "I must not create her from Adam's head, for she would be a proud person, and hold her head high. If I create her from the eye, then she will wish to pry into all things; if from the ear, she will wish to hear all things; if from the mouth, she will talk much; if from the heart, she will envy people; if from the hand, she will desire to take all things; if from the feet, she will be a gadabout. Therefore, I will create her from the member which is hid, that is, the rib, which is not even seen when man is naked."[2]

A variation with which I grew up renders a more tender attitude. It concludes with, "I will create her from the rib, that part of the man's body that is closest to his heart." This lore, which has no scriptural basis, seems to accept Eve as something of an afterthought.

On the contrary, Genesis 5:1, 2 says:

> This is the book of the generations of Adam. In the day when God created man, He made him in the likeness of God. He created them **male** and **female**, and He blessed them and named **them** Man in the day when they were created. *(Bold added for emphasis.)*

I believe when God created Adam, He included something that would become the basis from which Eve would later be formed. She was not an after-thought.

When God caused the deep sleep to fall upon Adam, He simply lifted that "side" of Adam out, placed it in a female body, and presented her to Adam. She was now a corresponding, suitable, mirror-like reflection of Adam, created in the image of God from the very beginning. There is little comparison between this Eve and the one tradition has told us was formed by taking one little bone and creating a whole new being.

The Septuagint

It is important to note that the Septuagint version of the Old Testament translated these verses "side" rather than "rib."

The Septuagint version is one of the most important documents that we have as a reference on this or any other biblical subject. This translation from the Hebrew to the Greek was produced by seventy-two Jewish scholars in 285 B.C. Many consider it the most important of all versions. It is among the most ancient manuscripts and was translated at a time when more was known about the ancient Hebrew than at any time since.

The Septuagint was much in favor among the Jews until Christians began using it to prove that Jesus was the Messiah. From that time it began to fall under Jewish displeasure. This is the text that was very probably used by the Lord Himself as well as the Apostles.[3] As Jesus read the Old Testament in the synagogue and taught against the traditions that had been handed down which nullified the Word of God (Mark 7:13), it is never recorded that He took exception to this translation, or any part of it.

The importance of the Septuagint translation must not be undermined. As we proceed in this discourse, other references will be made to its translation of certain important portions.

Conclusion

Based on this analysis of the creation story, one must conclude that the original plan God had in mind when He created man and woman was for unity, mutual support, and submission to each other – not for the subjugation of one over the other. I have come to agree with Faith Martin who has made the following statement in her book *Call Me Blessed:*

> A woman is an adult female human and, by reason of the honor and position granted her by God at Creation, stands beside the adult male human as his equal in all concerns of life.[4]

I am convinced that there is too much in Scripture supporting this statement for anyone to put and keep women in a lesser position. Nor did God change that through anything He said to Eve after the Fall. Let's return to the Garden and consider what really happened.

Chapter One Notes

1. R. David Freedman as quoted in Marvin R. Wilson, *Our Father Abraham* (Grand Rapids: Wm. B. Eerdmans Publishing Co. and Center for Judaic-Christian Studies, 1989), 201.

2. Katherine C. Bushnell, *God's Word to Women* (privately reprinted by Ray B. Munson, P.O. Box 417, North Collins, NY, 1923), 43. Also reprinted by Christians for Biblical Equality; 122 W. Franklin Ave. #218; Minn. MN 55404.

3. Ibid., 130. For further reference: Merrill F. Unger, *Unger's Bible Dictionary* (Chicago: Moody Press, 1957), 1147-49.

4. Faith Martin, *Call Me Blessed* (Grand Rapids: Wm. B. Eerdmans, 1988), 12.

Questions For Study or Discussion

1. According to Genesis 1:26-28, who was to rule over the creation?
2. Was Eve an after-thought on God's part? (Genesis 2:28; 5:1,2)
3. What does the Hebrew word "kenegdo" mean?
4. What does the Hebrew word "ezer" mean?
5. How should Genesis 2:18 be translated with a proper understanding of kenegdo and ezer?
6. What is the accurate translation of "tsela"?
7. How should Genesis 2:21-22 be translated?
8. What have you learned so far in this study about God's plan for woman? How does it compare with any previous understanding you have had?

TWO

What Really Happened in the Garden?

Satan Entered

Let's go back to the Garden scene and anaylze exactly what happened. Genesis 2:15 tells us, *"Then the Lord God took the man and put him into the garden of Eden to cultivate it and keep it."* According to *Gesenius' Hebrew-Chaldee Lexicon to the Old Testament,* "keep" means "to keep, to watch, to guard."[1]

I have this nagging question in the back of my mind: if Adam was guarding the Garden as God had instructed him, how did Satan get in there in the first place? It appears to me that Satan was the only thing from which the Garden needed protection. This was a responsibility given to Adam alone, since Eve had not yet been formed.

We know, of course, that Satan did enter the Garden and tempt Eve. She responded to that temptation, partook

of the fruit, and gave to her husband who also ate of it. I used to think that Eve was all alone when temptation came to her and that when she partook of the fruit, eager to share it with Adam, she ran all over the Garden looking for him. Not so! Genesis 3:6 says, *"And she gave also to her husband with her and he ate."* He was there all along! Yet Scripture does not indicate he said anything to keep her from eating or to correct her deception.

Thus the Fall took place. A careful analysis of the scenario that followed between God and Adam and Eve is very important for one who desires to know whether the traditional teaching is fact or fiction. Let's follow it.

Beginning with Genesis 3:9, both Adam and Eve partook of the forbidden fruit. Then God came to deal with them. First, God asked Adam, *"Hast thou eaten of the tree?"* Some would say the fact that God went to Adam first indicates the role of authority Adam held. I believe the reason God went to Adam first was because the prohibition had been given to Adam before Eve had been taken out of man and placed in her own body. Therefore, Adam was in the place of full accountability to God.

Anytime God (or anyone else for that matter) gives you something to do or commands you not to do something, He is going to hold you accountable to His directions, not your spouse. If God told me to make restitution to a certain person and I failed to do it, God would not go to my husband and ask him whether I had obeyed. He would come to me, the one to whom He had given the directive, and ask, "Joanne, did you do what I asked you to do?" And if not, "Why?"

When God asked Adam, *"Hast thou eaten of the tree?,"* Adam replied, *"The woman whom Thou gavest to be with me, she gave me of the tree, and I did eat."* Then God questioned Eve. Her reply was, *"The serpent beguiled me and I did eat."*

Notice the difference in their replies. Eve blamed Satan. Adam blamed Eve, and ultimately, God. Adam made an evil choice. He blamed God and in so doing, moved to the side of Satan. Eve, on the other hand, fully exposed the character of Satan before his very face. By so doing, she caused Satan to hate her, and all woman-kind that followed her, with intense hatred.

Since that moment, Satan has done everything he could to put and keep woman down — and quite successfully. He also knew, however, from the very beginning how God had created woman as the counterpart (mirror-type, equal to) to Adam, and that God's plan at Calvary was to totally restore woman back to her original position.

This restoration began with God's elevating women in the Old Testament to places of leadership and was completed with the death and resurrection of Jesus Christ. And with each new reviving move of the Spirit from the Acts of the Apostles to the present, God has again and again called His daughters forth. Where the Spirit is there is liberty; and in the initial years of each revival, women have begun to rise to their God-given position. However, Satan, in turn, has launched new attacks to bring women down again.

Satan's Counterfeit

By the 1960s, even though equality existed in some parts of the Church, it was sadly lacking in others. At the beginning of what has come to be known as the Charismatic Renewal in the mid-60s, there began a new thrust by the Holy Spirit to lead women forward to their position of equality with man before God. This time, Satan raised up a counterfeit movement labeled the Women's Liberation Movement. This movement pushed

the issue beyond equality of the sexes to a dominant role for the female, and acceptance of unnatural, ungodly male and female roles. This movement rose to its height in the 1970s and angrily continues to this day. I believe Satan instigated this movement, not because he wanted to see women liberated, but rather as a method of further dividing the Church and alienating women from men. Unfortunately, it worked! It caused those with a die-hard hierarchical understanding of the Scriptures, mistranslated as they were, to dig in their heels and fight for the male hierarchical beliefs more than ever. The result? More controversy and more feelings of alienation and lack of importance and validation among women in the Body of Christ.

Sadly, the Church has not been able to recognize the enemy's tactics and separate this plan and its true source from God's genuine plan, as outlined in Scripture.

I believe that Satan's goal in dividing the Body of Christ was much broader than the causing of multitudes of women to experience feelings of being lesser human beings than their counter part, as abomidable as that was. Rather Satan knows all too well the power the Church will have when women, with men, take their God-ordained positions to stand in unity as one in Christ. Satan has, therefore, continued to do all he can to keep God's house divided. He has diminished its power by keeping half of the family of God displaced, out of position, out of joint.

Consequently, much of the Body of Christ limps along, even at a time when we hear the Spirit echoing Jesus' prayer, *"Father, make them one;"* (John 17:21-23), and He continues to prepare Himself *"a glorious Church without spot or wrinkle or any such thing"* (Ephesians 5:27).

Between the counterfeit women's movement and the traditional position, we find our energies used up fighting each other rather than Satan. Oh, that women would be

allowed to take their position (along with men) in Christ so that the world might see a true reflection and demonstration of Him through His entire Body in the world today!

The Messiah Promised

Adam blamed God. Eve blamed Satan. Both, however, acknowledged their sin by saying *"I did eat."* One has to acknowledge that the heart-attitude of one who blames God for his own sin is different from the one whose heart-attitude puts the blame at the feet of Satan. There is no spirit of repentance in one who is still blaming God for his sin.

What follows next is that marvelous first Messianic promise in Genesis 3:15. God speaks to Satan and says,

> And I will put enmity between you and the woman, and between your seed and her seed; He shall bruise you on the head, and you shall bruise him on the heel.

This is the first prophecy of the coming Messiah, Jesus.

It is important to note here that Eve believed in the coming Messiah, and she acknowledged that belief by her statement in Genesis 4:1. When she had her first child, she said, *"I have gotten a man-child with the help of the Lord."* The word for Lord here means "Jehovah - the Coming One." So Eve really was the first to acknowledge faith in the promised Messiah.

In summary:

1. Eve sinned, laid the blame at Satan's feet, and yet acknowledged her sin.
2. She believed in the promise of the One who would conquer her enemy for her, as was prophesied in Genesis 3:15.

3. She even accepted that One by faith as indicated in Genesis 4:1.

It seems to be very clear that all of this could have counted to her for righteousness. Abraham believed and it was counted unto **him** for righteousness (Genesis 15:6), why not Eve? Jesus is the same yesterday, today, and forever!

This does not make Eve superior to Adam, just forgiven. But because of this, she certainly does not deserve the curse that tradition has told us she received from the hand of God.

Sin Entered the World Through Adam

After the fourth chapter of Genesis, Eve is never referred to again in the Old Testament. Adam is mentioned two times, once in Job 31:33, *"If I, like Adam, covered my transgression by hiding my iniquity in my bosom,"* and again in Hosea 6:7, *"They, like Adam transgressed the covenant."* Both of these references mention his transgression.

In the New Testament, it is plainly stated that Adam's conduct brought sin into the world:

- Romans 5:12, *"By one man sin entered into the world."*
- Romans 5:14, *"Nevertheless, death reigned from Adam to Moses, even over those who had not sinned in the likeness of Adam's offense, who is a type of Him who was to come."*
- 1 Corinthians 15:22, *"In Adam all die."*

Eve indicates, as recorded in Genesis 3:13, that the serpent deceived her when he tempted her. 1 Timothy 2:14 states, *"Adam was not deceived – but the woman being quite deceived fell into transgression."* We don't know all that transpired to allow this deception, but it is important to understand that the word "deceive" means to fool

someone so completely that he accepts what is false as truth.

This does not negate the sin, but it would seem that there is an even greater measure of mercy shown to those who sin out of deception. Paul said, in 1 Timothy 1:13:

> . . . even though I was formerly a blasphemer and a persecutor and a violent aggressor. And yet I was shown mercy, because I acted ignorantly in unbelief.

So even though tradition lays the blame for the Fall at Eve's feet, Scripture very clearly says that Adam willfully sinned; and that it was, in fact, through Adam that sin entered into the world.

Again, this does not make Eve superior, but certainly does not put her in line for the kind of curse that tradition claims was placed on her by God. The traditional doctrine concerning Eve has placed an inferior light upon woman's stature in God's sight; and, thus, greatly curtailed her spiritual activity. This has caused the entire Church of Jesus Christ to suffer, having been deprived of the full ministry of anointed women.

Did God Curse Eve?

One of the most controversial verses in the Bible relating to this whole issue is Genesis 3:16:

> To the woman He said, "I will greatly multiply your pain in childbirth, in pain you shall bring forth children; yet your desire shall be for your husband, and he shall rule over you."

It is the pivotal verse upon which the whole male/female relationship rests. Its accurate translation is crucial to the entire subject.

Most modern translations inaccurately render Genesis 3:16. However, it has been traced in history to the time when a calculated change was made in the translation of certain words. This change gave man the authority over woman as if ordained by God. Ancient manuscripts verify this calculated error.

So what does Genesis 3:16 really say? Let's begin with the first phrase, *"To the woman he said 'I will greatly multiply your pain in childbirth'"* (KJV – *"Thy sorrow and conception"*).

The ancient Hebrew word in this verse lacks two letters which it needs in order to be translated "childbirth" or "conception." Without those two letters, the word becomes "sighing" instead.[2] The Septuagint has translated that phrase "A snare hath increased thy sorrow and thy sighing."[3] The snare is Satan. He was the source of sorrow introduced into the world. God did not multiply woman's pain. Satan increased her sorrow and sighing.

The next phrase, *"in pain you shall bring forth children;"* or as the New International Version more accurately translates it, *"in pain you will bring forth children;"* has been interpreted to mean that, because of God's judgment, the birth process would always be accompanied by pain. However, one must keep in mind that in the beginning bringing forth children was to have been a blessing (Genesis 1:28). So the grief or the pain does not lay alone in the birth process, but, also in the whole rearing and raising process. God, in using the word "will," was warning Eve that pain and sorrow would accompany bringing children to a place of maturity in a world full of evil.

I recently asked an obstetrician if he ever has patients who give birth painlessly. He said, "Not totally painlessly, but there are women who give birth easily." I also have a

friend who has testified to having had two almost painless births. This confirmed my conviction that if God had decreed that a woman was to have great pain in childbirth, based on this verse, then there could be no exceptions. God's decrees have no exceptions.

The Bible does have many references to women in travail or painful labor leading up to their time of delivery. And more times than not, most of us mothers can testify to having experienced that kind of pain. However, I do not believe this is due to a "curse" having been placed upon woman by God. Rather, as He warned, it is the result of sin in general and its accompanying pain and sorrows.

The translation of the last part of the verse, *"Yet your desire shall be for your husband, and he shall rule over you,"* seems to rest on two words: "desire," and whether the correct verb form is "will" or "shall."

Let's look at the verb form first. "Shall" is an imperative. "Will" is a simple future verb indicating a warning. Shall declares that something **must** be done. Will is simply a prediction of something in the future. This phrase is written in the subjunctive, or conditional, tense which never implies a sense of obligation in the Semitic languages. Since the "wills" and the "shalls" are supplied by the translator, the word to be used can be proven only by the context and the tense in which the context is written. All the ancient manuscripts render this word as a simple future – a warning, not an imperative.[4]

Now what about that word "desire"? The Hebrew word *teshuqua* has traditionally been rendered as "desire" and interpreted as meaning "appetite" or "lust" in the modern translations. The concept of sensual desire can be traced back to the teaching of the rabbis in the *Talmud*.

The *Talmud* contains regulations and traditions handed down orally from one generation to another. These teachings gradually became law and were accepted to be

as authoritative as the five Old Testament books of the Law, referred to by the Jews as the *Torah*. In fact, by the time Jesus began his ministry, the *Talmud* had almost entirely replaced the commandments of the Old Testament. Included in the *Talmud* are the "Ten Curses of Eve." Within these "Curses," rather crude language was used by the rabbis to depict woman's sensual desires.

Some of those today who hold to the traditional understanding, still believe "desire" to be the strong sexual desire that woman will have for man. This is not born out in reality since, generally speaking, a man has a stronger sex drive than a woman. There are those, however, who believe it is referring to the desire or appetite woman would have to rule over man (rather than allowing man to rule over woman as they believe God intended).

Teshuqua is used three times in the Old Testament: Genesis 3:16, Genesis 4:7, and Song of Solomon 7:10. Genesis 3:16 and Genesis 4:7 have been translated into Greek in the Septuagint as the word *apostrophe,* meaning "turning away." Song of Solomon 7:10 has been translated into the Greek with the word *apistrophe* in the Septuagint, meaning "turning to." Again, referring to the Septuagint, this verb was translated "thou art turning away to thy husband and he will rule over thee." The meaning seems to imply that Eve would be turning away from God (this new-found relationship with God) toward her husband. Consequently, because of this defection, Adam would rule over her.

In his book *Hard Sayings of the Old Testament,* Walter Kaiser says,

> Of the twelve known ancient versions (the Greek Septuagint, the Syriac Peshitta, the Samaritan Pentateuch, the Old Latin, the Sahidic, the Bohairic, the Ethiopic, the Arabic, Aquila's Greek, Symmachus's

> Greek, Theodotion's Greek, and the Latin Vulgate), almost every one (twenty-one out of twenty-eight times) renders these three instances of *teshuquah* as "turning," not "desire."[5]

Kaiser goes on to say,

> Bushnell traced the change in translation to an Italian Dominican monk, Pagnino, who translated the Hebrew Bible. His version was published in Lyons in 1528. Now, with the exception of Wycliff's 1380 English version and the Douay Bible of 1609, both of which were made from the Latin Vulgate, every English version from the time of Pagnino up to the present day has adapted Pagnino's rendering for Genesis 3:16.[6]

Thus, the modern day translation "desire" comes from Pagnino's rendering, not from the ancient Hebrew.

A friend recently shared with me her experience which bears this out. I was explaining this concept regarding the accurate translation of the word *teshuqua*, turning away from God to her husband. Her response was very interesting.

She said,

> Joanne, you know, that is exactly what I did. When I was first converted, my only desire was to please God. Anything He told me to do, I did it. I had a very intimate relationship with Him. Then when my husband found the Lord, I turned to him and did everything I thought he wanted me to do, anything that would please him. Many times I did what I knew my husband wanted even when, in my spirit, I didn't have peace about a given situation. That is what I have been taught a good Christian wife should do. Now I see that in that turning, I forfeited a very precious and intimate relationship with the Lord in order to please my husband.

Based on this verse, it is part of the carnal nature of a woman to please her husband. As in the case of my friend, that carnal desire was broken at her conversion and her desire then moved to that of pleasing the Lord. Now, we all know that if she is pleasing the Lord she is going to be a super wife to her husband which should bring him much pleasure. When a believing husband is introduced into this picture with the traditional "ruler husband" teaching, the wife is basically taught to revert to the natural or carnal way of living. This way of living implies the view of "don't listen as closely to God as you listen to your husband. Give up that intimacy with God." What a travesty it is when women are either never allowed to develop this intimacy with God or when women are forced to forfeit it in order to "properly" submit to their husbands.

Having an intimate relationship with God, where listening intently to His voice and obeying His every command is important above all else, is the greatest gift a wife can give her husband and the most valuable contribution she can make to her marriage. If women would only understand this principle, what wives they would be! They would then be free to be that "helper suitable" that God intended them to be.

Of course, the ideal is for both husbands and wives to have that same kind of relationship with the Lord. This kind of marriage can't fail. These families won't fall apart. That kind of a relationship is as near to heaven on earth as is possible to experience.

Many Christians believe that:

1. God originally placed Adam over Eve.
2. The result of sin entering into the world through Adam destroyed Eve's natural, pure response to his authority.

3. Because of the Fall, Eve then "desired" to rule her husband.

Of these three, I believe Scripture confirms only that sin entered the world through Adam. However, even if they **all** were true, God still **never** would have placed on fallen man the responsibility of restoring his so-called "God-given" position of authority which was destroyed by the Fall. This would have established man as his own savior — humanism in its rankest form. God also would not have given that authority to an unregenerate man, as Adam was. It would have been difficult enough for a regenerate man to have handled that kind of authority, as we have watched so many men try to do. Given to an unregenerate man, that command would surely have been abused, as time also has sadly proven.

God always gives His command directly to the one whose responsibility it is to carry it out. Remember, God was speaking to Eve in Genesis 3:16, not Adam. If man ruling over woman had been the edict pronounced by God at that time — a responsibility that Adam was to carry — God would have spoken this directly to Adam rather than to Eve.

If the Hebrew verb in Genesis 3:16 were a command rather than a warning, then the more forcefully a man domineered his wife, the more spiritual he would be. However, it seems that the closer a man walks with God, the more mature and secure he becomes, the more whole he is, and the less he seems to need or desire to rule his wife (or anyone else for that matter). The spiritually mature husbands I have observed openly honor and cherish their wives and release them completely from any sense of bondage to their husbands.

Although God's plan for husbands and wives was mutual submission, He warned Eve that, as a result of the Fall, the natural (carnal) instinct of man would be to rule

over her. He also warned her that her turning away from God to her husband would make that "ruling" a greater temptation. I believe man's carnal instinct to rule over woman has caused the erroneous translation of Genesis 3:16. This, in turn, has perpetrated the traditional teaching and practice.

We will look next at how God did, in fact, use women in leadership both in the Old and the New Testament, during the centuries when women experienced extreme suppression from the hands of men.

Chapter Two Notes

1. *Gesenius' Hebrew and Chaldee Lexicon to the Old Testament* (Grand Rapids: Baker Book House, 1981), ref. 8104.
2. Walter Kaizer, *Hard Sayings of the Old Testament* (Downers Grove, IL: InterVarsity Press, 1988), 31-32.
3. Katherine C. Bushnell, *God's Word to Women* (privately reprinted by Ray B. Munson, P.O. Box 417, North Collins, NY, 1923), 121.
4. Ibid., 127.
5. Kaizer, op. cit., 34.
6. Ibid., 34.

Questions For Study or Discussion

1. Put in your own words your understanding of what happened in the encounter of the serpent with Adam and Eve.

2. Whom does the Word of God hold responsible for the Fall?

3. Whom did Adam blame for the Fall? Whom did Eve blame?

4. What were the consequences of the Fall? For the serpent? For Eve? For Adam? For Adam and Eve?

5. What is the difference between Old Testament law and Talmudic law?

6. Is there any basis in Genesis for the husband ruling his wife? Explain.

7. What response would you give to someone who insists that Genesis 1-3 teaches that a husband is to rule his wife?

THREE

Women in the Old Testament

As Men Began to Rule

What did life hold for women after the Fall and throughout the Old Testament? As we proceed, we'll see to what extent women were generally held in low esteem. At the same time we will observe how God raised up certain women to places of leadership and blessed them.

It's important to recognize the blessing of God upon these women. Scripture records many things that were not part of God's plan. When, however, we can read His pronouncement of blessing upon someone we can know that their actions were inspired of God.

As we discussed in Chapter Two, God warned Eve that man would rule over her. This "ruling" first became apparent with a man by the name of Lamech. Genesis 4:19

says that Lamech "took" for himself two wives. This is the first evidence of polygamy and the first indication that God's intended plan for marriage had been reversed.

Lamech's "taking" of a wife is in direct opposition to the first scriptural law of society and marriage. In Genesis 2:24 God said,

> For this cause a man shall leave his father and his mother, and shall cleave to his wife, and they shall become one flesh.

This is not some archaic law that was mentioned once way back in the beginning of the Bible never to be heard again. On the contrary, this verse is quoted a total of four times in the Bible. First, by God the Father in Genesis 2:24; then God the Son in Matthew 19:5 and Mark 10:7; and finally by God the Holy Spirit through Paul in Ephesians 5:31. Obviously there was a very important point God was wanting to make, as all three in the Godhead stated it.

I believe God was setting down guidelines which indicated first to Adam, at the time Eve was formed, the extent to which he was to give himself to his wife to love her, cherish her, and nourish her. And in order to give himself to her to that degree he had to "cleave" to her, attach himself to her in such a way that they would become one flesh. For succeeding generations, this would require that a man leave that which he had previously "clung" to, namely his father and mother.

For the most part, in earliest human history, it would appear that this law was acted upon.[1] It was customary for the husband to leave his family and either live under the roof of his wife's parents or live in close proximity and make frequent visits. This gave the parents of the wife the opportunity to "eye" this man to see if he was properly caring for their daughter. The mother and father of a daughter are her natural protectors, totally different from the mother and father of a son.

But, there is a part that the parents of the husband plays in this "leaving and cleaving." They must totally release their son from any possessive ties they have to him. Doing this will free him to cleave to his wife and become one with her. This kind of releasing is not to be confused with a parental love that will always exist between parents and their son. Rather, it is a heart attitude on the part of the parents that conveys to the son, perhaps even verbally as part of the wedding ceremony, his right to shift his deepest allegiance from them to his wife.

God brought this about in my heart in a rather interesting way. Let me relate to you my own experience.

We have a son, Gerry, and a daughter, Beth, both of whom I absolutely adore. Yet, as adults, my mother's heart protects, surrounds, and goes out to Beth in a different way than it does to Gerry. When Gerry was young and approaching his courting and marrying age, I really did not know if there was any woman alive worthy of him. Somehow, I didn't worry about Beth in the same way. As I pondered the difference in my feelings regarding them, I concluded that there was a built-in sense that when Gerry left, I would be transferring his care over to his wife. I knew he would be "leaving" my care in order to "cleave" to his wife. I knew this was "right" but I wasn't sure there was a woman alive to whom I could entrust this precious son of mine.

It didn't take long for us to fall in love with Wenda after we met her, so as their wedding approached, we were truly at peace regarding this union. Any remaining fears were allayed the last time he was home before his wedding with what might appear to be a very insignificant detail.

I had cut Gerry's hair from the time he was a toddler until he went away to college where he met his future wife. After he and Wenda began seeing each other, she

began cutting his hair. As it turned out, he needed a haircut when he was on that college break and visiting us at our home in Oregon. So out came the clippers and I went to work. As I was nearing the completion of the job, Gerry very matter-of-factly informed me that he liked Wenda's haircuts better than mine. (Mine weren't that bad, but without question, Wenda's had a finesse about them that mine lacked.) When he said that, a sweet peace came over me and my heart was joyful. God used that statement by Gerry to give me the assurance that not only was I turning my son over to a woman who could possibly do as good a job taking care of him as I, but she was, in actuality, going to do a better job. I was set free to fully release Gerry to do the "cleaving" with Wenda that was God's plan.

So it was with great joy that Nate and I were able to give our blessing to their marriage. Our love for Gerry has not decreased one iota, neither has his love and respect lessened toward us. But the "leaving" and "cleaving" has definitely taken place.

With Beth, there was a built-in sense that my care and concern for her would always be needed. Granted, it took on a different form as we joyfully released her to be joined in marriage with her wonderful husband Greg and allowed them the freedom to establish their own family. Even though we no longer live close to them geographically, as we did for a number of years, the natural desire to protect her will always be there.

The extended family in one locality can be of immeasurable blessing to the grandchildren growing up, even when the immediate family unit is strong. The older generation adds a dimension of wisdom and security to the younger generations.

In this mobile world that we live in, where parents and children alike are constantly moving around, the logistical

reality of this concept is almost non-existent. We all know of situations among believers today where it is the wife who has left her home to go with her husband and the outcome has been joyously blessed by God. But is there Scripture to support this? I believe there is.

In Genesis 24, when Abraham's servant went back to Abraham's family to find a wife for Isaac, Rebecca was given the choice as to whether or not she wanted to go. She was not forcibly "taken" or coerced into going. But she chose to go – with God's blessing.

In the New Testament, it would appear, based on 1 Corinthians 9:5, that someone had brought a wife along on that missionary journey. It would be assumed that she had been led by the Holy Spirit to accompany her husband. Also in Acts 18, Aquila and Priscilla relocated twice. They were first forced to leave Italy because they were Jews. Then they went to Ephesus with Paul for the sake of the Gospel. They were simply living out Jesus' command in Mark 16:15 to *"Go into all the world and preach the gospel to all creation."* Many of us have been led of the Lord to relocate, leaving parents and family in order to fulfill His call on our lives.

But for the wife to leave her parents in order to, with her husband, follow the will of the Lord for their lives is far different from the "taking" of a wife as Lamech did. So what should be the reality of the "leaving" and "cleaving" command of the Lord in our lives today?

This "leaving" and "cleaving" must become a reality in the heart of a husband whether or not he ever leaves the locality where his parents reside. When a young man marries a wife, he must determine in his heart that he is going to devote his life to loving and cherishing her above all other humans, including his mother and father. We sometimes jokingly refer to this as "cutting the apron

strings," but it really is no laughing matter. It is a very serious step that a man must take.

We know that the custom had been reversed by the time of the New Testament. When Christ was on earth, it was customary for the groom to go to the bride's home, fetch her, and take her to his father's house. Jesus' parable of the ten virgins, however, tells no such story. Jesus never violated the laws of God. When the bridegroom arrived at the home of the bride, he went in and the door was shut. There is no mention of his "taking" the bride away.

When Lamech "took" wives, he began the reversal of God's original plan. Wickedness prevailed, and then came the flood.

After the flood came the story of Abraham and the beginning of the Hebrew nation. Some have asked, "Why did God establish the patriarchal system (through Abraham, Isaac, and Jacob) if man was not to rule?" God didn't establish the patriarchal system. Ancient civilizations had been ruled by patriarchal systems for generations. Women had been ruled over and subservient to men since the Fall.[2]

When God began establishing the nation of Israel, He was actually setting the stage — preparing a people — for the coming of the Messiah Who would restore all things. This included the lifting up of women to their God-given status in life. Thus, He would do away with the patriarchal system.

With the beginning of the nation of Israel, under the patriarchs Abraham, Isaac, and Jacob, God began setting boundaries. He began laying ground rules to move society back to the place which He originally intended. God always uses what He has, or what exists, to move people to the next place He has for them. He starts with people where they are and moves them onward.

Women's Low Estate in the Old Testament

To show just how far God had to bring society, let's look at some examples that portray the less-than-second-class citizenship experienced by women in the Old Testament.

Genesis 12:10-20 and 20:1-13 are two examples involving Abraham and Sarah where Abraham told Sarah to say she was his sister. In so doing, Sarah made herself vulnerable to be taken into other men's harems. Abraham obviously was more concerned for his own safety than for his wife's virtue.

Even in our society today only the most depraved of men would set his wife up for such treatment. Yet, Abraham, the one with whom God had made a covenant, saw his wife not as one to be loved and cherished, but as one to be used that he might be spared.

Genesis 19:1-8 gives a clear picture of the abhorrent status of women in that day. It relates the story of Lot and his willingness to give his own virgin daughters to the wicked men of Sodom in order to protect the male guests in his home.[3]

Judges 19-21 tells the story of a young girl who was so raped and abused by the Benjamites in the town of Gibeah that she died. As a result, the rest of the sons of Israel set out to avenge the girl. In the ensuing battle, it was feared that the tribe of Benjamin would be completely annihilated. Not wanting to see that happen, the rest of the sons of Israel devised a plan whereby the Benjamites could "kidnap" women to be their wives. This story shows not only the lack of respect for women, but portrays the utterly degraded state in which they existed.

God's Blessing on Women

However, as God revealed Himself to His people, a gradual change came over Hebrew society. Women began to be used and blessed by God in various ways and situations. Let's look at some examples, beginning with Sarah.

We have covered how Sarah suffered as a woman, but she had some positive experiences as well. Her name was taken from the Hebrew word *Sar* meaning "chieftainess." It would appear that she had her own independent residence at Hebron (Genesis 23:2) and lived there while Abraham lived at Beersheba (Genesis 22:19). Abraham went to Hebron when Sarah died to mourn for her and bury her.

> Her position, therefore, during her wanderings and in later life was not by any means that of secluded dependence, but rather that of an independent head of the tribe, or "tribal mother."[4]

Miriam, in Exodus 15:20, is described as a prophetess. In Micah 6:4, God said, *"I sent before you Moses, Aaron, and Miriam."* God set Miriam as one of the leaders over Israel.

Numbers 27:1-11 is another example of how God was easing the Children of Israel into the acceptance and recognition of women. This is the story of the Daughters of Zelophehad who stood before Moses and all the people and requested possessions from among their father's brothers, since their own brothers were dead. Moses went to God Who said, "Give it to them." Furthermore, God said that from that day forth, if a man died with no sons, the inheritance was to be given to his daughters. This was a tremendous change in the whole life of the Hebrew nation. Up to this time, women were not allowed to own property. These women were extremely bold and brave to stand before Moses and say, "Hey, look, this isn't fair. We

don't have any male to receive our inheritance. Why should we not receive what is rightfully ours?" God told Moses to honor their request, which changed the course of history.

Judges 4:4-23 tells of Deborah, a prophetess, who was one of several judges of Israel whom God raised up to lead His wayward people back to Him and against their enemies. God chose to use Deborah to lead and encourage the Children of Israel in the battle against Jabin, King of Canaan. She gave Barak the "word of the Lord" concerning the battle. Barak was willing to do as Deborah said, but only if she would accompany them to battle. God honored His word and delivered the Canaanites into their hands. This included Sisera, the commander of Jabin's army, who was killed by a woman Jael. The battle was won; victory was theirs; and in Judges 5 we have the lovely, victorious song that is sung by Deborah and Barak. Her words are recorded in the Scriptures, the significance of which we'll touch on later. Israel was desolate until Deborah arose, a "Mother in Israel" (Judges 5:7).

Abigail, in 1 Samuel 25, is one who operated contrary to her husband Nabal's wishes. Upon hearing of David's request, without consulting her husband, Abigail took provisions to David and his men. She knew full well that Nabal had just refused to give David anything. I do not believe Abigail was operating out of a rebellious heart just for the sake of defying her husband. Her heart told her David's needs should be ministered to, and she was simply taking what she felt was the right course of action. God clearly honored her decision. He smote Nabal ten days later, and he died. The Word says Abigail was *"a woman of good understanding"* or *"intelligence"* (1 Samuel 25:3).

Huldah was a prophetess (2 Kings 22:8-20) sought out by the king's priest to inquire of the Lord concerning His

Word for the king and the people. This course was taken, not because there was no male prophet available at this time, for both Jeremiah (Jeremiah 1:1, 2) and Zephaniah (Zephaniah 1:1) were her contemporaries. This resulted in tremendous reform by Josiah the king including the celebration of the Passover which had not taken place for many years. It was a real revival! Huldah is an excellent example of a woman giving a man (the king) "the word of the Lord."

Hannah made a vow to the Lord without consulting her husband (1 Samuel 1:9-23). Eli the priest blessed her, and Elkanah her husband obviously agreed with her. This vow resulted in their first-born, Samuel, being taken to the temple at a very early age to be raised by the priest and to serve God. Not a small vow to make.

The traditional teaching regarding women in ministry discourages or even prohibits women from being in spiritual leadership. The Word of God is our guide for truth. Truth has no exceptions. Truth is unchangeable. Only one example is needed of a woman who ruled or exercised authority or initiative, without being granted permission by her male guardian, and was clearly blessed by God for doing so, to undermine this traditional teaching. We have cited not one but four such examples in the Old Testament: Deborah, Abigail, Huldah, and Hannah. The New Testament contains examples as well which we will examine in Chapter 10.

Important Old Testament Scriptures

There are several Scriptures in the Old Testament which can not be overlooked as it relates to the role women are to play in the Kingdom of God.

Psalm 68:11 – *"The Lord gives the command (Word). Great is the company of women who proclaim it"* (KJV). NASB

says, *"the women who proclaim the good tidings are a great host."*

One can not silence the half of the human race to whom God has given the command to "proclaim."

Joel 2:28, 29 tells us:

> And it will come about after this that I will pour out My Spirit on all mankind; and your sons and daughters will prophesy, your old men will dream dreams, your young men will see visions. And even on the male and female servants I will pour out My Spirit in those days.

This is Joel's prophecy to Judah which is later quoted by Peter on the day of Pentecost (Acts 2:16-18). It is a clear indication that the Holy Spirit was to be poured out upon women as well as men. The significance of this will be dealt with in Chapter 10.

Jeremiah 9:17, 18, 20 says,

> Thus says the Lord of hosts, "Consider and call for the mourning women, that they may come; and send for the wailing women, that they may come!" (vs. 17).

> "And let them make haste, and take up a wailing for us, that our eyes may shed tears, and our eye lids flow with water" (vs. 18).

> Now hear the word of the Lord, O you women, and let your ear receive the word of His mouth; teach your daughters wailing, and every one her neighbor a dirge (vs. 20).

Today's counterpart to the "wailing" or "mourning" woman in the Old Testament is the intercessor. The Lord's call for the "wailing women" is a distinct call of God upon women for intercession. We are seeing this call of God being answered today as never before. Great numbers of

women all over the world are responding to the call to give themselves to the ministry of intercession.

I believe the one who attempts to silence or control the ministry of women is on dangerous ground. As we have just seen, God used women in the Old Testament in powerful ways as they acted totally independent of men, yet with His blessing.

Now let's see what we find in the New Testament.

Chapter Three Notes

1. For further discussion on female kinship including numerous ancient historical examples, see Katherine C. Bushnell, *God's Word to Women* (privately reprinted by Ray B. Munson, P.O. Box 417, North Collins, NY, 1923), 415-464.

2. Faith Martin, *Call Me Blessed* (Grand Rapids: Wm. B. Eerdmans Publishing Co., 1988), 34.

3. We know that these guests were angels, vs. 1, but they came in the appearance of men and were referred to as men in vss. 5, 8, 10, 12, and 16.

4. Bushnell, op. cit., 59.

Questions For Study or Discussion

1. When a man and a woman are married, are they to leave the husband's parents or the wife's?

2. How do we know this plan was so important to God?

3. What affect has the ignoring of this decree had upon society world-wide?

4. Were there any Biblical exceptions to Genesis 2:24 that had a positive outcome? (See Genesis 24 and 31.) How were each of these situations handled that made it acceptable to God?

5. Summarize these four situations which show the low estate of women in the early pages of the Old Testament: Genesis 12:10-20; Genesis 20:1-13; Genesis 19:1-8; Judges 19-21.

6. Describe the leadership each of these women exerted with God's blessings: Miriam (Exodus 15:20, Micah 6:4); the daughters of Zelophehad (Numbers 27:1-11); Deborah (Judges 4:4-23); Abigail (1 Samuel 25:1-42); Huldah (2 Kings 22:8-20); Hannah (1 Samuel 1:9-23).

7. What do these passages further tell us about God's plan for women? Psalms 68:11; Joel 2:28-29; Jeremiah 9:17-20; Proverbs 31:10-31.

8. Based on God's releasing and blessing of Old Testament women into places of leadership, what conclusions can be drawn regarding God's view of women in leadership in Old Testament times?

FOUR

Jesus' Attitude Toward Women

In His Steps by Charles Shelton, written a number of years ago and considered a classic, is centered around a group of people who pledged for one year to do nothing without first asking, "What would Jesus do in this situation?" As those who made this commitment followed through, lives were changed, relationships were healed, peace reigned. If Christians would follow Jesus' example and respond to women as He did, I'm convinced the atmosphere in the Church would be different today.

Let's take a look at the Gospels and see what Jesus did in relation to women. How did He respond and relate to women while He was on earth? There is much to be learned simply by observing His actions and responses toward women in light of Jewish laws and traditions of that day.

Even the way the news of the coming of the Messiah was delivered to Mary is in direct opposition to the traditional viewpoint as it relates to the husband being "in charge." If such rulership had been ordained of God from the beginning, Mary would not have been the first to learn of the coming "blessed event." God would have sent the message through Joseph because, as her betrothed, he would have been over her in the line of authority. However, to the contrary, the angel appeared to Mary first (Luke 1:26-38), and she agreed to be the mother of the Messiah without even consulting her husband. Joseph knew nothing about it until after the fact (Matthew 1:18-25). It was only when he wanted *"to put her away"* (vs. 19) that the angel appeared to him and clued him in on what was happening.

As we look into the Scriptures and discover how Jesus and women interacted, we need to remember that according to the Babylonian *Talmud*:

1. Women were considered mere chattel, and the possessions of men;
2. It was Jewish law that the woman's voice was not to be heard in public; and
3. She could not be used as a witness in any situation.[1]

When we examine specific scenarios involving Jesus (or anyone else in the Bible for that matter), we must remember many stories in the Bible include Eastern customs that were (and are today) readily understood by the Eastern mind. Unfortunately, few of us from Western culture know much about them. Therefore some, if not much, of the meaning behind a narrative or parable can be lost to us. The Holy Spirit, in His faithfulness to "teach us all things," reveals to us the overall spiritual truths; but I wonder how many deep nuggets we have missed because

we lack knowledge about the customs that precipitated various biblical situations.

Mary and Martha

For instance, in the story of Mary and Martha (Luke 10:38-42) the emphasis is usually placed on Martha's being so busy making preparations for Jesus and, no doubt, others who were traveling with Him, that she didn't have the time to sit at Jesus' feet and learn. The lesson projected then is that we should not get so busy with the mundane things of life that we don't have time to be with the Lord.

What is overlooked is that the Jewish oral law forbade the teaching of the law to Jewish women. They were not to sit at anyone's feet to be taught spiritual truths.[2] For Mary to have placed herself in this position was, to say the least, unusual. Jesus was attempting to put Mary at ease even as He spoke to Martha when He said, *". . . Mary has chosen the good part, which shall not be taken away from her."* This response was in direct opposition to the custom of the day, but Jesus was in the process of turning "customs" around to conform to God's plan for women. He came *"to set the captive free,"* and that included Mary.

Woman with the Issue of Blood

In Matthew 9:20-22 the story is told of the woman with the issue of blood. One needs to review Leviticus 15 to fully appreciate what Jesus did here. The children of Israel were taught the importance of cleanliness. Great detail was given as to how these procedures were to be carried out. Leviticus 15 specifically dealt with a woman who had an issue of blood. Anyone touching her, or anyone she

touched, was made unclean until proper washings took place and time periods elapsed.

However, Jesus disregarded these laws when dealing with the woman in this story. Her faith told her that she only needed to touch Jesus' garment and she would be made whole. Upon doing so, did Jesus reprimand her and ask her why she was not following the Levitical law regarding uncleanness? Did he remind her that she should not even be mingling in a crowd of people? No! He healed her, called her "daughter," and acknowledged her faith.

Woman Bent Over by a Spirit

In Luke 13: 10-17, Jesus healed a woman bent over by a spirit. He singled her out, called her to come to Him, and healed her. Afterwards she glorified God. It would appear there was some audible manifestation of praise to the Lord contrary to the Jewish law of public silence for women. And Jesus called her a *"daughter of Abraham,"* a blessing the Lord Jesus gave because of her faith (Galatians 3:7). Jesus did not differentiate between her, a woman, and men referred to as *"sons of Abraham"* (Luke 19:9) because of their faith.

Woman Taken in Adultery

The woman taken in adultery in John 8:3-11 is a classic example of the depths to which society had gone in its prejudice against women. Again, one must compare this situation with the law that had been given in Leviticus 20:10. This law specifically said that both the adulterer and adulteress were to be put to death. Yet when the Scribes and Pharisees brought this woman caught in the

act of adultery, they totally misquoted that law to Jesus. They said only that Moses commanded them to stone such women. Not one word was said about the adulterer. However, the Lord would have no part of their scheme. He placed the responsibility back upon them, and He forgave the woman. Finally someone had appeared on the scene to take the woman's side in this society of injustice.

The Samaritan Woman

The significance of Jesus' conversation with the woman at the well in John 4:3-42 is increased not only because he was conversing with a woman, but she was also a Samaritan with whom the Jews had had trouble, even bloodshed, for years. Not only did Jesus ask her, a Samaritan, for a drink of water, a practice that is acceptable as long as there is no further conversation, but he continued on, engaging her in the dialogue in which He revealed that He was the Messiah.

Jesus broke all the rules:

1. Jews avoided Samaria if at all possible;
2. He asked water of her, a Samaritan woman (even she was amazed, vs. 9); and
3. He conversed with this woman, a totally unacceptable behavior for that day and situation.

The result of this conversation was that she became the first woman to bring men to Christ. She went back into the city to tell about this man who knew everything about her. Jesus was persuaded to stay there for two days and many believed on Him.

Mary Magdalene

A scene often overlooked in the New Testament is the one in the garden after Jesus' resurrection. To whom did He first appear after emerging from the grave? Mary! And what did He say to her? "Go, tell!" He commissioned her with the responsibility of telling His disciples the greatest story ever told — Jesus is risen (John 20:11-18)!

So Jesus proceeded to revolutionize a number of Jewish laws and traditions regarding women:

1. He encouraged a woman to learn about Him.
2. He spoke with women publicly. (A Jewish Rabbi would not even speak to his wife in public.)
3. He did not rebuke an unclean woman for touching Him.
4. He did not rebuke a woman who spoke in public (praising God).
5. He prevented the stoning of an adultress.
6. He conversed with a Samaritan woman.
7. He gave a commission to a woman — "Go, tell!"

Indeed, Jesus shocked all who observed His personal attention and appreciation toward women in every station of life. As Jesus walked on earth as the Son of Man, He became the first man to defend, uphold, and honor womanhood. His shocking behavior was continued by the apostle Paul.

Many say that there are New Testament Scriptures where Paul takes a chauvinistic stance regarding women, going so far as to silence them completely. Not so, as we will see.

Chapter Four Notes

1. Charles Trombley, *Who Said Women Can't Teach?* (North Brunswick, NJ: Bridge Publishing, 1985), 31.

2. Katherine C. Bushnell, *God's Word to Women* (privately reprinted by Ray B. Munson, P.O. Box 417, North Collins, NY, 1923), 202, 335, 610.

Questions For Study or Discussion

1. Describe how Jesus related to women, often contrary to custom, in each of these situations. Matthew 9:20-22; Luke 10:38-42; Luke 13:10-17; John 4:3-42; John 8:3-11; John 20:11-18.
2. What conclusions can be drawn regarding God's plan for woman based upon the way Jesus responded and related to women?

FIVE

Introduction to Paul's Writings

The apostle Paul is the one most often credited with giving directives regarding the subordinate role of women. However, I'm convinced Paul would never have made a statement which would have silenced a group of people whom God says are to proclaim the Word of God (Psalm 68:11), and whom God said in the last days would be anointed to prophesy (Joel 2:28, 29). Neither should spiritual leaders today assume that authority.

One can not take an isolated social issue, use a few proof texts and make them say what one wants them to say, disregarding all previous principles and moral imperatives that have already been laid down. Psalm 119:160 declares, *"The sum of Thy word is truth."* As it relates to our issue, all biblical teaching in the Old Testament, the Gospels, and the Acts of the Apostles tell of

woman's place before and after the Fall. They show how God accepted, released, and anointed women, thereby reaffirming His plan for equality. To isolate and interpret Paul's writings for what they appear to be saying would negate all that the Scriptures have taught previously, which we simply do not have the liberty to do.

Throughout the Old Testament, the Gospels, and the Acts, not one word has been said about the authority role of husbands over wives — not one (keeping in mind the proper translation of Genesis 3:16).

To attribute to Paul the total reversal of the heretofore mentioned principles and moral imperatives laid down in the Bible is to undermine Paul's intelligence, spiritual acumen, and his credibility. Remember, Paul was a well-educated man, highly skilled in his knowledge of the Old Testament. Also, keep in mind, the Word of God, including Paul's writings, was inspired by the Holy Spirit and does not contradict itself.

However, one can not ignore 1 Corinthians 11, 1 Corinthians 14, Ephesians 5, and 1 Timothy 2. So what was Paul saying? There is a very adequate explanation and interpretation for each of these Scriptures which does not contradict the theology laid down in previous Scriptures. However, one must adhere to proper rules of interpretation.

Rules of Interpretation

There have been rules of interpretation accepted by biblical scholars for over two thousand years. Here is one form of those rules:

> 1. Rule of Definition - Define the term of words being considered and then adhere to the defined meanings.

2. Rule of Usage - Don't add meanings to established words and terms. What was the common usage in the cultural and time period when the passage was written?

3. Rule of Context - Avoid using words out of context. Context must define terms and how words are used.

4. Rule of Historical Background - Don't separate interpretation and historical investigation.

5. Rule of Logic - Be certain that words as interpreted agree with the overall premise.

6. Rule of Precedent - Use the known and commonly accepted meaning of words, not obscure meanings for which there is no precedent.

7. Rule of Unity - Even though many documents may be used there must be general unity among them.

8. Rule of Inference - Base conclusions on what is already known and proven or can be reasonably implied from known facts."[1]

What we have discussed so far is that man and woman had a perfect relationship of unity and equality in the Garden. After the Fall, because of sin, man had a desire to, and therefore did, rule over woman. We have seen this tendency to rule exemplified quite strongly in the Old Testament, yet we have also seen the number of situations where women were called by God to be leaders, and their leadership was blessed by God. We have seen situations where wives went against the will of their husbands or did things that might be considered to be

undermining their husband's authority, yet were blessed by God.

The question raised is this: If God had desired to lay down the law of male authority for all time, would He ever have blessed something contrary to that principle? The answer is "No." Truth is truth, and there is no exception to truth. It would be totally contrary to the character of God to lay down a law and establish a pattern that He had intended to be carried out through all time and then to violate His own law by blessing someone who had operated in a contradictory manner.

Progression, not Regression

Another important aspect is the progression of Scripture, or the evolving of Scripture from the Old Testament to the New Testament. We move from the law of the Old Testament to the grace of the New. Indeed, from the bondage of the Old Testament to the freedom in Christ in the New. We are moving from the first Covenant which called for the blood of bulls and goats to the New Covenant where Christ's shed blood paid for our sin once and for all. This is the progression of the Bible, not regression. To move women from a state of freedom which included opportunity to exercise a leadership role in the Old Testament, to the bondage of the subservient role that many would have us believe the New Testament teaches, is simply not in keeping with the overall biblical pattern of progression.

Neither Male nor Female

Paul said in Galations 3:28, *"There is neither male* (and most translations say) *nor female."* This is an incorrect

translation. It should read *". . . there is neither Jew nor* (oude) *Greek, there is neither slave nor* (oude) *free man, there is neither male AND* (kai) *female."* Paul is saying Jew and Greek are opposites, bond and free are opposites, but concludes with male AND female. They are considered equals, not opposites, but a mirror-like reflection of each other.

Some traditionalists would say that Paul is referring here only to the fact that salvation is available to everyone no matter their lot in life. However, the word "salvation" means "wholeness," "completeness" in every area of life, and the means of the restoration of all things. This restoration must include the kind of relationship God ordained for man and woman in the Garden of Eden. Furthermore, this work of salvation does not stop with what Christ can do for women, but also includes what Christ can do through them by way of ministry. **Everything that is available to men who are "in Christ" is also available to women.** This is born out in the correct understanding of Paul's writings, which we will see in the following chapters.

Chapter Five Notes

1. Charles Trombley, *Who Said Women Can't Teach?* (North Brunswick, NJ: Bridge Publishing, 1985), 135-36.

Questions For Study or Discussion

1. Summarize in your own words each of the Rules of Interpretation of Scripture given on pages 54-55. (1) Rule of Definition, (2) Rule of Usage, (3) Rule of Context, (4) Rule of Historical Background, (5) Rule of Logic, (6) Rule of Precedent, (7) Rule of Unity, (8) Rule of Inference.

2. How should Galations 3:28 be translated?

3. Explain the danger of taking a few "proof texts" to form a whole dogma or doctrine, such as has been done with some of Paul's writings.

SIX

What About Submission and Headship?

Ephesians 5:21-33

One of the most important and misunderstood New Testament passages dealing with husbands and wives is Ephesians 5:21-33. It is a rare occasion when one sees Ephesian 5:22-33 written in its proper context. It is amazing to me that Bible teachers, who should know better, often lift out and expound upon verses 22-33, while leaving behind the verse just previous, verse 21, which is of utmost importance to the totality of this portion of Scripture.

To be completely accurate one needs to go back to the beginning of Ephesians 5 and get the full picture of what Paul is saying to the Ephesians. In fact, this particular teaching does not stop at the end of Chapter 5,

but goes on to the tenth verse of Chapter 6 to complete Paul's thoughts.

In these chapters he is telling the Ephesian Christians how they are to conduct their lives now that they are children of light and not children of darkness. There were specific areas in which there needed to be drastic changes.

This crucial portion of Scripture, as it relates to the women's issue, actually begins with verse 18, where Paul says, *"Do not get drunk with wine, but be filled with the Spirit."* He then moves on, in verses 19-21, to describe how one who is filled with the Spirit will respond. They will speak to one another in psalms and hymns; they will sing and make melody in their heart; they will give thanks for all things; and they will be subject to one another in the fear of Christ.

Then in what follows, from verse 22 through 6:10, he deals with three separate areas of society in which there has been gross inequity and abuse of power: husbands and wives, fathers and sons, and slaves and masters.

The pivotal verse is verse 21, the one that is so often omitted when quoting the portion in Ephesians 5 having to do with the submission issue. It says, *". . . be subject to one another in the fear of Christ."* One simply can not single out one portion of society, that is, one-half of the human race, and say that this Scripture tells them, and them alone, to submit. Rather, Paul is saying there needs to be a general spirit of submission to one another on every level: wives to husbands, husbands to wives; children to parents, fathers to children; and slaves to masters, masters to slaves.

To quote Ephesians 5:22-33 without including verse 21 is a gross exegetical error (Rule #3, Rule of Context, p. 55). Furthermore, to quote verse 22 in its original state would not make sense without verse 21, because the verb in the Greek text was not included in verse 22. The original text

of verse 22 actually reads, *"wives to your own husbands as to the Lord."* So when most of our translations say, *"Wives,* (be subject) *to your own husbands,"* they're having to insert words that are not in the original in order to make a complete sentence.[1] When quoting this portion in Ephesians, verse 21 must be included to give true integrity to the subject.

Marriage in the First Century

To understand the necessity for Paul's Ephesians discourse here, one needs to understand what marriage was like in the First Century. Marriages in three nationalities were represented and addressed in this chapter. There was the Jewish marriage, the Greek marriage, and the Roman marriage.

Marriage was held in high regard among the Jewish people. It was thought that everyone should be married. However, the Old Testament laws to protect women had been ignored, or made ineffective, making it very easy for a man to obtain a divorce. All the wife had to do to constitute grounds for divorce was to burn his dinner, go out with her head uncovered, or speak negatively about his parents. Or, if a Jewish husband saw a prettier woman he wanted to marry, he was free to do so. Women could not divorce, but if a wife chose to leave her husband, she had to leave her children with him. In general, women were considered inferior to men and held in very low esteem.[2] They were considered possessions on the level of animals and had no voice whatsoever in the relationship.

Among the Greeks it was considered necessary to marry in order to provide legitimate heirs to a man's property, but marriage was not considered particularly satisfying otherwise. Women were very young, about 14, when they married. The men were much older, in the

neighborhood of thirty-seven years old. Since it was the responsibility of a Greek wife to manage her husband's household affairs, it was considered prudent for a man to marry a very young girl so he could teach her the way he wished his household to be managed. Eroticism being part of Greek life, a husband did not need a wife for companionship, love, or sexual fulfillment. It was not considered immoral for husbands to have affairs. However, there were serious penalties for an adulterous wife. The wife's legal position to her husband was much like a child or a slave. She actually went from the rule of her father to the rule of her husband and, if her husband died, to the rule of her son, if he was old enough. Consequently, in the Greek marriage, there was little common ground between the husband and the wife.[3]

The Roman marriage was much like the Greek, but Roman wives had more freedom. They could own property, and a wife could obtain a divorce. However, the power over the family clearly rested in the hands of the husband and/or father. Some wives, especially among the upper class, were able to find ways around both the law and their husbands in order to do with their money and themselves as they wished.[4] Many Roman women were well educated, and there is historical evidence indicating that a number of them reached highly responsible positions in government.

Because of the general imbalance in the marriage relationships of that day, one can readily see the necessity for Paul to instruct these Ephesian believers as to how husbands and wives were to relate to each other. Women had been forced to outward obedience. However, Paul needed to exhort them to have an attitude of submission in their hearts toward their husbands (their head) even as the Church is to have a heart of submission to Christ (her Head).

Then Paul talked about the reversal, that is, how a husband was to submit to his wife. He taught that a husband's submission to his wife involved loving her. That concept was totally foreign to that age and society; husbands knew little or nothing about loving their wives. Paul needed to deal in depth with the subject. He proceeded to explain the kind of love a husband was to have for his wife, that is, a sacrificial love that goes beyond what the word "submission" alone denotes. He even went so far as to compare it with the love Christ has for His Bride, the Church; a love that made Him willing to die for Her.

The Meaning of Submission

Submission! What in the world does it really mean? The verb, "to be in subjection," is from the Greek word *hupotasso* and means "to place, arrange, or rank under; to subject, to subordinate, to obey; to submit to one's control; to yield to one's admonition or advice."[5] Although the word includes a dimension of obedience, it is more a heart attitude of yieldedness than a blind obedience.

One author has this interesting comment:

> Two words are constantly confused in reference to woman's duties, "subjection" and "obedience." . . . The noun "subjection" is not found (in Classical Greek) outside the New Testament, and we are left to infer that it was coined to describe a relation peculiar to believers. Had the word merely meant "obedience," such an invention would have been needless. . . . The true sense of the word describes the Christian grace of yielding one's preferences to another, where principle is not involved, rather than asserting one's rights.[6]

When submission between Christians is referred to in the New Testament, it generally means an open attitude of mutual acceptance, sharing ideas, and yielding to the desire of the other, not mindless obedience. Never would one be expected to blindly **obey** every other Christian, yet, Ephesians 5:21 says we are to **submit** ourselves to one another.

The apostles plainly taught "subjection" to the civil authorities or powers that be,[7] however, they were constantly disobeying those powers when they conflicted with God's commands in order to *"obey God rather than men"* (Acts 5:29). They weren't being inconsistent. They simply understood "subjection" to mean an attitude of flowing, yielding, and preferring, or respecting, the God-granted positions of civil authority, not absolute obedience.

In 1 Corinthians 16:16, Paul says: *". . . be in subjection to such men and to everyone who helps in the work and labors."* Now if this meant blind obedience, this would also mean that the men in the church at Corinth must obey women because those who helped in the work and labor of the Gospel included Phoebe (Romans 16:1, 2); Priscilla (Romans 16:3); Junias, whom many scholars agree was a woman (Romans 16:7); and Tryphaena and Tryphosa (Romans 16:12). Those with a traditional understanding would find this command difficult, to say the least.

One can not arbitrarily decide that when the word "subjection" or "submission" is used referring to wives, it means absolute obedience, unless one is ready to place that meaning upon every other similiar reference. And that would be both unbiblical and unthinkable.

The husband and wife, in "being subject to one another" (verse 21) are to place themselves second to the other, they are to honor the desires and advice of the other.

Ephesians 5:23 speaks of Christ as not only the Head of the Church but also Her Savior. How deep our worship and submission should be to Him. If the husband is truly laying down his life for his wife, as verse 25 teaches, he will, in effect, be a "savior" in life to his wife, exemplifying a deep level of submission to her. The response from his wife should be one of deep honor and submission. I believe Paul was explaining a deeper level of submission exchanged between husbands and wives than that which should be between all other believers.

However, Jesus Christ is the master of a believing wife just as He is of the believing husband, and He meant what He said when He said, "No one can serve two masters." All believers are called upon to exercise forbearance, yield one's preferences, and respect one another's opinions and desires, but no one, except Jesus Christ Himself, should be master over another human being!

1 Peter 3: 6 – Sarah and Abraham

Another Scripture often interpreted as meaning absolute obedience on the part of a wife to her husband is 1 Peter 3:6,

> Thus Sarah obeyed Abraham, calling him lord, and you have become her children if you do what is right without being frightened by any fear.

This verse must be looked at in light of the context in which it is found beginning with 1 Peter 2:12 and going through to 3:12.

The key verse is 2:13. Peter said, *"Submit yourself for the Lord's sake to every human institution."* The Greek word for "institution" is *ktis'is* and is used nineteen times in the New Testament. This is the only time in the NASB it is translated institution. Every other time it is translated

"created thing," "creation," or "creature." To be consistent and correct in the context of this Scripture, I believe *ktis'is* should be translated "creature" here as well.

Following verse 13, from 2:14 to 3:7, Peter dealt with several areas of society where there was considerable inequity (much as Paul did in Ephesians 5 and 6), but in spite of that inequity, they were admonished to submit. They are to submit to kings (vss. 13, 17) and governors (vs. 14). These were not human institutions, but God ordained. *"For there is no authority except from God, and those which exist are established by God"* (Romans 13:1). However these places of authority are held by human creatures. They were also to submit to all men (vs. 17), the brotherhood (vs. 17), servants to masters (vs. 18), wives to husbands (3:1), and husbands to wives (3:7). I don't believe husbands and wives are part of a human institution as NASB says. Marriage is ordained of God, but husbands and wives are human creatures.

Again, this submission spoken of in 1 Peter 2:13 can not mean abject obedience. Remember, Peter was one of the apostles who said, *"We must obey God rather than men"* (Acts 5:29). So even as he teaches submission to civil authorities, Peter was one who recognized a higher Authority Who must be obeyed.

When Peter begins his discourse to wives in 3:1, he prefaces it with *"in the same way."* In what same way? One must read the verses immediately preceding this to get the flow of Peter's thought. He has just explained how Jesus was reviled and suffered yet did not retaliate, but, sinless though He was, bore our sins in his body meekly and without threats trusting *"Him who judges righteously."* Peter is saying, "Wives, this is the spirit and attitude with which you should submit to your husbands." Then he used the holy women in former times as an example.

These former times were times when women were held at an even lower place in society than when this letter was written. Peter said they, like Jesus, were reviled (remember our discussion of the treatment of Old Testament women in Chapter 3) and suffered at the hands of men. Then Peter used Sarah as an example. Even though Abraham told her to place herself in two situations, first with Pharoah and then with Abimelech, where she could very easily have been taken into their harems, yet because her hope was in God, she submitted to the point of obedience. As God protected Sarah of old when women had few, if any, rights, so God will honor a woman whose attitude leads her to live a submissive lifestyle.

Sarah was one who submitted to her husband's directive, unjust as it was, even as Christ had submitted to revilings and death, unjust as they were. Sarah's *"gentle and quiet spirit"* is given as an example of what pleases God in a woman. But not in women only because in 3:8 and 9, where Peter sums up his comments, he admonishes all to be *"humble in spirit."*

Sarah's calling Abraham "lord" or "master" was indicative of the authority men held over women (predicted in Genesis 3:16) at that time. Remember, with Abraham, God was just beginning to establish His people, a nation into which some semblance of godly order in this otherwise pagan world could be established. That would prepare the way for the coming Messiah Who would restore all things.

One can not deduct from this one verse that God's plan for women was to include blind obedience to her husband any more than one could say that men should always obey their wives because God told Abraham one time to do as Sarah had said (Genesis 21:12). I do not believe this verse negates a woman's personal

accountability to God, or can be taken to supplant the references to wifely "submission" with the word "obedience."

In Matthew 23:8-12, we are told,

> But do not be called Rabbi; for One is your Teacher, and you are all brothers. And do not call anyone on earth your father; for One is your Father, He who is in heaven. And do not be called leaders; for One is your Leader, that is Christ. But the greatest among you shall be your servant. And whoever exalts himself shall be humbled; and whoever humbles himself shall be exalted.

This was the New Testament humility Jesus was teaching and exemplifying.

It is intriguing to discover that all the Greek words for rabbi, master, and teacher reflect the meaning of one word. They are all synonymous with one another. Rabbi means master; master means teacher. Those men who insist on being master, both in word and action, are in direct disobedience to the command of Jesus.

In Hosea 2:16, God is speaking of the kind of relationship He longs to have with the children of Israel,

> "And it will come about in that day," declares the Lord, "That you will call Me Ishi *(my husband)* and will no longer call Me Baali *(my master)*."

We can see from this Scripture that the husband/wife relationship is not to be that of a master and his subordinate, but one of mutual intimacy and love.

1 Peter 3:6 is an example of when the teachings of Jesus and the overall biblical principles take precedence over what one might misconstrue one single verse to say.

Mutual Submission

So how does submission work practically in a Christian marriage relationship? Doesn't someone have to be boss? Absolutely! Jesus Christ, by the Holy Spirit! Paul made it very clear in Ephesians 5:18 that the key to joyful, harmonious living is to be filled with the Spirit.

I am absolutely convinced that if a husband and wife are both filled with the Spirit, walking closely with Him and listening to His voice, there will be no need for an earthly "boss." When a decision needs to be made in a family, both the husband and wife need to make it together. Both should go to the Lord and listen for His direction. If there isn't unity at first, they should continue to seek the Lord until there is.

You say, "Oh, brother, that will take forever!" I can assure you it will, if the couple is not being controlled by the Holy Spirit or not willing to "in honor prefer" the wisdom and understanding of each other.

Even when the Holy Spirit is in charge, important decisions should not be made hastily, but only after the husband and wife have jointly or separately sought the Lord. Many impulsive decisions made by husbands without consulting their wives (and decisions made similarly by wives) which have negatively affected the family (sometimes for many years), could have been prevented if this form of decision making was followed.

In family decision-making, a couple also needs to consider the matter of "domain." A husband and wife need to work out together, before the Lord, the areas of responsibility each will shoulder. Each one's interests and giftings should figure into the dividing of these responsibilities. Once they have been established, each of these responsibilities is an area of "domain" and he or she is free to make decisions relating to that segment of their lives. However, even in each one's area of domain, the

other is at some time or another going to be affected. Therefore, one should never be selfish in making any decision, but always keep the husband/wife (and children) in mind. However, each must release the other to manage that area of life as he/she sees fit.

As the years go by, husbands and wives should take time to reassess and make changes if necessary. Different periods of life have different sets of responsibilities. For example, a mother who is raising a family and is carrying the load for the children's daily care and other homemaking responsibilities might find that her "domain" would change drastically when the children are grown, and she would decide (prayerfully with her husband) that she should take a job outside of the home. This new arrangement might call for a shifting of the husband's "domain" as well. He might need to help shoulder housekeeping chores that up to this time had been in the wife's "domain."

Nate and I do quite a lot of traveling in connection with our ministry. Not long ago as we were preparing for another ministry trip that would have us on the road for a considerable time, Nate came to me about some detail of our itinerary to get my advice. He recognized that I would be affected by the decision since I would be with him. Although we had never actually sat down and spelled it out, it was at this moment I acknowledged to him that our travels were largely centered around his ministry. (I do some teaching at most locations where we go, but he carries the greater responsibility.) Unless he specifically felt he needed counsel or confirmation, the travel decisions were his "domain."

Conversely, things having to do with the running of the house are in my "domain," and I am free to make decisions and keep it running as I see fit, always keeping in mind that many things around the house affect him. I

dare not be selfish in those areas. It is often necessary to confer.

Now suppose there is a family decision that needs to be made and made immediately. It affects everyone in the family so it must be made by both husband and wife (and there are times when the children should be included), but you are not in agreement. Let me hasten to say, Satan is the master of haste and will do everything he can to convince us a decision just has to be made **now**. Most of those decisions do **not** have to be made immediately. If God is in the situation, He will wait and give one time to pray about it. However, from time to time, there are decisions that need to be made more or less immediately.

These are the times when each has to take his/her turn at submitting. Some of these times the wife will have to yield to her husband something like this: "Honey, I don't really agree with that form of action, but it doesn't violate my principles. I could feel comfortable with our proceeding your way since I recognize that you know more about the matter than I do." Likewise, the husband needs to be just as willing to yield to his wife in just the same manner at times when she is more "in tune" with the situation.

A few years ago, our finances were such that both Nate and I felt we could not continue carrying health insurance. For many years, while our children were growing up, we had been without health coverage, trusting God for protection. Now we were at a place where we needed to walk by faith again. About a year after dropping the insurance, the Lord began strongly impressing upon me the need to get coverage again and get it now. Nate never did feel as I did. Nevertheless, because I felt so strongly about it and knowing I am often more "in tune" with the practical things of life, he graciously submitted to my "leading."

Most insurance plans have a 3-month waiting period before your policy becomes effective. Less than a year after our 3-month waiting period was over, Nate had to spend over a week in the hospital and receive care from two different specialists. With today's astronomical costs of medical care, his bill ran into the multiple thousands. He would be the first one to acknowledge how grateful he is that I pressed to get our insurance re-instated and that he submitted to my urging.

However, the bigger decisions of life that greatly affect the whole family such as "Do we go to the mission field?" or "Where do we go on vacation this year?" or "How do we spend the income tax return?" need to be made jointly under the leadership and direction of the Holy Spirit in humility before one another.

I am saddened as I observe some husbands who seem to totally ignore their part in Ephesians 5:25-31. They conduct themselves as if life was made to revolve around them and their wishes. What does it mean to love one's wife so much that a husband would lay down his life for her? Husband, when was the last time you did something for your wife that cost you? I'm not just talking about bringing her a bottle of perfume or a bouquet of flowers, although either would be nice sometimes. I mean it cost you:

1. Time you wanted to spend in some activity of your choice;
2. Energy you expended to give of yourself to her when you were exhausted (knowing full well she was equally as exhausted and yet on-going household demands forced her to keep going);
3. Sacrificing some gadget you had been wanting in order that you could buy

something for her instead knowing your budget couldn't afford both; or

4. Your comfort, in order to increase hers.

It is interesting to me that some husbands seem to think it was written in their marriage vows that they be allowed time to "play," that is, participate in some activity just for the fun of it even though this takes them away from the home and children for hours at a time. I am not opposed to that (within reason). I think it is great when a husband can have a good time "unwinding" at some sport or activity with his friends. The question I have is, is he equally as concerned that his wife have a comparable amount of time away from the responsibility and pressure of home and children? This involves more than just being there in body so that the children are not alone. It involves stepping in and filling the "gap" left by mom's absence, such as getting dinner started (or finished as the case may be), helping with homework, or lovingly tucking them in at bedtime. It seems to me that if that didn't fall into the category of mutual submission (or if a husband couldn't accept that scriptural understanding) that it certainly would fall into the category of laying down his life for his wife as taught in Ephesians 5:25.

Undoubtedly the underlying reasons for this one-sided thinking are:

1. The erroneous interpretation and translation of the Scriptures as it relates to the woman and why God placed her on this earth; and
2. The license the traditional teaching, subconsciously, gives men to insist on having their way.

I am afraid that many husbands don't have the kind of love for their wives that would lead them to lay down their lives for them.

As husbands allow God to reveal His will to them in this area of their marriages, it will take real humility to acknowledge it and courage and discipline to make the appropriate adjustments.

All of us, both husbands and wives, need to re-evaluate our reasons for marriage. Was it just to get love, affection, sex, security, companionship; or was it to give and share these, with a desire to see one's spouse become all God has called him/her to be?

The "Weaker Vessel"

In 1 Peter 3:7, speaking to husbands, Peter admonishes them to exercise restraint, not authority, towards their wives, living with them *"as with a weaker vessel."* To what was he referring? He can not be speaking of emotional weakness. Women are notorious for their emotional strength. He surely isn't referring to mental weakness. There are too many female PhD's to support that. Nor can he be talking about spiritual weakness. To say a woman can not hear God's voice as well as her male counter-part or have as close a walk with God is absurd.

Peter is either referring to the fact that she is physically weaker or perhaps is referring to her legal weakness. Even though womanhood had come a long way since "the days of old," pagan influences upon society still kept her in a weaker state legally. Peter may have been saying husbands needed to live with their wives in a way that indicated their understanding of her lot in life. He should grant her honor since, even though society didn't recognize her as a believer, she was a fellow heir of the grace of life.

It is also possible that Peter is using the "weaker vessel" as an example of how a husband is to treat his wife. Vessels were made of clay in Peter's time and

although they had little monetary value, they were guarded carefully because of their sentimental value. "Orientals feel that the clay of the pot is analogous to the clay which is our body; the water within the pot corresponds to God's spirit within us."[8] So it is possible Peter is comparing the way one would handle a vessel that was cracked or for some other reason fragile and "weak" with the way a husband should live with his wife – with care and tenderness.

Verse 7 goes on to speak of the honor that a husband is to grant his wife. How can that be done? It has been said that the greatest gift a father can give his children is to love their mother. Make sure your children know that you, father, love their mother. Show affection to her in their presence. Our son Gerry remembers as a boy coming in from playing and very often finding Nate and I in the kitchen "huggin' and kissin'." He says this gave him a great sense of security because it demonstrated to him that our marriage, and therefore his family, was solid.

Speak well of her in public. Don't keep your accolades just for the privacy of your home or bedroom. The public touching of one another, the arm around the shoulder, the holding around the waist, even the holding of hands as you walk together down the street, all indicate oneness. It is very lovely to see. The onlooker gets a warm feeling of the joy and unity of marriage. Your demonstration becomes a living witness of God's intention for husband and wife. (This would not be as applicable in some cultures as it is in the West.)

Show her honor by helping her with her chair as she is being seated at a table. Open the door for her to a building as well as to a car. Some may call that chauvinism; I call it honor. Ask God to show you ways to honor your wife.

Whether or not a husband chooses to grant his wife honor does not seem to be an option. Apparently God felt this was a message that badly needed to penetrate the hearts of the early Christian husbands to whom honoring wives was foreign. In fact, He attached a serious consequence for those who failed to comply. Verse 7 ends with: *". . . and grant her honor as a fellow heir of the grace of life,* ***so that your prayers may not be hindered."*** There seems to be a direct connection between husbands receiving answers to prayer and the honoring of their wives.

In far too many cases today, honoring wives is no less foreign than in the early church. Husbands, examine your prayer life. Have you been getting answers? If not, perhaps it's because God has not witnessed your honoring your wife as a fellow heir.

Understanding "Headship"

By now you are, no doubt, asking the question, "But isn't the husband the **head** of the wife?" Keep reading.

The answer to that question hinges on the translation of the Greek word *kephale* translated "head" in Ephesians 5:23 and 1 Corinthians 11:3, and whether it means "authority over" or "source of life."

In the New Testament the word "head" (*kephale*) is used the same way as the word "head" (*ro'sh*) is in the Old Testament. It stands for "chief" in speaking of Christ as "head of the corner." Matthew 21:42, Luke 20:17, Acts 4:11, Ephesians 2:20, and 1 Peter 2:7 are all referring to Psalm 118:22, *"The stone which the builders rejected has become the chief cornerstone."* To understand that verse one must understand the significance of the "chief cornerstone" of a building when the Psalmist penned those words.

In ancient times a huge stone was used as the headstone or cornerstone to give support to the entire building. The walls of the building were built in such a way that they wrapped around that chief cornerstone, giving the building the support that it needed. Christ is just that kind of support to the Church, binding its members together. Ephesians 4:15, 16 says,

> But speaking the truth in love, we are to grow up in all aspects unto Him who is the head, even Christ, from whom the whole body, being fitted and held together by that which every joint supplies, according to the proper working of each individual part, causes the growth of the body to the building up of itself in love.

Colossians 1:16-18 reminds us,

> **For in Him all things were created** (He gave life), both in heaven and on earth, visible and invisible, whether thrones or dominions or rulers or authorities - all things have been created through Him and for Him. And He is before all things, **and in Him all things hold together.**

There is that chief cornerstone, again, holding things together. Then those verses go on to say that even as He is the One who holds everything else together, *"He is also head of the body, the Church."* In other words, He gives life to the Church and holds it together. This whole passage is not talking about "authority" but "source of life."

Colossians 2:18, 19 tells us to

> Let no one keep defrauding you of your prize by delighting in self-abasement and the worship of angels, taking his stand on visions he has seen inflated without cause by his fleshly mind, and not holding fast to the head from whom the entire body being supplied and

> held together by the joints and ligaments grow with a growth which is from God.

Ephesians 1:20-23 speaking of Jesus, tells us that God

> . . . seated Him at His right hand in the heavenly places, far above all rule and authority and power and dominion, and every name that is named, not only in this age, but also in the one to come. And He put all things in subjection under His feet, and gave Him as head over all things to the church, which is His body, the fulness of Him who fills all in all.

But the Church is not there under His feet in this Headship of government, but, rather, is at His side. As Ephesians 2:6 says we are *"seated with Him in the heavenly places, in Christ Jesus."* Furthermore, in Revelation 3:21, Jesus didn't say, "This is My throne; keep away." He said, *"He who overcomes, I will grant to him to sit down with Me on My throne, as I also overcame and sat down with My Father on His throne."*

All through these passages, Jesus is using the head/body metaphor and is speaking of the "head" as that which gives life to the body. None of these passages refer to Christ's government. They represent Him as the supporter, nourisher, and builder of the body, not Her ruler. **It is in this same way that man is the "head" of the wife.**

Recent scholarship has increasingly concluded, after continued study of ancient biblical, secular, and medical writings, that *kephale* means "source of life" rather than "authority over."[9]

There are about 180 times in the Old Testament when the Hebrew word *ro'sh* clearly did mean "ruler," "commander," or "leader," but the Septuagint translators rarely used *kephale* in translating these portions. They used other Greek words that more accurately defined "chief" when meaning a person of authority.

> *Kephale* would have been the natural word to use in all the 180 instances if the word had been commonly understood to mean "leader or chief." Its rare usage indicates that translators knew that *kephale* did not carry this meaning.[10]

Furthermore,

> Examination of the seven passages where Paul used *kephale* in reference to Christ indicates that, when they are read with common Greek meanings of *kephale,* we see a more exalted Christ than when we read "head" primarily with the meaning of "authority over".[11]

Colossians 2:19 points to Christ as the source of life. Ephesians 4:15, 16 emphasize the unity of head and body and present Christ as the nourisher and source of growth.

Just as Christ personally brings His Church to perfection (Ephesians 4:11-13) by means of the five-fold ministry (apostle, prophet, evangelist, pastor, teacher) *"for the equipping of the saints for the work of service, to the building up of the body of Christ,"* so the husband's desire should be to build up his wife until she becomes all God intended her to be.

There is a certain energy a husband is to infuse into his wife. Remember the last time you went to a party and there was one, or perhaps two people, who brought "life" to the party, and without them it would have been rather boring and dull? In fact, they were even referred to as the "life of the party." There was an influence they brought to the party that sparked life and vibrancy and joy.

Life is not a party, certainly, but there is an energizing element that the husband is to infuse into his wife that gives life to her and results in her being joyfully fulfilled and released to become all God intended for her to become as an individual. This is an extremely vital ingredient in any marriage.

It has been said, and I believe rightly so, that the wife and mother sets the tone or atmosphere for the home. 1 Timothy 5:14 (see pgs. 128-130) seems to indicate that the home is her domain, regardless of whether or not she works or has a career outside of the home. So, as she naturally exudes who she is and how she feels, she will strongly affect the atmosphere in the home. The ingredient of "life" in the form of love, encouragement, praise, and release from her husband is of utmost importance in helping her be the relaxed and fulfilled wife and mother that will set that tone.

This ingredient is missing in far too many Christian homes. However, before some wife finds herself wallowing in self-pity while reading these pages, let me remind you that even if this dimension is missing in your husband, you can and must find your fulfillment in Jesus. None of us can blame our husbands, or anyone else for that matter, for our lack of joy. Jesus is our joy! It is possible to give up that joy by choosing to walk in discouragement and unbelief, but no one can take it away. Each of us must "abide in the vine" that we might "bring forth fruit."

Nevertheless, the relationship of a husband and wife who have become one flesh must contain this "life-giving" dimension on the part of the husband if the marriage is to fulfill God's overall plan. There is nothing in this that gives him the right to dominate, rule, or control, but only to love, encourage, and release.

Whom Should We Obey?

Aren't we supposed to obey Christ? Yes, absolutely, because He is God! He is **KING OF KINGS** and **LORD OF LORDS!** But that is not what these verses are talking about. These verses aren't dealing with His Lordship as

One Who should be obeyed, but with the headship of Jesus, the One Who is the "Source of Life" for His Body.

The Greek word that clearly means authority is *exousia,* not *kephale.* Christ's authority over the Church and over the world is established in other passages of Scripture which use this Greek word *exousia.* Some examples are:

> "But in order that you may know that the Son of Man has **authority** on earth to forgive sins" – then He said to the paralytic, "Rise, take up your bed, and go home" (Matthew 9:6).

> And Jesus came up and spoke to them, saying, "All **authority** has been given to Me in heaven and on earth " (Matthew 28:18).

> For just as the Father has life in Himself, even so He gave to the Son also to have life in Himself; and He gave Him **authority** to execute judgment, because He is the Son of Man (John 5:26, 27).

In all three of these passages, the Greek word used is *exousia,* a word that does carry a clear meaning of authority.

However, a husband is not King of Kings and should not take Christ's position as lord of his wife. A woman must answer to her spiritual Master in exactly the same way as a man must. A husband, as the matrimonial head, is a fellow-servant of the King and the one to whom God has given the responsibility of infusing into his wife the fullest life possible.

Jesus, in Matthew 20:25-28, made it very clear how fellow-disciples were to relate to one another. He said the Gentiles exercised authority over one another, but that it was not to be so among His followers. Rather, *"whoever would be first let him be your servant."* This is the key to every relationship.

Philippians 2:3-8 admonishes,

> Do nothing from selfishness or empty conceit, but **with humility of mind let each of you regard one another as more important than himself**; do not merely look out for your own personal interests, but also for the interests of others. Have this attitude in yourselves which was also in Christ Jesus, who, although He existed in the form of God, did not regard equality with God a thing to be grasped, but emptied Himself, taking the form of a bondservant, and being made in the likeness of men. And being found in appearance as a man, He humbled Himself by becoming obedient to the point of death, even death on a cross.

Jesus is the perfect example of One Who came to serve mankind, unworthy as we are. The problem with humanity, and even the Body of Christ today, is that there is more interest in having authority over people — that is, being "in charge" — than a desire to live in a position of humility and servanthood.

Each of us, as Christians in general and husbands and wives in particular, so desperately need to follow Jesus' example and embrace the brokenness of servanthood rather than revel in the selfishness of being served.

Chapter Six Notes

1. Ruth Tucker and Walter Liefeld, *Daughters of the Church* (Grand Rapids: Zondervan Publishing House, 1987), 81-82.

For further reference: Charles Trombley, *Who Said Women Can't Teach?* (North Brunswick, NJ: Bridge Publishing, Inc., 1985), 151-52.

2. Patricia Gundry, *Heirs Together* (Grand Rapids: Zondervan Publishing House, 1980), 72-73.

3. Ibid., 73-75.

4. Ibid., 75-76.

5. Joseph H. Thayer, *Greek-English Lexicon of the New Testament* (Grand Rapids, MI: Baker Book House, 1977), no. 5293.

6. Katherine C. Bushnell, *God's Word To Women* (privately reprinted by Ray B. Munson, North Collins, NY, 1923), 292.

7. Romans 13:1, 5; Titus 3:1; 1 Peter 2:13.

8. Bishop K. C. Pillai, *Light Through an Eastern Window* (NY: Robert Speller & Sons Publishers, 1963), 95-96.

9. Ruth Tucker and Walter Liefeld, op. cit., 455.

For further reference: "Does *kephale* (head) Mean 'Source' or 'Authority Over' in Greek Literature?: A Rebuttal." This 19-page paper by Richard S. Cervin, doctoral candidate for the degree in Linguistics from the University of Illinois, Urbana-Champaign, is available from Christians for Biblical Equality, 122 West Franklin Avenue, Suite 218, Minneapolis, MN 55404-2451.

10. Alvera Mickelsen, ed., *Women, Authority & the Bible* (Downers Grove, IL: Inter Varsity, 1986), 102-04.

11. Ibid., 104-05.

Questions For Study or Discussion

1. Discuss the importance of Ephesians 5:21 as it relates to Ephesians 5:22-33.
2. Describe each of these marriages: Jewish, Greek, Roman.
3. What does the Greek word "hupotasso" mean?
4. How does this apply to the husband-wife relationship?
5. What does the Greek word "kephale" mean?
6. How does this affect the husband-wife relationship?
7. How is the husband to work out "mutual submission" in his relationship with his wife as taught in Ephesians 5:25-32?
8. How is the wife to work out "mutual submission" in her relationship with her husband as taught in Ephesians 5:22-24, 33?
9. According to 1 Peter 3:1-6, how is a wife to relate to her husband?
10. According to 1 Peter 3:7, how is a husband to relate to his wife?
11. According to 1 Peter 3:8-9, how are the husband and wife to relate to each other?
12. What does the Greek word "exousia" mean?
13. Whom is the Christian (male and female) to obey?

14. Describe how all Christians should relate to one another – Philippians 2:3-8.

15. What have you learned in this study about God's plan for the husband-wife relationship?

16. How should you apply this to your marriage?

17. What changes do you need to make?

SEVEN

Shall Women Keep Silent?

I Corinthians 14:34-40

> Let the women keep silent in the churches; for they are not permitted to speak, but let them subject themselves, just as the Law also says. And if they desire to learn anything, let them ask their own husbands at home; for it is improper for a woman to speak in church (1 Corinthinians 14:34, 35).

For those who have not been comfortable with the total silencing of women, the most commonly accepted explanation of these verses is that it was customary for the women to sit on one side of the room and call out their questions to their husbands who were on the opposite side. This explanation is acceptable and satisfactory to many people. I, personally, have not been totally content with it.

If Paul is demanding silence, he is contradicting his own teaching of 1 Corinthians 11 where he allows women to pray and prophesy. This makes the issue not a feminist one but an exegetical one and affects the integrity of the Scripture as well as Paul's credibility.

One of the most important rules of interpretation in our list of rules is #3, Rule of Context (see page 55). It is very important to interpret Scripture in light of the Scripture surrounding it.

The Context of 1 Corinthinians

What does the rest of 1 Corinthians tell us that will shed light on these verses?

We know the Corinthian Christians had written Paul a letter (7:1) and that in that letter a number of issues were raised that Paul needed to address.

In Paul's letter, as he addressed a question or issue that had been raised by the Corinthians in their letter to him, sometimes he simply referred to the subject in question, and then responded to it, as in the following examples:

7:1 — Paul says *"now concerning the things about which you wrote . . ."*

7:25 — *"now concerning virgins . . ."*

8:1 — *"now concerning things sacrificed to idols . . ."*

9:1 — he asks questions to bring up the next subject, *"Am I not free?" "Am I not an apostle?,"* etc. He is obviously referring to their questions regarding his being called an apostle.

12:1 — *"now concerning spiritual gifts . . ."*

Other times Paul repeated the Corinthians' erroneous statements and then proceeded to correct, or bring balance to, their thinking.

6:12 — Paul seems to be quoting them - *"All things are lawful for me,"* then he counters with *"but not all things are*

profitable." Then he repeats again what probably was their statement to him, *"All things are lawful for me,"* and again balances that statement with, *"but I will not be mastered by anything."* The Corinthians were justifying license by their words because Paul had taught, *"Ye are not under the law, but under grace."*

The portion in question here, 1 Corinthians 14:34, 35, finds Paul describing in some detail how the gifts of the Holy Spirit are to be in operation in a church assembly, and specifically the gift of prophecy. At this point a new subject is being introduced. Paul seems to shift to the subject of women in the assembly.

It is very much in keeping with the pattern of this letter for Paul, in verses 34 and 35, simply to be repeating the words of the Corinthians,

> Let the women keep silence in the churches; for they are not permitted to speak, but let them subject themselves just as the law also says. And if they desire to learn anything, let them ask their own husbands at home; for it is improper for a woman to speak in church.

What follows in verse 36 seems to rebut their statement when he says, *"Was it from you that the Word of God first went forth? Or has it come to you only?"* Then he closes this chapter with a few more remarks concerning prophecy and speaking in tongues.

Which Law

The key phrase in verse 34 is *"just as the law also says."* Remember, Paul was an educated man. He called himself a Pharisee of the Pharisees. Certainly he knew the law. There is no Old Testament law or Scripture that either silences women or subjects them – none whatsoever.

Check the cross reference notes in your Bible for verse 34, and you'll find no cross reference in the Old Testament. Rather, Psalms 68:11 says, *"The Lord gives the command; the women who proclaim the good tidings are a great host."*

Does Paul have the right to silence that "great host of women?" Inconceivable!

However, the Jews were living according to the *Talmud,* not according to the Old Testament Law. Remember the *Talmud* contains regulations and traditions that had become more important than the Old Testament books of the Law.

In "The Ten Curses of Eve" listed in the Babylonian *Talmud,* the sixth is summarized this way:

> "He shall rule over thee," the wife being in total submission and subjugation, since the wife is the personal property of the husband.[1]

When he quotes their statement back to them in verses 34 and 35, which makes reference to the law, he is attempting to show them that they are still living and operating by the oral law of the Jews or Jewish traditions.

> The great German lexicographer, Schleusner, in his Greek-Latin Lexicon, declares the expression "as also saith the law" refers to the Oral Law of the Jews. Here are his words: "The oral laws of the Jews or Jewish traditions . . . in the Old Testament no precept concerning this matter exists," and he cites Vitringa as showing that it was "forbidden by Jewish traditions for women to speak in the synagogue."[2]

Paul would never have made a statement such as is quoted in verses 34 and 35 attributing something to Old Testament law that simply did not exist. Not only that but all through his letters he tried to free believers from the bondage of the law, not hold them to it (Romans 6:14; Galatians 2:16, 5:1).

By Paul's response in verse 36, he is saying, "Who do you think you are, setting yourselves up to proclaim something as from God that is not supported by Scripture?"

We are doing Paul a disfavor and discrediting his intelligence by accusing him of originating this statement rather than understanding that he was simply quoting theirs. Paul is not attempting to establish the silencing of women in the New Testament Church. On the contrary, he is chiding the Corinthians for their attempt to keep women silent and thereby prevent them from freely ministering as the men were free to do.

Paul released women to speak within the church in this chapter, but did he require them to cover their heads while doing so?

Chapter Seven Notes

1. Charles Trombley, *Who Said Women Can't Teach?* (North Brunswick, N J: Bridge Publishing, Inc., 1984), 30. Summarized from *Genesis with a Talmudic Commentary* by Herson.

2. Johann Friederich Schleusner as quoted in Katherine C. Bushnell, *God's Word to Women* (privately reprinted by Ray B. Munson, P. O Box 417, North Collins, NY 14111, 1923), 201.

Questions For Study or Discussion

1. What has been your previous understanding of 1 Corinthians 14:34-40?
2. Put this passage in your own words now that you have studied it further.
3. Did Paul have the right to silence women? Explain.
4. Has your understanding of this passage changed as a result of this study? If so, what is your new understanding?

EIGHT

The Head Covering

I Corinthians 11:3-16

A great portion of the Church today has leanings toward male domination, because it feels that certain passages in the Bible, including Genesis 3:16, establish this. However, only a small segment of the Church adheres to the head covering for women as the biblical sign of that male authority. Even Anabaptist groups, who have historically followed this conviction, such as the Mennonites and the Brethren In Christ, are moving away from the practice.

I have great admiration for Christians who live by their convictions no matter how stringent they may be. At the same time, I am saddened by the bondage some of these convictions have kept them in. I am concerned that they are basing their salvation on the living out of these convictions, rather than the grace of God through faith in the shed blood of Jesus. My own church background was

one that, historically, was conservative regarding dress, although it did not include the head covering for women. I know from experience how easy it is to measure one's spirituality by how closely one is adhering to established standards, rather than by one's personal relationship with Jesus.

On the other hand, one wonders if male domination is biblical and if 1 Corinthians teaches that there should be a sign on a woman's head acknowledging that domination, why are there so many Christians who do not follow that teaching? Shouldn't we be consistent? Either the Bible teaches male authority and women need to accordingly cover their heads, or there is no biblical basis for male authority, and 1 Corinthians 11 is saying something else.

I am convinced there is no biblical basis for male authority and, therefore, 1 Corinthians 11 is addressing an issue that was a source of controversy in the Corinthian church at that time.

Another of the rules of interpretation is needed here: Rule #4, Rule of Historical Background (see page 55). One dare not separate interpretation and historical investigation. Remember, in our Western civilization we are trying to amalgamate into our way of thinking all of Scripture which was written by and for the Eastern mind. Cultural practices were either referred to or otherwise connected to many portions of Scripture. Without knowing and understanding these cultural practices we can not accurately interpret what the writer is attempting to say. I believe such is the case with 1 Corinthians 11.

Cultural and religious dogma (especially for the Jews who were by this time living throughout the Roman Empire) held strongly to the practice of a married woman having her head covered in public. This was directly related to the male domination tradition. As new believers became part of the Church and were being

discipled, freedom from the bondages of the law was being taught. As a part of this new-found freedom, the whole subject of whether or not heads should be covered when praying had become an issue in the Corinthian church. In this chapter, as in 1 Corinthians 14, Paul is responding to arguments a contentious group of believers apparently had been holding onto and which had been related to Paul in their letter to him.

He begins this portion in verses 1 and 2 by challenging them to imitate him as he imitates Christ. He praises them for holding firmly to the traditions he (Paul) had taught them and not yielding to that faction who insisted upon clinging to former rules and regulations.

Next, we need to observe that in verses 3-10 there seems to be one tone followed by verses 11-16 which takes on quite a contradictory tone. It is an insult to Paul's coherency to assign to him the origination of these statements. I believe in verses 3-10 of this chapter, as in 1 Corinthians 14, Paul is referring to the arguments the "contentious" Jews were making which was causing the controversy in the Corinthian church.

Is There a Hierarchy?

Verse 3 is the basis the striving Corinthians were using to support their argument for the woman's head covering. However, I believe their understanding of "head" was more accurate than today's traditional understanding.

There are those who believe that verse 3 in 1 Corinthians 11 is talking about a hierarchical structure:

> But I want you to understand that Christ is the head of every man, and the man is the head of a woman, and God is the head of Christ.

Nothing else in the passage suggests this. The only time *exousia,* which was a well accepted and understood word for authority at that time, is used in this portion (verse 10) is in reference to the woman's own authority. The Septuagint, when translating *ro'sh* ordinarily used *kephale* when the physical "head" was intended and almost never did where "ruler" was intended.[1] So the Corinthians would have naturally accepted Paul's "head" as "source" – more specifically "source of life."

If Paul had wanted to convey the idea of a chain of command, he surely would have used a word that everyone would have understood to mean authority, such as *exousia*. He also would have arranged it in proper order: God, Christ, man, woman.

Also, Paul could not be talking governmentally or hierarchically because God and Christ are equal in authority. Even while on earth Jesus said, *"I and the Father are one"* John 10:30. The Jews understood this to mean equality because in verse 33 of the same chapter they said, *" . . . because you, being a man, make yourself out to be God!"* And Jesus said in John 8:42, *"I proceed forth and have come from God . . . "* So "head" here means "source of life."

Even the "contentious" Corinthians understood "head" to be "source of life" and, in fact, were using this truth to support their arguments since so much is said in verses 8 and 9 about the source of life of man and woman. This group of Corinthians were using all of these arguments to support keeping women "in their place." I believe Paul, in making this statement in verse 3, is showing that the Corinthians were using the "headship" truth as a foundation for their following arguments. In other words, Paul was saying, "Yes, that is true, but when you get to verse 11 you will see how I bring balance to the erroneous statements you have made (verses 4-10) based on that 'headship'."

> Verses 4-6: "Every man who has something on his head while praying or prophesying, disgraces his head. But every woman who has her head uncovered while praying or prophesying, disgraces her head; for she is one and the same with her whose head is shaved. For if a woman does not cover her head, let her also have her hair cut off; but if it is disgraceful for a woman to have her hair cut off or her head shaved, let her cover her head."

Verses 4-6 are so full of legalism and bondage that it is virtually impossible to attribute those words to the one who wrote, *"It was for freedom that Christ set us free; therefore keep standing firm and do not be subject again to a yoke of slavery"* (Galatians 5:1). Rather Paul is still referring to the arguments of the "contentious" Corinthians.

In the Image of God

Verse 7:

> For a man ought not to have his head covered, since he is the image and glory of God; but the woman is the glory of man.

Paul, who knew the Old Testament Scriptures would never have made such a statement as this. He knew that Genesis 1:27 says,

> And God created man in His own image, in the image of God He created him; male and female He created them.

And Genesis 5:1, 2:

> This is the book of the generations of Adam. In the day when God created man, He made him in the likeness of God. He created them male and female and

> He blessed them and named them Man in the day when they were created.

Man and woman together were created in the image (and glory) of God and Paul knew this very well. He was schooled in the Law (Acts 22:3 and Philippians 3:5) and would never have taught that only man was made in the image of God.

The arguments that are presented in verses 8 and 9, although having some thread of truth in them, are so contradicted by Paul's words beginning with verse 11 that one can not attribute them to Paul.

Verses 8, 9:

> For man does not originate from woman, but woman from man; for indeed man was not created for the woman's sake but woman for man's sake.

These verses contain some truth in that woman was formed from man and, indeed, was given to man as a "helper suitable." However, verse 9 must be looked at in light of Genesis 2:18, keeping in mind the scriptural meaning of "helper." Remember man was not created because woman **needed** man, but because man **needed** woman.

Then comes the Corinthians' statement in which they attempt to put the bondage of a head covering onto the women.

Verse 10:

> Therefore the woman ought to have a symbol of authority on her head, because of the angels.

This statement is totally contradicted in verse 16 which we'll discuss later.

Paul's Rebuttal

It is at this point that the tone of this passage changes as Paul, in verses 11 and 12, begins his rebuttle and brings the balance to the male dominance arguments that had been referred to previously.

Verses 11, 12:

> However, in the Lord, neither is woman independent of man, nor is man independent of woman. For as the woman originates from the man, so also the man has his birth through the woman; and all things originate from God.

In these verses Paul is teaching an interdependence and equality of man and woman culminating in the fact that we all come from God. He is the source of life for all mankind.

A key phrase here is **"in the Lord."** "Religion," whether in New Testament times or today, contains many "laws," rules, and bondages. But they all pass away when one comes under the New Covenant. To be "in the Lord" is to be set free from all legalism and religious mores. To be "in the Lord" is to be walking in relationship with Him and with fellow believers, made possible by Jesus' shed blood. One's value is no longer measured by who you are or what you do, and definitely not your gender (Galatians 3:28). This means there is no need for any "veiling."

2 Corinthinians 3:16 says, *"But whenever a man turns to the Lord, the veil is taken away."* In other words, the veil, whether referring to Jewish law, hardness of heart, or condemnation for sin, is removed when one turns to the Lord. And what liberty is described in 2 Corinthians 3:17, 18:

> Now the Lord is the spirit, and where the Spirit of the Lord is, there is liberty. But we **all**, with **unveiled**

> **face** beholding as in a mirror the glory of the Lord, are being transformed into the same image from glory to glory, just as from the Lord, the Spirit.

This truth applies to women as well as to men. Paul would **never** teach the removal of a spiritual veil and at the same time place redeemed women under the bondage of a literal veil.

> It was for freedom that Christ set us free; therefore keep standing firm and do not be subject again to a yoke of slavery (Galatians 5:1).

A number of years ago, I went through a short period when I felt I should cover my head whenever I prayed (especially in public). We were fellowshipping with Christians who actually did this, and having great respect for their walk with the Lord, I began to feel that I should follow their practice. It was devastating to my spirit. Every time we would get ready to have prayer with someone, I couldn't listen to God or pray freely. I was too concerned about my having, or not having, something on my head.

One day the Lord in His faithfulness spoke to my heart. He said, "Joanne, anything that keeps you from freely and openly coming into My presence is bondage. That is not of Me." I was immediately set free! It was not until I was immersed in this study that I came into a clear understanding of this Scripture; but I was set free at that earlier time by the Holy Spirit.

Nature And Hair Length

Some Greek scholars are quite convinced that 1 Corinthians 11:13-15 should not be translated in the form of questions as they are:

> Judge for yourselves: is it proper for a woman to pray to God with head uncovered? Does not even nature itself teach you that if a man has long hair, it is a dishonor to him, but if a woman has long hair, it is a glory to her? For her hair is given to her for a covering.

There are no interrogative words in the Greek text nor, of course, were there any question marks. And, no, in fact nature does not teach us anything regarding men and long hair. A man's hair will grow just as long as woman's if left to nature. The Bible has several references to the vow of the Nazarite, which included not cutting one's hair (Numbers 6:1-21). Samuel's mother vowed that Samuel's hair would never be cut; that he would be dedicated or separated unto the Lord all his days (1 Samuel 1:11). Paul let his hair grow at one point in accordance with a vow he had made (Acts 18:18).

Nature has never taught the Chinese that long hair is shameful: millions of men in China have long hair. The Native American woman is attracted by long flowing hair on her brave. So it is clearly not a fact of nature that long hair is shameful for a man. Whether long hair on a man is shameful or acceptable seems to be a cultural matter.

Some think verses 14 and 15 could be one continuous sentence. When translated in the form of statements rather than questions these verses would then read, "Nature does not even itself teach you that if a man has long hair it is a dishonor to him, but if a woman has long hair, it is a glory to her for her hair is given to her for a covering." In other words, one can not draw any conclusions regarding long or short hair based on what nature teaches or shows one.

Finally, Paul sums up his whole argument against enforced headcoverings for women in verse 16 where he says, *"But if one is inclined to be contentious, we have no such practice, nor have the churches of God."* The NASB and NIV

render the verse *"we have no other practice,"* which would cause one to believe Paul is advocating the head covering for women as being the general practice of all the churches. However, the Greek word is *toioutos* which actually is the word for "such." When accurately translated, this verse wipes out any possibility that Paul is requiring or even advocating the head covering for women.

Now that we have allowed women's voices to be heard in the Church and have "removed" the head covering, should they be allowed to teach or have any leadership role?

Chapter Eight Notes

1. Alvera Mickelsen, ed., *Women, Authority & the Bible* (Downers Grove, IL: InterVarsity, 1986), 101-102.

Questions For Study or Discussion

1. Is 1 Corinthians 11:3 talking about a spiritual chain-of-command? Why or why not?
2. How does Paul counter the "image of God" and "origination of woman" statements the Corinthians made in verses 7-9?
3. Explain the importance of the phrase "in the Lord" found in verse 11?
4. What was Paul's summary regarding the head covering spoken of in verse 10?
5. How should you apply 1 Corinthians 11:3-16 to your life?

NINE

Can Women Teach?

1 Timothy 2:8-15

Paul addresses the subject of women teaching in the church in 1 Timothy 2:8-15. But it would be impossible to fully understand this passage without looking at and understanding the historical situation to which Paul was writing.

Just as Paul had to deal with old Jewish laws and traditions that Jewish converts to Christianity were still clinging to, he also had to deal with pagan doctrines that were being carried over into the Christian Church. The mixing of Christian and pagan ideas, called syncretism, was taking place in the church at Ephesus at that time. Paul was dealing here with former pagans who had not made a clean break with their past and who needed to renounce and disassociate themselves from their former practices.

Ephesus, a Pagan City

It is helpful in understanding this chapter to recognize the depths of immorality that prevailed in the pagan religions of the day, especially in Ephesus. Some of the new believers had come out of an immoral, lewd lifestyle. Greek and Roman mythology controlled the society of that day. The worship of Diana (known among the Greeks as Artemis) was the accepted cult of the day. A great part of that worship involved sexual promiscuity – temple prostitution where women were actually the leaders of the cult.

Much can be learned about what was going on in the Church as well as in society by the ancient writings which date back to that period of time. At the time this letter was written, the religion or cult of Gnosticism was on the rise. Early Christian literature indicates that there was a great deal of debate regarding Gnosticism in the early Church.

Gnosticism, which literally means "higher knowledge," had many forms. Some taught that Eve was created first, partook of the fruit willfully and, subsequently, became enlightened with "higher knowledge," thereby becoming a channel through whom God could reach mankind. Some of the other teachings where women were concerned included liberal sexual behavior with no birth control and even the avoidance of marriage altogether.

Paul Refutes False Doctrines

As one looks at 1 Timothy, it is quite obvious that false doctrine was definitely a problem at Ephesus. Paul was simply addressing the different aspects of that false doctrine. In fact, if one understands Gnosticism and

the gross errors it embraced as well as the pagan religion that was coming into the Christian church and all the horror that that involved, it makes 1 Timothy 2 very understandable. It all falls right into place as Paul in verse after verse refutes the gross error that was being taught. This explanation, however, is totally different from the traditional interpretation that has been taught for centuries in many Christian circles.

So let's look at 1 Timothy 2:5: *"For there is one God, and one mediator also between God and men, the man Christ Jesus."*

Remember they were teaching that the woman was the mediator[1], and Paul was saying, *"Not so, but the man Christ Jesus."* When Jesus came in the flesh, He came as a man. Paul was pointing out here that it was a man and not a woman, as the heathen taught, who became the mediator between God and mankind.

Verse 8: *"Therefore I want the men in every place to pray, lifting up holy hands, without wrath and dissension."*

The dominance of the women, having been carried over from the worship of Diana, may have caused a hesitancy on the part of men to participate in prayer. In fact, it would even appear that there was wrath and dissension between the men and women over the participation of men in prayer. Paul is simply correcting this by telling the men that they are to pray and that there should be no argument over the issue.

Verses 9, 10:

> *Likewise, I want women to adorn themselves with proper clothing, modestly and discreetly, not with braided hair and gold or pearls or costly garments; but rather by means of good works, as befits women making a claim to godliness."*

Here, Paul is trying to counteract the seductive way in which some of the women were still dressing. Their whole pattern of life was not totally unlike that which is often seen today in a woman who is converted to Jesus out

of a worldly lifestyle. She does not immediately equate her new-found faith in Jesus with her standard of dress. Paul was simply saying that women should dress more discreetly if they were going to call themselves Christians. He was saying that they would have to leave behind the lewdness, the gaudiness, the worldliness that was a part of their former religion. They should dress more modestly and discreetly. It is this form of dress that befits a woman who desires to be an expression of godliness.

The Importance of the Outward Appearance

We women, in this day, need to be prayerful as to how we apply this teaching to our lives. I would not suggest that a Christian woman should look like a rummage sale reject. I'm sorry to say I've seen a few who do. However, I'm equally sorry to say that some Christian women have taken their freedom in Christ too far towards the worldly side, and in so doing, do not exemplify a life of humility and purity.

I am particularly saddened to observe women who have come from church backgrounds where conservative dress was rigidly monitored. As the rigidity has lifted in recent years, the pendulum has swung the other way.

Not long ago I was in conversation with a woman who apparently had come from such a background. She and her husband were involved in Christian ministry. She made a comment which indicated her understanding of the release of women meant women were now free to wear earrings. Observing her appearance, it was obvious that along with the freedom to wear earrings (and hers were huge) came the freedom to wear long acrylic nails, over-done make-up, and excessive jewelry. Her appearance struck me as being more gaudy than godly.

Thank God, a woman is free to dress as she feels led of the Lord and not as she is told by a certain church or group. However, one whose desire is to exemplify godliness needs to be very prayerful in setting her own standards.

So what should be our philosophy of dress? Here's mine. A Christian woman should not dress to call attention to herself but should dress in such a way that if anyone looks her way, what they see will be both pleasing and attractive. Remember, even though God looks on the heart, man(kind) **does** look on the outward appearance (1 Samuel 16:7). This involves color (yes, even a little on the face) that is properly coordinated; hair that is well groomed; styles at least in keeping with the decade (not necessarily the last word in fashion); nylons when appropriate; and shoes that are clean and polished. It should also include well-groomed nails which may or may not be polished, and might include some tastefully-added jewelry.

There will be those who will argue that their budget does not allow for such detail. Everything I have mentioned above can be done on a "shoestring." I know. I've done it. What started out to be a necessity in our early married life – going to garage sales – is still a necessity, but has also become my biggest hobby. The buys one can find at resale shops, garage sales, and flea markets is unbelievable, and so much fun! I once had a lady, who knew we operated on a modest budget, tell me that I looked like a wealthy woman. I thanked her and then informed her that the dress I was wearing had been purchased at a garage sale for three dollars. She was amazed!

I have seen some women whose dress and general demeaner exemplify the subordinate role in which their husbands are keeping them. Their lack of self-esteem is

apparent. In some extreme cases I'm afraid the husband is too insecure to allow his wife to look lovely and has convinced her that dowdiness is synonymous with godliness.

You don't have to be rich and go to extremes to look lovely. Neither should one use the excuse of spirituality or poverty for looking unattractive.

The Instruction of Women

Verse 11: *"Let a woman quietly receive instruction with entire submissiveness."*

Since Paul was dealing with certain women who had brought their pagan doctrines with them into the Christian Church, he, of necessity, had to address the fact that they had not been properly taught the truths of the Kingdom of God. He was addressing a particular group of women in a specific setting and was telling that group of believers to allow these women to be taught and instructed properly. Remember, this was contrary to the Jewish tradition in which women were not allowed to be taught the Scriptures. Paul was reversing that tradition. Historically, women would have been told to sit down and be silent. Paul was saying they should be instructed and allowed to learn if they were willing to sit down, be quiet, and learn in a non-disruptive manner and with the right attitude. Remember, he was dealing with a rather brazen bunch of women.

The Greek word used here is *hesuchia* and means to lead a "quiet, non-disruptive life." NASB says *"quietly receive instruction."* I believe this rendering is more in keeping with the spirit of what Paul is saying than the KJV, for instance, which seems to take a harder line when translating *hesuchia* in this verse. It says *"learn in silence."* It is really stretching the issue to say that in this verse Paul

was directing women not to open their mouths while going through the learning process. Dialogue and asking questions are very important aspects of learning.

Authentein

Verse 12: *"But I do not allow a woman to teach or exercise authority over a man, but to remain quiet."*

This is the verse most often referred to by those who believe the Bible forbids women to teach or exercise authority over men. And the modern translations would seem to indicate that. However, it contains a very interesting Greek word *authentein* that has tremendous bearing on the proper translation of this verse. This is the only place in the New Testament where this word is used. The modern translations render it *"exercise authority over a man."* That is not the translation in the ancient manuscripts. It had a totally different meaning when originally written.

When 1 Timothy was written, this Greek word *authentein* was more closely associated with Greek pagan worship and sometimes meant "to commit murder" or, in some cases, to pantomime murder. Human sacrifices were made in the worship of Diana. Priestesses were sometimes required to put men to death, although sometimes it was just acted out. But the message conveyed implied the death of the man. Greek mythology tells of religiously inspired murders of men by women.[2]

Coupled with this, *authentein* also often had sexual connotations which included promiscuous rites by which women went about teaching men religious truths. Proverbs 5:3-5 seems to indicate there is a real connection between this promiscuity and death. This Scripture teaches that seduction by a woman is considered the pathway to death.

Remember, Paul is still addressing the existing problem of syncretism which included pagan practices. It is conceivable that Paul used this word because he was saying, "We will not allow this kind of seductive teaching going on in the Church by these women."

In his book *Who Said Women Can't Teach?*, Charles Trombley states,

> It was long after Paul wrote his epistle to Timothy that *authentein* came to mean "to exercise authority," "to bear rule over," or "to domineer." John Chrysostom (A.D. 347-407) was one of the dominant Greek Church fathers and patriarchs of Constantinople. In his commentary on 1 Timothy 5:6, he used *authentia* to express "sexual license" nearly two centuries after Paul wrote Timothy. *Authentein* had not yet taken on the meaning "to usurp authority.[3]

Paul did speak of authority or superiority of rank in other passages, but there were three other Greek words in the New Testament that were accepted words for authority and superiority:

- 2 Corinthians 10:8 – *exousia*
- 1 Timothy 2:1, 2 – *huperoche*
- Titus 2:15 – *epitage*[4]

All of the above would have been well understood and accepted words to convey the meaning of authority, if that had been Paul's thought. Instead he chose to use the rare word *authentein.*

To say that Paul, in verse 12, directed that women were never to teach men, would be to say that Paul had the right to negate all other Scriptures which clearly give women not only the right but the directive to do so. No one has that right, including the apostle Paul.

No Special Enlightenment for Eve

Verses 13, 14: *"For it was Adam who was first created, and then Eve. And it was not Adam who was deceived, but the woman being quite deceived fell into transgression."*

Remember, some Gnostics were saying that Eve was the first created, not Adam. Furthermore, they taught that Eve willfully partook of the fruit and Adam was the one who was deceived. So Paul was telling Timothy that these Ephesians had it all wrong. He's setting the record straight regarding the Creation order and the Fall so as to refute the Gnostic teaching of Eve's so-called special enlightenment.

Bearing Children and Preservation of Women

Verse 15: *"But women shall be preserved through the bearing of children if they continue in faith and love and sanctity with self restraint."*

This is probably one of the least understood and most often misinterpreted verses in all of the Bible. The best that most traditional scholars can do is to somehow relate this verse with Mary and the bearing of the child Jesus. However, Jesus is the Source of Salvation for men as well as women. It makes no sense to single out women in this verse as the sole recipients of the blessings of Christ's birth.

Nor is it credible to believe this verse to be saying that bearing children in general will be the means of a woman's salvation.

This verse, however, does become understandable when given the facts regarding the Gnostic teaching about womanhood and sexual promiscuity. Given this understanding, there are several possible explanations, any of which are very plausible.

The Gnostic ethics which often took the form of free love (without contraceptives) resulted in children being born illegitimately. One possible reading of verse 5 might be, "Women will be preserved even though they have born illegitimate children, if they continue in faith, love, and sanctity with self restraint." That is, if they no longer involve themselves in promiscuity but follow the Lord in faith, love, and sanctity, they will be saved even though their previous involvement has resulted in illegitimate childbirth.

Another possible explanation is that Paul was refuting a part of the Gnostic doctrine which taught that women were to become males[5] and that Jesus had come to do away with the works of women, specifically childbearing.[6] Paul was saying that the role of womanhood would be preserved, reproduction would see to that, but the woman must also live a life of holiness, faith, and purity, using self restraint.

A third possible explanation is this. Women who have been involved in illicit sex and who have had abortions – and no doubt these Gnostic women had – have a greater chance of contracting sexually transmitted diseases, miscarriages, still births and even childbirth-deaths. This could mean that if such a woman has entered into a life of faith in Jesus, is filled with His love, and is now walking in purity, she can claim God's protection.

The purpose of 1 Timothy 2: 5-15 was to refute the error in doctrine (a combination of pagan religion, Gnosticism, and Christianity) that was quite prominent in the church at Ephesus. Furthermore, Paul was encouraging the women who were perpetuating the false teaching to settle down and submit to learning the correct Christian doctrine, as well as to set their moral standards in accordance with righteousness. To put any other

interpretation upon these verses is to disregard the setting and situation to which Paul was writing.

So, if this Scripture does not put a restraint on women teaching or having a leadership role, as has been traditionally taught, what examples are there in the New Testament of women who were involved in ministry and leadership?

Chapter Nine Notes

1. Charles Trombley, *Who Said Women Can't Teach?* (North Brunswick, NJ: Bridge Publishing, Inc., 1985), 164-165.

2. Catherine C. Kroeger, *Ancient Heresies and a Strange Greek Verb,* Reformed Journal. (March 1979), 12-15.

3. Trombley, op. cit., 176.

4. Faith Martin, *Call Me Blessed* (Grand Rapids: Wm. B. Eerdmans, 1988), 141-142.

5. Gospel of Thomas (II, 2) Saying 114 (Robinson, 130); Zostrianos (VII, 1), 131; (Robinson, 393). In Alvera Mickelsen, ed. *Women, Authority & the Bible* (Downers Grove, IL: InterVarsity, 1986), 243.

6. Clement of Alexandria, "Miscellanies," 3.45, 63, 64. In Alvera Mickelsen, ed. *Women, Authority & the Bible* (Downers Grove, IL: InterVarsity, 1986), 243.

Questions For Study or Discussion

1. What is a brief definition of Gnosticism?
2. What forms did the worship of the goddess Diana take?
3. Define syncretism. How did it affect the Ephesian church?
4. Why was 1 Timothy 2:5 so important in light of the setting? How does it relate to verses 12 and 14?
5. Explain how Christian women of today should apply verses 9 and 10?
6. Paraphrase verse 11.
7. What did the Greek word "authentein" mean at the time of the writing of 1 Timothy?
8. Put verse 12 in your own words as it should be translated.
9. Give one plausible explanation for verse 15.
10. Does 1 Timothy 2:11-12 limit the ministry of women? Explain.

TEN

Women in Leadership

Were women in places of spiritual leadership in the New Testament? Certainly! However, before we look at several examples, we need to look at a very crucial portion of Scripture.

Acts 2 is a foundational chapter for the entire Church Age. In it we have the outpouring of the Holy Spirit on the Day of Pentecost (vs. 1-13), Peter's explanation of that event (14-21), Peter's preaching the Gospel to the assembled crowds (22-40), the mass conversion of three thousand (41), and a description of the life of the early Church (42-47).

In Peter's explanation of the outpouring of the Holy Spirit, he quotes Joel 2:28-32. This prophecy of Joel was quoted in Acts 2:17-21. It is God's foundational truth for the entire Church Age.

Verses 17 and 18 read,

> And it shall be in the last days, God says, that I will pour forth of My Spirit upon all mankind; and your sons and your daughters shall prophesy, and your young men shall see visions, and your old men shall dream dreams; even upon My bondslaves, both men and women, I will in those days pour forth of My Spirit and they shall prophesy.

As we look at this passage, we discover God is pouring forth His Spirit equally upon both men and women. All other New Testament Scriptures dealing with the subject of men and women must be interpreted in light of this truth: **God's purpose for the Church Age is to pour His Spirit out equally upon men and women alike.**

Now let's see how God anointed women for ministry and leadership and how the early Church viewed women in these roles.

Priscilla

In Romans 16:3, Paul says, *"Greet Prisca* (spelled Priscilla in other passages) *and Aquila my fellow-workers in Christ Jesus."* Whenever names are listed in the New Testament, the more prominent one is listed first. Since Prisca is listed first in this verse, it indicates that she was considered the leader of this husband and wife ministry team. Also in Acts 18:26, Priscilla is mentioned first before her husband Aquilla, again indicating that of the two she had the more prominent role in teaching. Paul calls them his fellow-workers, not Aquilla his fellow-worker. They both were well known in all the churches of the Gentiles (Romans 16:4).

Phoebe

In Romans 16:1-2, we read about a woman by the name of Phoebe,

> I commend to you our sister, Phoebe, who is a servant of the church which is at Cenchrea; that you receive her in the Lord in a manner worthy of the saints, and that you help her in whatever matter she may have need of you; for she herself has also been a helper of many, and of myself as well.

In verse 1, the word translated "servant" is the Greek word *diakonos*. This is the same Greek word used in 1 Corinthians 3:5 referring to Apollos and Paul. The KJV translates it "ministers" and NASB and NIV translate it "servants." Also in Colossians 1:7, concerning Epaphros who took the Gospel to Colossae, the word *diakonas* is translated "minister" in the KJV and NIV and "servant" in NASB. In Acts 21:19 this word is translated "ministry" in all three versions in describing the work of Paul. In 2 Timothy 4:5, Paul admonishes Timothy to do the work of his "ministry" and is thus rendered in all three translations. These are but a few of the many different references where the Greek word *diakonos* is often translated "minister" rather than "servant."

It seems very strange that the one time when this word is used directly referring to a woman, all three translations render it "servant." However, when *diakonos* is used when referring to men, it usually is translated "minister" which denotes teaching or preaching. There is no problem with Phoebe being called a servant; that is what the word *diakonos* means. It seems, however, that the translators were trying to restrict Phoebe to a lesser role as evidenced by the inconsistency in the translation of *diakonos*. She was "a minister" in the same way that Paul was "a minister."

In Romans 16:2 another word is used in describing Phoebe. This word is *prostatis* and is "the feminine word for a person set over others, a female guardian, protectress, patroness, caring for the affairs of others and aiding them with her resources."[1] Yet in the NASB and NIV this word is translated "helper" and "a great help" respectively. The modern translations are not allowing Phoebe to be recognized for the leadership role the word *prostatis* indicates she actually fulfilled in her work with Paul in Cenchrea.

Other New Testament Women

1 Corinthians 1:11 refers to "Cloe's people" ("people" being in italics). This was most probably "the church meeting in her home" and not her family or servants. Historical writings suggest to us that when Scripture refers to a particular woman "and the church that meets in her house," these women were not just hosting the meeting but had a prominent place of leadership within the group.[2]

In Romans 16:7, Junias is referred to as an apostle. Present day translations and authorities are about equally divided on whether this is a female name "Junia" or a male name "Junias." However, a number of the Church fathers understood it to be feminine, including Origen (A.D. 185-253), Chrysostom (347-407), and Jerome (304-419). Dr. Leonard Swidler, in his book *Biblical Affirmations of Women* says, "To the best of my knowledge, no commentator on the text until Aegidus of Rome (A. D. 1245-1316) took the name to be masculine."[3]

In Philippians 4:3, Euodia and Syntyche are mentioned in the context of "fellow-workers." Paul describes them as *". . . these women who have shared my struggle in the cause of the gospel. . ."*

1 Timothy 5:1 is referring to male elders; 5:2 to female elders. A female form of the word *presbyter* is used, although, most translations try to obscure this by rendering it to be referring simply to "older men" and "older women." Likewise, some scholars believe that Titus 2:3, where the Greek word *presbytidas* was used, is speaking of women elders, not "older women."[4] The office of presbyteress was abolished by the Council of Laodicia in A.D. 363, which indicates that at some prior period there must have been such an office.[5]

2 John was written "*. . . to the chosen* (elect - KJV) *lady.*" Many commentators believe that since the church has been called the "Bride of Christ," John was actually writing to a local church and its members. But it is the whole church which is the "Bride" not each local group. Nowhere else in Scripture is this term "elect lady" used. Furthermore this sentence is almost exactly parallel to that in 3 John where he addresses a man named Gaius. It would appear, therefore, that this elect lady is actually a lady who has converts under her leadership.

The ministry of the women mentioned above may seem insignificant compared to that of Peter and Paul. It is certainly true that the majority of Christian workers in the New Testament were men. However, there is actually more said about a number of these women than about the majority of the Twelve Apostles, most of whom are not mentioned after the resurrection.

Considering the Jewish status of women in Paul's day, the number of women noted in Scripture is actually remarkable. Both Paul and John appreciated these women. They were not just the hospitality committee or the church secretaries, as important and valuable as those roles are. They were hard workers in the Gospel with places of responsibility and leadership.

Those who say women should never teach men, based on a traditional understanding of Paul's letters, have neglected to consider one other very important point. Many places throughout the Bible women are quoted: Exodus 15:21, 2 Kings 22:15-20, Judges 5, and Mary's Magnificat in Luke 1:46-55, to name a few. There is no higher form of teaching than that which is found in Scripture. Everywhere a woman is quoted is inspired teaching. It is equally binding on both men and woman. 2 Timothy 3:16 says,

> All Scripture is inspired by God and is profitable for teaching, for reproof, for correction, for training in righteousness.

Does "Keeping House" Involve Leadership?

What about women in leadership in their homes? Do they have any such role? Traditionally we have been taught that the husband / father is the final authority in the home. But a careful study of another Greek word used throughout the New Testament places a whole new light on that subject.

We get our English word "despot" from the Greek word *despotes*. It means exactly the same in Greek, "absolute ownership and uncontrolled power:"[6] as in English "an absolute ruler; an autocrat."[7] This word is translated "master" in the following verses: 1 Timothy 6:1, 2; 2 Timothy 2:21, Titus 2:9, 1 Peter 2:18, 2 Peter 2:1; and it is rendered "Lord" in Luke 2:29, Acts 4:24, Jude 4, and Revelation 6:10.

Another Greek word, *oikos* is the common word for "house." When "oikos" and the noun form of "despotes" are combined into one word, it is "oikodespotes." When used with reference to Beelzebul, or men, "oikodespotes"

is translated "head of the household" in NASB; "master of the house" in KJV, and "head of the house" and "owner of the house" in NIV (Matthew 10:25, Luke 13:25, 14:21).

However, when "oikodespoteo," a verb form, is used in 1 Timothy 5:14, a verse specifically referring to women, it is translated "guide the house" (KJV), "manage their homes" (NIV), and "keep house" (NASB). After comparing the different passages that use some form of this Greek word, it becomes obvious that Paul, in these verses, gave the wife/mother a much greater level of authority and, yes, even rulership in the home than these three translators have allowed. It is unfortunate that the translators could not release all wives and mothers to the full authority that should have been given them by a proper rendition of Paul's word.

Does that give any woman the right to flagrantly flaunt that authority before her family? On the contrary! She should be released to: organize her home, plan the meals, set rules for proper care of the rooms, keep the children's time and efforts properly directed with full release to discipline as necessary, and otherwise make sure her home is running smoothly. However, this should all be done in the context of flowing with the needs of her husband and family. This does not make her a law unto herself, but frees her to flow in her area of domain while at the same time submitting to her husband and family, thereby endeavoring to make the home a haven from the world. A woman can not do this unless her husband takes his hands off and acknowledges the role she has been given in the New Testament, letting her freely "rule" her household.

I have been in more than one home and observed how well the wife has the home and family organized, including five to seven children. These were capable women. However, I noticed a change come over them

when the husband was around. These wives went from running a house like clockwork to not being able to make simple decisions, such as what silverware to use or whether or not to put the baby to bed. It didn't take a genius to figure out that in those homes it didn't matter how well she had things under control in the husband's absence, when he arrived on the scene her domain was taken away from her. Scripture does not support this practice.

The Proverbs 31 Woman

Proverbs 31 describes the "virtuous woman" (KJV) or "excellent wife" (NASB) as one who would put most of us wives to shame by her accomplishments. However, the Hebrew word *chayil* has, as part of its definition, words that are much stronger than "virtuosity" and "excellence" would convey. The word means "to show oneself strong, to display valour."[8] This Proverbs 31 woman was, no doubt, virtuous (full of integrity, uprightness) and excellent (she was terrific!). However, to only use these English words to translate a Hebrew word that contained so much more, displays a reluctance to acknowledge the strength, and valour and, yes, even authority, women can handle.

Why is it that, for some men, to release a woman to do something where strength, courage, and organizational ability is needed, would be to destroy their stereotypic picture of womanhood — weak, inept, quiet? I'm afraid that, in many cases, it is because of their own insecurities. In order to maintain some semblence of security, many men find it necessary to keep women in a lesser role.

Working Women

One of the bigger decisions within a family, and one that should be arrived at jointly, is whether the wife/mother should work outside the home. This unfortunately is often considered by the world as a litmus test as to how truly "liberated" a woman is.

I was very angry in the 1970s when the feminists told me I was a lesser human being since I stayed at home and devoted my time to my family and home rather than pursuing a career. I was a college graduate with teaching credentials, and with a husband in full-time Christian ministry, we could have used the extra money that my teaching would have provided. I chose not to, however, because Nate and I placed time with the children — my being there when they came home from school — above money and things. I did not want my husband and children to come home to an exhausted wife and mother who had taught school all day and had nothing left to give her family.

As a result we lived on a shoestring, but we lived well. We didn't have money for a lot of extras, but we had everything we needed and more. We had a modest but lovely, well-furnished home. We all dressed nicely, and our daughter even had the braces she needed for her teeth. This called for planning, watching for sales, lots of sewing, and in general, being creative.

What is my reward? I could write a book on that alone. I can look back with tremendous satisfaction knowing that I established a secure, well-run haven for my family to come home to each day and that I had the time to give my children the nurturing they needed. I was there for them. Our daughter Beth once made the comment, "Mother, I loved coming home from school and knowing you would always be there."

Is it wrong for a woman to work outside of the home? One can not arrive at a definite "yes" or "no" from the Scriptures. 1 Timothy 5:14 and Titus 2:5 would seem to indicate that home is where the mother belongs. However, Proverbs 31 describes a woman who had business interests far beyond the confines of her home. The important question is, "What does God want for you?" The decision should not be based on what a mother **wants** to do to feel "fulfilled" or to have more money to spend. Nor should it be based on what a husband **wants** the wife to do, because he either **wants** her to bring more money in for the things he **wants** to buy, or he doesn't **want** her working outside of the home in an attempt to keep her in a more submissive position.

The decision should be based solely on what God is saying to you as a couple. Earnestly seek His guidance. And, of course, whatever He says to do is what will be best for the family in general and the children in particular. I'm convinced many wives are working outside the home not because the Lord has led them to or because the husband makes too little, but because the family spends too much.

I know a family in which the husband and wife are both working full-time. As a result, their children spend far too much time alone, the results of which are being evidenced in their oldest child. This child needs more supervision and, in fact, has needed this supervision for several years. Recently the wife was sharing with me a bit of what they were experiencing with this child. She acknowledged she should not be working but added, "I don't have any choice." Red flags immediately went up in my mind. I don't pretend to know all the details of their lives, but I am aware of money that they have spent on things — big things — that are far above the "need" category. Nothing — no job, no career, no home, no car —

is worth having or doing if it means the children will suffer to the point of making wrong choices that could affect them for the rest of their lives. The sad thing is that this family is only one of millions just like them.

When parents, particularly Christian parents, choose to bring a child into the world, they should do so with a personal commitment to make any sacrifice, material or otherwise, necessary for that child. No stone should be left unturned in order to be able to give themselves to that child for the nurturing, training, guiding, and molding he or she so desperately needs. If that means less material comfort — so be it.

It is far too easy to look around at the material society in which we live and slip into that mind-set that says we have to have two pay checks. I'm convinced that with a tightening of the belt, a reigning in of the high-living dreams, and a rearranging of priorites, one paycheck would suffice. God would bless those families, and their children will thank them. As someone once said, "No one ever came to the end of their life and said, 'I wish I'd spent more time at the office.'" Why do we have to learn that lesson when it's too late?

Of course, there are the single parent or family illness situations that understandably make it necessary for the mother to work away from the home. Those are situations that offer tremendous challenges filled with lots of stress for those families. While they need to draw heavily upon God's grace and strength, we as Christians need to come alongside with our encouragement. For some who are able, that encouragement might include some financial assistance. "Visiting the orphans and widows in their distress" doesn't just mean going to their house for a cup of coffee.

Sooner or later most couples will be faced with the decision of whether or not the wife/mother should work.

Above all, (1) seek the Lord for His wisdom and guidance and, (2) husbands and wives, **be in unity** in this decision. It is one of the biggest decisions you will make as a couple.

In this day and age, some families have chosen to have the wife work outside of the home and the husband stay at home and care for the children. That, again, is a decision the husband and wife should make in unity after earnestly seeking the will of the Lord. It is interesting to observe that for couples who make that arrangement, they are acknowledging that at least one parent needs to be at home with the children.

Unbiblical Clichés

There are a number of clichés we as Christians use that actually have no scriptural basis. One is that the husband is "the priest of the home." There is no verse in all of the New Testament to support this idea. On the contrary, 1 Peter 2:5, 9 says,

> You also, as living stones, are being built up as a spiritual house for a holy priesthood, to offer up spiritual sacrifices acceptable to God through Jesus Christ. . . . But you are a chosen race, a royal priesthood, a holy nation, a people *(men and women)* for God's own possession, that you may proclaim the excellencies of Him who has called you out of darkness into His marvelous light.

Couple these verses with Revelation 1:6, *"And He has made us to be a kingdom, priests to His God and Father."* One clearly finds that we are all (men and women) part of that holy, royal priesthood. Each of us is privileged to stand as a priest before God in repentance and accountability. No wife can hide behind her husband when accounting to God for some action – or lack of it.

Both parents should accept the responsibility of the spiritual training of their children. Mothers can not hide behind the erroneous idea that the father as the "priest of the household" is to bear the responsibility alone. Proverbs 1:8 says, *"Hear, my son, your father's instruction, and do not forsake your mother's teaching."* Both must accept their own role in the children's training. Because of the time a mother spends with her children and because, in some homes, the mothers are more gifted and anointed for teaching than the fathers, the spiritual training in those homes flows more readily from the mother. (In other homes, the opposite would be true.) This does not free fathers to abdicate their responsibility as described in Ephesians 6:4. However, those gifted and anointed mothers/teachers should not suppress the burden and desire they have to teach their children because of some erroneous idea that the father is "supposed to do it."

Timothy learned the Scriptures at the knees of his mother and grandmother. Susanna Wesley, mother of John and Charles Wesley, taught her children. She gave birth to a total of nineteen children. Although only six lived to adulthood, she spent hours with each one privately, indelibly imprinting on their hearts and minds the truths of God's Kingdom.

Some time ago, I taught on this subject to a group of ladies in Montana. At the close of the session a young mother approached me with a joyous expression on her face. She was one of those mothers who had the desire and gifting to teach her children the things of God. However, because she had always been told that was the father's role, she quite regularly prodded her husband regarding his responsibility, which he had no inclination to fulfill. He, on the other hand, recognized her desire to teach the children and encouraged her to do so. She laughed as she said to me, "My husband is going to be so

happy that I will no longer be goading him into doing something that is no more his responsibility than mine."

Both mothers and fathers have a God-given mandate to train their children in the ways of God. Both will have to answer to Him as to how well they fulfilled that commission.

Another word that is taken completely out of context and misapplied is the word "covering." Much is said in some quarters of the Church today about one's "covering," whether implying that every woman needs a man to cover or protect her, or whether referring to the organizational protection many feel is needed in ministry.

The place in Scripture where the word "cover" is mentioned with this possible implication, is Ruth 3:9. Here Ruth asks Boaz to spread his cover over her as an acknowledgment that he is her next of kin. This had to do with the Jewish custom regarding redeemer marriages where the nearest of kin to a deceased husband was to marry the widow and raise up children in the name of the deceased husband. It had nothing to do with New Testament church life or the protection of a wife by her husband.

Shouldn't the husband protect his wife, the weaker vessel? Yes, there would certainly be times when the husband should be a protection to his wife, such as helping to lift an object beyond her strength and ability, performing a task that would be a hazard to her with her limited physical strength, and even protecting her from an intruder or assailant.

Then there are times, when the wife is stressed "to the max" with her daily responsibilities of home and children (and maybe a job), when a loving husband and father should step in and relieve her pressure.

(Equally, there are times when it is necessary for the wife to do the same for her husband.)

Who Are We to Set Limits?

With all that has been said to this point and with the biblical references where God released women to be involved in the Kingdom at all levels both in the Old and New Testament, who are we to say to a woman who is clearly gifted and anointed by God for some ministry, "This far and no farther!"? Paul nor any other New Testament writer said that. Likewise, we do not have the liberty to say that either.

So what about women in leadership today?

Chapter Ten Notes

1. Joseph H. Thayer, ed., *Greek-English Lexicon Of The New Testament* (Grand Rapids: Baker Book House, 1981), ref. 4368.

2. Richard and Catherine Kroeger, *Women Elders . . . Sinners or Servants?* (100 Witherspoon Street, Louisville, KY 40202-1396: Council on Women and the Church, The United Presbyterian Church in the U.S.A., 1981), 10-11.

For further reference:

Faith Martin, *Call Me Blessed* (Grand Rapids: Wm. B. Eerdmans, 1988), 19.

Charles Trombley, *Who Said Women Can't Teach?* (North Brunswick, NJ: Bridge Publishing, Inc., 1985), 189.

3. Leonard Swidler, *Biblical Affirmation of Women* (Philadelphia: Westminster Press, 1979), 299.

4. Kroeger, op. cit., 11.

For further reference: R. K. McGregor Wright, *A Response to the Danvers Statement* (Minneapolis, MN 55404: Christians for Biblical Equality, 1989), 9-11.

5. Katherine C. Bushnell, *God's Word to Women* (privately reprinted by Ray B. Munson, P. O. Box 417, North Collins, NY 14111, 1923), 244.

6. Thayer, op. cit., ref. 1203.

7. Clarence L. Barnett, ed., *The American College Dictionary* (New York: Random House, 1951), 329.

8. *Gesenius' Hebrew and Chaldee Lexicon to the Old Testament* (Grand Rapids: Baker Book House, 1979), ref. 2428.

Questions For Study or Discussion

1. What does Acts 2:14-18 say about the place of women during the Church Age?

2. Priscilla and Aquila are mentioned six times in the New Testament. Her name is mentioned first in Acts 18:2, 18:18, 18:26; Romans 16:3; and 2 Timothy 4:19. What is the significance of this?

3. Who is a female example of each of the following ministries: Apostle – Romans 16:7; Prophet – Acts 21:9; Evangelist – Psalms 68:11; Shepherd – 2 John 1; Teacher – Acts 18:26.

4. Who were the women to whom Paul was referring as "fellow-workers" in Romans 16:3? In Philippians 4:3?

5. What is the significance of 2 Timothy 3:16 as it relates to the quoting of women in Scripture?

6. What is the significance of the phrase "Cloe's people" in 1 Corinthians 1:11?

7. In light of the word "presbytery" used in 1 Timothy 4:14, what do 1 Timothy 5:1-2 and Titus 2:2-5 show about the possibility of female elders?

8. What do these Scriptures show about the possibility of female deacons? Romans 16:1-2; 1 Timothy 3:11?

9. What can we learn from early Church history about the possibility of female elders and deacons?

10. What is the meaning of "oikodespoteo" in 1 Timothy 5:14 and how does it apply today?
11. What are the two most important ingredients needed when a decision is being made regarding a wife/mother working outside of the home?
12. Can limitations can be put on the ministry of women during the Church Age? Explain.
13. What are two clichés often referred to in the Body of Christ which have no Biblical basis? Can you think of others?

ELEVEN

Woman Throughout Church History

Looking back in Biblical history we can see how God used women in both the Old and New Testaments, in spite of the obstacles they had to overcome. We will now see how God has used women throughout Church history.

Early Centuries

Following the recorded New Testament letters which tell us of the development of the early Church and the role that women played, women continued to occupy a prominent place in the Church. ". . . even limited historical evidence witnesses to the fact that the ministry of women flourished during the first six hundred years of Christianity."[1]

Several writings in the early Church indicate that there was even an office of female elder until it was eliminated in A.D. 363 at the Council of Laodicea.[2]

Women's service to God took the form of poverty in the Fourth to Eighth centuries. There were a number of women, not the least of whom was Constantine's mother, who gave up their wealth and nobility to go into the hearts of the cities that they might minister to the poor. As this ministry developed, other women joined them. A simple garb was developed, and before long an order was formed which became the beginning of various Roman Catholic orders of nuns. Their influence was felt mostly by the poor and the women who joined their efforts. Man's leadership in the Church was in no way threatened.

In the Eastern Orthodox Church there was an ordained office of woman deacon — an equivalent to the male deacon — that was quite active from the early Church at least until 1200 A.D. They had a full range of ministries: traveling, evangelism, pastoral care, ministering to the poor and needy, preparing women for adult baptism, assisting the bishop, leading the female portion of the congregation, and founding and overseeing monasteries. In recent years, the Orthodox Church has been moving toward restoring this office.[3]

13th - 18th Centuries

In 1212, the female arm of the Franciscans was founded by **Clare of Sciffi**.

> Clare was only a teenager when she first heard Francis of Assisi preach. His message was compelling, and with his assistance she fled the security and wealth of her noble family and took a vow to live her life in the service of Christ. Soon afterward the order of Poor

Clares (or Clarisses) was officially organized and she headed that order for some forty years.[4]

The most famous of all medieval Church women was **Catherine of Siena** who lived during the 1300s. As a very young child she made a vow of virginity and, though coming from a large family (twenty-five children), managed to find time to spend in contemplation. As she grew older, not only did she dedicate her life and ministry to the poor, sick, and dying, but she fought ardently against the corruption and immorality that existed within the Catholic Church.

During the 1600-1700s, the mystics became quite prominent. **Madam Jeanne Guyon** was a French mystic who, although a Catholic, had a good deal of influence among the Protestants. Because of this, she suffered condemnation by the Catholic Church officials. John Wesley called her a true woman of holiness.

Susanna Wesley is an example of a woman whose ministry was directed to men as well as women — a practice not acceptable in that day. She was a woman of tremendous discipline. Her husband Samuel was away from the home much of the time. They did not agree on the law of Divine Right of Succession to the British throne which caused quite a rift between them. Their marriage was not very smooth, and Susanna was virtually left alone to raise the children for extended periods of time.

During one of those times, the Wesleys were still living in the parsonage of the parish which Samuel was supposedly pastoring. Susanna had become known for the excellent job she was doing in teaching her own children the things of God. As a result, people started coming to her home for teaching — women first and then men. The man who was preaching in Samuel's absence was not nearly as interesting to listen to as Susanna, and that word got around. She had as many as two hundred

people coming to her home. At one point, Samuel came home and told her she had to stop these meetings. Although she was not trying to assert "women's rights," she felt she could not deny her God-given gift to teach the people who were begging her to continue. So she continued.

More and more women began taking on the role of teaching. The early Sunday School movement, originally founded in England in the 1780s by Robert Raikes, had more women than men teaching the classes. Although their teaching met with much opposition, there is little evidence that this in any way discouraged them from continuing.

Nineteenth Century

When **Joanna Bethune** and her husband felt it was time to organize a similar Sunday School movement in America, he began contacting businessmen in an attempt to stir up interest. This not being successful, he encouraged Joanna to go ahead with some of her female friends. This she did in January, 1816, forming the Female Union for the Promotion of Sabbath Schools. However, the men, not wanting to be outdone, met and formed their own New York Sunday School Union just one week later under the leadership of Joanna's husband. Before long the Female Union for the Promotion of Sabbath Schools became just an auxiliary of the New York Sunday School Union.[5]

In the mid-1800s, **Charles Finney** was one of the first to permit women to pray and testify in public. The door to public ministry for women was slowly beginning to open.

About that same time, women began writing hymns. Some of the greatest hymns that have blessed the

Church were written by women. These include "Just As I Am," "Take My Life and Let It Be," and "I Gave My Life for Thee." **Fanny Crosby**, one of the best known and best loved song writers of all times, wrote over nine thousand hymns including "Blessed Assurance," "Rescue the Perishing," and "I Am Thine, Oh Lord." Preachers and theologians who wouldn't think of allowing a woman to stand up in a pulpit, would sing these songs every week and be blessed by them.

Also in the Nineteenth Century, women began to be full-fledged preachers. Some of them began talking about having been "called" to preach, and they didn't know what to do with it.

There were three well-known women of that time. One was **Phoebe Palmer** who was called the mother of the Holiness Movement. The other two were **Hannah Whitall Smith**, who is known for her devotional classic, *The Christian's Secret of a Happy Life*, which was published in 1875; and **Catherine Booth**.

Catherine Booth, wife of William Booth, was a very interesting woman. We usually think of William Booth as being the founder of the Salvation Army. We hear very little about the fact that Catherine was every bit as involved in starting the Army as was William. They founded it together.

Catherine's preaching began one Sunday morning in her husband's church where there were about one thousand in attendance. God spoke to her and told her she was to get up and say something when her husband finished preaching. In obedience to the Lord, she did. What came forth from her mouth was so anointed that upon completion of her remarks, William got up and promptly announced, "Catherine will be preaching tonight." This was the beginning of her

preaching ministry, and she was so fulfilled in it that her only regret was that she had waited so long.[6]

Contrary to other women who just wanted to preach, Catherine was committed to seeing women released to an equal status with men in every area of life. It was said that she made William agree to their marriage being an egalitarian marriage before she would agree to marry him.[7]

The Salvation Army welcomed women. In fact, the Foundation Deed submitted in 1875 included the following clause:

> Nothing shall authorize the conference to take any course whereby the right of females to be employed as evangelists or class leaders shall be impeded or destroyed or which shall render females ineligible for any office or deny to them the right to speak and vote at all or any official meetings of which they may be members.[8]

So confident was William Booth in the ministry of women that he made the statement, "My best men are women."[9] The Army met with much opposition and was literally scorned by virtually every segment of society during its early years. This gradually changed, but as the Army gained the desired respectability, the role of women declined. (Recent years have seen a restoration of the role of women in the Salvation Army.)

This seems to have been the pattern in other movements as well. As men moved into leadership, women found themselves slowly relegated to non-leadership roles.

During the Nineteenth Century, cults were being founded by women — Christian Science by **Mary Baker Eddy** and the Shakers by **Mother Ann Lee**. **Ellen G. White** was another prominent woman who was the prophetess of Seventh-day Adventism.

There are those who would say this indicates that women have a weakness for sects or cults. History does not prove this to be true as the majority of the many sects in existence today, including the Mormons, Jehovah's Witnesses, The Way, and the Children of God, were founded by men. However, because of the male domination that was firmly rooted in the institutional Church, women who had a desire to be involved in meaningful ministry found much more openness in these movements developing on the fringes.

The Church And Women Today

In the late Nineteenth and early Twentieth Centuries, the established denominations would not tolerate women ministering from the pulpit, whereas the emerging Holiness and Pentecostal movements were just the opposite. They were open and ready to accept women in ministry.

Although the Holiness movement is still relatively open to women ministers today, the positions of the mainline denominations and much of the Pentecostal movement have reversed. Partly due to the Feminist Movement, mainline churches have been forced to work through this issue, deal with it, and are now much more open to women ministers, even the practice of ordaining women. However, in many charismatic churches, there is a great deal of reluctance, even deep antagonism, towards women being involved in a preaching/leadership ministry.

However, God's plan for women's involvement in the work of the Kingdom has been emerging. It will continue to grow as the restoration of women's God-ordained status in life comes to fruition.

As for modern-day women who have been greatly used of God, there are several that deserve to be recognized. **Aimie Semple McPherson** founded the Church of the Foursquare Gospel. **Henrietta Mears** founded Gospel Light Publications and the Hollywood Christian Group, was director of Christian Education at Hollywood Presbyterian Church, and developed Forest Home Conference Center. She was one of the most influencial Christian women of the mid-Twentieth Century. **Kathryn Kuhlman** was well-known for her thirty-year healing ministry. **Vonette Bright** has played a major role in the present-day, world-wide prayer movement. **Joy Dawson's** *Steps to Intercession* and prophetic-teaching ministry around the world has affected countless Christians. Other women whom God is greatly using in the area of teaching in this 21st Century are: Joyce Meyer and Beth Moore.

These women, along with many others who could be mentioned, were and are, living proof that when God places His hand upon a woman with a specific ministry in mind, no human hand can stop her.

Chapter Eleven Notes

1. Ruth Tucker and Walter Liefeld, Daughters of the Church (Grand Rapids: Zondervan Publishing House, 1987), 90.

2. This can be verified by checking the following: Katherine C. Bushnell, *God's Word to Women* (privately reprinted by Ray B. Munson, P. O. Box 417, North Collins, NY 14111, 1923), 244; R. K. McGregor Wright, *A Response to the Danvers Statement* (St. Paul, MN: Christians for Biblical Equality, 1989), 11; and Richard and Catherine Kroeger, *Women Elders . . . Sinners or Servants?* (100 Witherspoon Street, Louisville, KY: Council on Women and the Church, The United Presbyterian Church in the U. S. A., 1981), 11.

3. Kyriaki Karidoyanes FitzGerald, *Women Deacons in the Orthodox Church* (Brookline, MA: Holy Cross Orthodox Press, 1998).

4. Tucker and Liefeld, 14, 155.

5. Ibid., 249-250.

6. Ibid., 264.

7. Ibid., 265.

8. Ibid., 265-266.

9. Ibid., 266.

Questions For Study or Discussion

1. Tell about five women whom God has used significantly throughout Church history.
2. Tell about five women (other than those mentioned in WOMAN) whom God is using today.
3. If you are a woman, how do you think God wants to use you? If a man, how?

TWELVE

What Should Our Response Be?

It is important to spend time considering how one should respond to truth such as this. How does one receive this releasing revelation and teaching?

Response of Women

If God has been speaking to you as you have been reading this book and you believe He is in the process of revealing truth to you, do your own study of the Bible until God assures you of His truth. Then allow God to make it yours and to release you by His Spirit to be the woman He designed you to be.

Accept this freedom whether or not your husband, your pastor, or spiritual leaders are ready to agree. You can be set free in your own heart even if the visible

"chains" are still on. Many is the prisoner who has found Jesus while behind bars who declares he's freer than he ever was before his physical imprisonment. Rejoice in who you are in God's plan.

I remember as I was getting into this subject and discovering the mutual submission and equality taught in the Word, I began sharing it with Nate. He had come a long way during our married life where women were concerned. In fact, he had made a 170 degree change in his attitude from having difficulty with any woman in spiritual leadership, to himself releasing women to be in ministry and spiritual leadership. However, he was still of the opinion that the Bible said he was to rule his wife. Although his form of "ruling" did not include controlling my every move, he was still the one "in charge." (He still had 10 degrees to go!)

Since Nate wanted to obey God's Word above anything, he was committed to sticking with his understanding. In fact, he expressed to me very clearly one day that he was concerned that I was getting into heresy. However, he agreed to read Katherine Bushnell's book *God's Word to Women*. (Remember, this was the book he had felt I should read and the book that challenged me into doing this study. But, he had not yet read it.) As he read, God began dealing with Nate's heart and his understanding began to change. Until that change came, however, I still felt a release in my heart as to who I was as a woman before God. How my husband felt could not quench that which was God's revelation to me through His Word.

WITH GREAT HUMILITY, accept your position created by God and begin to move in it. Many Christian women believe if their husband tells them to do something, even if it violates their conscience, they are bound to obey. Not so! Every woman will stand before

God and give an account of her own actions. No husband will "stand in" for his wife.

I well remember a few years ago I was struggling over what I thought was a directive from God which was to give away a ring I had recently purchased. Not having much in the way of valuable jewelry, I wanted to make sure it was God and not the enemy robbing me of a blessing. So I said to myself, "Aha, I'll ask my husband. He's my 'head'. Whatever he says I should do, I'll do." (I realize now, to my shame, I was playing a game with God. I have sought the will of God over many issues and situations that were of a personal nature. This was a "cop-out" on my part, but one I thought was justified based on false "head-ship" teaching.)

To my surprise (because "things" mean little to Nate), he said, "Absolutely not. God gave you that ring for you to enjoy. I don't believe you're to give it away." I was greatly relieved and the matter was settled — temporarily. However, I couldn't get lasting victory and that "tug" kept returning. I was willing to give up the ring as long as I could be sure it was God. Yet, somehow, I could not get clarity. A second time I went to Nate with my dilemma. A second time he admonished me to keep the ring. Again, I accepted his word.

It was not until a year and a half later, when I began this study, that the Lord made very clear to me that God deals with me personally as an individual and that I could not hide behind my husband's convictions or opinions. I realized I had to battle this one out all by myself. So I set about doing just that.

God showed me very clearly that, indeed, He had been the One urging me to give away the ring. All along I knew who was to receive it, so, give it away I did! I said nothing to Nate until after the fact. He has never hindered my being obedient to any clear word I had from the Lord,

so it was no problem to him. However, with his understanding today of our mutually submissive relationship, under the control of the Holy Spirit, if I were to go to him again with a similar dilema, he would not be as inclined to make my decision for me, as he did before. His response would be something like this: "Honey, I can't tell you what to do. You'll have to ask the Lord." He would willingly join me in prayer regarding the matter and would give me his counsel but would never presume to play "God" in my life.

The release and victory I received in my spirit when I was obedient to God was indescribable. I had been living under a cloud for two years, not realizing that the ring was the root of it all. Had I not been lulled into lethargy regarding the issue by the erroneous teaching that my husband would hear from God for me, I would have "buckled down" earlier, sought Him more diligently myself, and avoided that lengthy cloud that robbed me of victory. (A year later the Lord miraculously replaced that ring with one of greater value. A gift "out of the blue." Isn't that just like Him?!)

Accept who you are before God and begin moving in it. Become a woman of God. Learn to hear His voice. Then when the Holy Spirit tells you that some form of action that your husband has decided to take that also involves you is wrong, you can go to him and humbly but honestly say, "Honey, I can not proceed as you have decided. God has spoken thus to me and I must obey Him." If he has a problem with this and he chooses to proceed as he had planned, God will not hold you accountable for the outcome. Don't ever disobey God to please your husband — or anyone else, for that matter. There are many husbands whose shoes I would hate to be in on the day of judgment. I am very serious when I say I

fear for them. *"But many who are first, will be last . . ."* Mark 10:31.

This, in no way, gives anyone license to respond or conduct oneself in a disrespectful way toward anyone — husband, spiritual leaders, or other fellow believers. But one should be able to move in the freedom of hearing and responding to what one believes to be the word of the Lord to them personally. The secret is **humility**. Don't flaunt your newfound freedom, but in humility before God, walk in it.

However, there are many husbands who will, when they observe that you really are a woman of God who hears God's voice, be willing to start praying together about decisions even before they are willing to accept the mutuality of your relationship.

It is of utmost importance that you ask God to search your heart for any bitterness you may have toward your husband, spiritual leaders who have kept you in bondage in one way or another, or men in general. Recognize it, admit it, and deal with it. This calls for true repentance before God for allowing the bitterness to creep in. It may even require going to the person or persons toward whom you are bitter and asking their forgiveness. Humbling? Yes, but an important step in the whole releasing process. One can not be totally set free to be the woman God made you to be while still under the bondage of bitterness.

Although God may lead you to share your new understanding with others, your husband included, don't feel responsible to change their thinking. It is very easy to consider it one's own personal responsibility to change everyone's thinking on any subject about which one has received new understanding. It is not! That always has been, and always will be, the role of the Holy Spirit.

I remember as I was beginning to teach on this subject, I soon realized it was not being received by everyone in the audience. I was really shaken. I had just rather expected that everyone would be just as thrilled as I was at this revealed truth and be eager to walk it out. Finding that not to be the case, I felt I had failed in my quest, and the enemy had a hay-day with me for a while. Then the Lord spoke to my heart that it wasn't my responsibility to "change" anyone. Rather, that was His. I just needed to humbly "speak the truth in love" and leave the results with Him.

There have been a number of times when Nate and I have come into a new situation and awareness of what I teach regarding women has preceded me. I don't have to be in that situation very long before it is obvious who is ready to welcome me and who wants little or nothing to do with me. God, in His faithfulness, has "thickened my skin" and given me the grace to realize that this is part of the battle.

On the other hand, I have no desire to battle it out with anyone. There was a time when I was willing to roll up my sleeves and go head-to-head with anyone on the subject. God had to do a humbling job on me. I now am blessed when I have an opportunity to share the truth regarding God's plan for woman. But that is where my role ends. The rest is up to the Holy spirit.

Response of Men and Spiritual Leaders

If you have been one — either man or woman, husband or spiritual leader — who has perpetuated the traditional doctrine regarding women, I believe there needs to be deep personal repentance on your part. If there are any women whom you have kept in bondage in one way or another, perhaps God would lead you to go

to them, seek their forgiveness, and personally release them to fulfill God's calling on their lives.

Some would argue, at this point, that Hebrews 13:17 instructs all believers, which would include women, to **obey** spiritual leaders. Furthermore, some spiritual leaders believe they have a right to assert that control. *Vine's Expository Dictionary* defines the Greek word *peitho* used in that verse this way:

> To persuade, to win over, in the Passive and Middle Voices, to be persuaded, to listen to, to obey, is so used with this meaning, in the Middle Voice, e.g., in Acts 5:36, 37 (in ver. 40 Passive Voice, "they agreed"); Rom. 2:8; Gal. 5:7; Heb 13:17; Jas. 3:3. The obedience suggested is not by submission to authority, but resulting from persuasion.[1]

So we, as believers, whether male or female, need to be open to input from spiritual leaders, or other mature brothers and sisters. We need to be teachable, willing to learn. But no one has been given the authority to counter, or block, what anyone believes to be God's clear word to them.

Surely, if you are a husband who has kept your wife in bondage by your unbiblical rulership, humbling yourself before God and your wife will be the first steps toward developing a relationship in keeping with God's plan.

How well I remember the day Nate took my hands in his, looked into my eyes and lovingly said, "Honey, will you forgive me for all the wounds you received from me because of my controlling approach to our relationship." Of course, I did. Nothing brings healing like repentance and forgiveness. On another occasion he even washed my feet.

We were then free to re-evaluate and re-work the way we relate to each other. This kind of change doesn't take place over night. It takes time, and we're

still in the refining process. Each must be free to make mistakes. We did. But each digression has been used as a learning experience to strengthen our skills at relating to one another as equals.

Our love and respect for each other has greatly deepened. For a number of years, Nate had recognized my ability to hear the voice of God and had sought my counsel and desired that we make most decisions in unity. However, he still reserved the "right" to exercise the authority he felt Scripture gave him, if he felt so led. My respect for him has increased as I have watched him humble himself before me, yielding in areas he would previously have "stood his ground" as the "head" of the house.

His respect for me has increased because his understanding of me, a woman, has been elevated by the new light he has received as to who women are in God's sight. He respected me as a godly woman but did not see women in general as on an equal par with men. This has all been a work of God as we have responded to revealed truth.

Response of the Church

I also believe the Church needs to repent corporately for the centuries of grief it has brought to women. The Church needs to repent for stifling the ministry of anointed women who have had much to offer to the Church and to the world. The world and the Body of Christ have been denied countless blessings because these gifted women have not been adequately released. May God have mercy upon us!

Pray

Last, but not least, pray. God is in the process of restoring woman to her rightful place, make no mistake about it. Be encouraged! It's happening! But, He has to do it. Our role is to pray that the Holy Spirit will be released to complete the restoration process He has already begun.

Pray for the Church of Jesus Christ that her eyes will be opened to the truth regarding God's plan for woman. And pray for those spiritual leaders who are bound by the traditional teaching and are unable to receive from or release women to minister from the wealth of insight and wisdom God has deposited within them.

God is in the process of preparing His Bride for His return. The enmity between Satan and woman may be the last demon that needs to be slain before that great event.

We are living in exciting days — and the best is yet to come!!

Chapter Twelve Notes

1. *Vine's Expository Dictionary of Old and New Testament Words* (Old Tappan, NJ: Fleming H. Revell Company, 1981), 124.

Questions For Study or Discussion

1. After thoroughly reading "WOMAN – God's Plan, not Man's Tradition", what is your understanding of God's plan for woman – in the marriage and in the church?

2. Explain the importance of humility as one would attempt to live out or share with others the understanding of God's plan for woman based on "WOMAN."

3. What changes do you need to make in your life as a result of this study? (Your answer might include your need to forgive someone or ones who have kept you in bondage, your need to repent if you have been one who has not released women to be whom God intended, or your need for a greater level of humility.)

Bibliography

Bilezikian, Gilbert. *Beyond Sex Roles.* Baker Book House, Grand Rapids, MI 49516, 1985.

Bristow, John Temple. *What Paul Really Said About Women.* HarperCollins Publishers, New York, NY 10022, 1988.

Bushnell, Katherine C. *God's Word to Women.* Privately reprinted by Ray B. Munson, P. O. Box 417, North Collins, NY 14111, 1923.

Cervin, Richard S. "Does *kephale* (head) Mean 'Source' or 'Authority Over' in Greek Literature?: A Rebuttal." Available from Christians for Biblical Equality, 122 West Franklin Avenue, Suite 218, Minneapolis, MN 55404-2451.

Cook, Barbara. *Ordinary Women, Extraordinary Strength.* Aglow Publications, Lynnwood, WA 1988.

Cunningham, Loren and Hamilton, David J. *Why Not Women?* YWAM Publishing, P.O. Box 55787, Seattle, WA 98155, 2000.

"The Danvers Statement." Council on Biblical Manhood and Womanhood, P. O. Box 1173, Wheaton, IL 60189.

Dayton, Lucille Sider and Donald W. "Women in the Holiness Movement." A paper presented at Christian Holiness Association Convention, 1974.

Deen, Edith. *All of the Women of the Bible.* Harper & Brothers Publishers, NY, 1955.

Deen, Edith. *Great Women of the Christian Faith.* Christian Herald Books, Chappaqua, NY, 1959.

FitzGerald, Kyriaki Karidoyanes. *Women Deacons in the Orthodox Church: Called to Holiness and Ministry.* Holy Cross Orthodox Press, Brookline, MA, 1998.

Foh, Susan. *Women and the Word of God.* Baker Book House, Grand Rapids, MI, 1981.

Fujita, Neil S., *A Crack in the Jar.* Paulist Press, NY.

Gesenius' Hebrew and Chaldee Lexicon to the Old Testament Scriptures. Translated by Samuel Prideaux Tregelles, Baker Book House, Grand Rapids, MI, 1979.

The Greek-English New Testament. Christianity Today, Washington, DC, 1976.

Gundry, Patricia. *Heirs Together.* Zondervan Publishing House, Grand Rapids, MI, 1980.

Gundry, Patricia. *Woman Be Free!* Zondervan Publishing House, Grand Rapids, MI, 1977.

Haubert, Katherine M. *Women as Leaders, MARC.* Monrovia, CA 91016-3400, 1993.

Hull, Gretchen Gaebelein. *Equal to Serve.* Fleming H. Revell, a division of Baker Book House, Grand Rapids, MI 49516-6287.

Johnson, Alan F. (Editor) *How I Changed My Mind about Women in Leadership: Compelling Stories from Prominent Evangelicals.* Zondervan, Grand Rapids, MI 49546, 2010.

Keener, Craig S. *Paul, Women & Wives.* Hendrickson Publishers, Peabody, MA, 1992.

Keizer, Walter. *Hard Sayings of the Old Testament.* InterVarsity Press, Downers Grove, IL, 1988.

Kroeger, Richard and Catherine. *I Suffer Not a Woman.* Baker Book House, Grand Rapids, MI 49516-6287, 1992.

Kroeger, Richard and Catherine. *Women Elders . . . Sinners or Servants?* Council on Women and the Church, The United Presbyterian Church, 100 Witherspoon St., Louisville, KY, 1981.

Krupp, Nate, *God's Simple Plan for His Church.* Destiny Image Publishers, P.O. Box 310, Shippensburg, PA 17257, 2018.

Krupp, Nate. *Leadership–Servanthood in the Church as found in the New Testament.* Destiny Image Publishers, P.O. Box 310, Shippensburg, PA 17257, 2018.

Lance, Fran and King, Pat. *Healing the Wounds of Women.* Free Lance Ministries, Seattle, WA, 1989.

Lee-Barnewall, Michelle. *Neither Complementation nor Egalitarian - A Kingdom Corrective to the Evangelical Gender Debate.* Baker Academic, Grand Rapids, MI,

2016.

Martin, Faith McBurney. *Call Me Blessed.* Wm. B. Eerdmans Publishing Co., Grand Rapids, MI, 1988.

Mathews, Alice. *Gender Roles and the People of God - Rethinking What We Were Taught About Men and Women in the Church.* Zondervan, Grand Rapids, MI 49546, 2017.

Mickelsen, Alvera. *Women, Authority and the Bible.* InterVarsity Press, Downers Grove, IL. 1986.

Mollenkott, Virginia Ramey. *Women, Men and the Bible.* Abingdon, Nashville, TN, 1981.

Pape, Dorothy R. *In Search of God's Ideal Woman.* InterVarsity, Downers Grove, IL, 1976.

Pawson, J. David. *Leadership is Male.* Oliver-Nelson Books, Nashville, TN, 1984.

Penn-Lewis, Jessie. *The Magna Charta of Woman.* Bethany Fellowship, Inc., Minneapolis, MN, 1919.

Pillai, K. C. *Light Through an Eastern Window.* Robert Speller & Sons Publishers, New York, NY, 1963.

Piper, John and Grudem, Wayne. *Recovering Biblical Manhood and Womanhood.* Crossway Books, Wheaton, IL, 1991.

Silk, Danny. *Powerful & Free: Confronting the Glass Ceiling for Women in the Church.* Red Arrow Media, Redding, CA 96001, 2012.

Strong, James. *Strong's Exhaustive Concordance.* Baker Bookhouse, Grand Rapids, MI, 1981.

Thayer, Joseph H. *Greek-English Lexicon of the New Testament.* Baker Book House, Grand Rapids, MI, 1977.

Thomas, Robert L. *New American Standard Exhaustive Concordance of the Bible.* Holman Publisher, Nashville, TN, 1981.

Torjesen, Karen Jo. *When Women Were Priests.* HarperCollins Publishers, New York, NY 10022, 1993.

Trombley, Charles. *Who Said Women Can't Teach?* Bridge-Logos Publishers, North Brunswick Corporate Center, 1300 Airport Rd., Suite E, North Brunswick, NJ 08902, 1985.

Tucker, Ruth A. and Liefeld, Walter. *Daughters of the Church.* Zondervan Publishing House, Grand Rapids, MI, 1987.

Van Leeuwen, Mary Steward. *Gender and Grace.* InterVarsity Press, Downers Grove, IL, 1991.

Wilson, Marvin R. *Our Father Abraham.* Wm. B. Eerdman Publishing Co., Grand Rapids, MI, and Center For Judaic- Christian Studies, Dayton, OH, 1989.

Woodrow, Ralph. *Women's Adornment.* Ralph Woodrow, P.O. Box 124, Riverside, CA, 92502.

Wright, R. K. McGregor. "A Response to the Danvers Statement." Christians for Biblical Equality, 122 West Franklin Avenue, Suite 218, Minneapolis, MN 55404-2451, 1989.

Young, Robert. *Analytical Concordance to the Bible.* Wm. B. Eerdmans Publishing Co., GrandRapids, MI.

Westfall, Cynthia Long. *Paul and Gender: Reclaiming the Apostle's Vision for Men and Women in Christ.* Baker Academic, Grand Rapids, MI 49516, 2016.

About the Author

Joanne Krupp is the youngest daughter of the late Dr. Harold K. Sheets, a General Superintendent of the Wesleyan Methodist Church. Although there was never a time when she didn't love Jesus, she dates her conversion to when she was twelve years of age.

She attended Marion College (now Indiana Wesleyan University) in Marion, Indiana, for two years and graduated from Asbury College in Wilmore, Kentucky, in 1958 with a Bachelor of Arts degree in Social Studies (Elementary Education).

She was the wife of Gerald Brannon, a Wesleyan Methodist pastor, until his death in 1959. A son, Gerry, was born to her two months after Gerald's death. Gerry and his wife, Wenda, have three grown children (Geoffrey, Alex, and Allison) and have been in pastoral ministry for 35 years.

She married Nate Krupp in 1961. A daughter, Beth, was born in 1962. Beth and her husband, Greg, have three married children (Jamie, Kelly, and Daniel), six grandchildren, and are ministering in the business world as well as involved in discipling through their church.

Joanne has had a Bible teaching and discipling ministry with women since 1971, ministering in North America, Europe, Africa, Asia, and the Pacific. She and Nate reside in Salem, Oregon. Their ministry, prior to retirement, was directed primarily to the church-at-large, emphasizing the restoration of the church to New

Testament Christianity, including the restoration of women to their God-given role.

What People are Saying

One of the significant trends in the Body of Christ in our day is the strong release of the female portion of that Body. For centuries they have been held back by wrong interpretations of certain Bible passages. Joanne Krupp, in her book *Woman,* writes to dispell these misconceptions and to set free more than half of God's army. – Robert, Hawaii

I highly recommend *Woman.* The revealed truth of God's Word regarding His plan for women has set me free from the bondage of man's tradition. I now walk in a new confidence of who I am in Christ. – Patricia, Arizona

Your book opened the door of my heart and mind to so many important insights, perhaps the least of which, the satanic darkness which had infected my own male mindset concerning women. It certainly helped me to see and better understand "... a great wonder in heaven: a woman ..." Once seen, she is reason enough for us to lay down our lives. – Jay, North Carolina

As a pastor's wife in rural Iowa, *Woman* brought an understanding to Scriptures that in the past seemed to contradict the very God-given gifts within me. With a new level of understanding and humility came a release and freedom to flow with my husband, becoming a more complete ministry to our local congregation. I consider this book a valuable resource tool, well written and easily assimilated. – Victoria, Iowa

Joanne Krupp has been an inspiration to me both by her study of the role of women and by her lifestyle of integrity and Christian love. No doubt the truth in this book will bring much needed understanding, freedom, and healing to the Body of Christ! – Cindy, Oregon

Joanne Krupp has brought insight to a controversial topic in a refreshing way. Her research and practical wisdom demonstrates her own walk with God. Her ministry partnership with her husband, Nate, lends credibility to the message of this book. – Bev, California

83743334R00106

Made in the USA
San Bernardino, CA
31 July 2018